OUTLINE OF
MEDIEVAL HISTORY

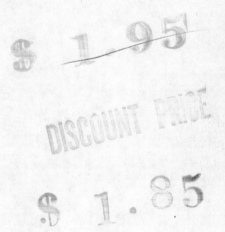

OUTLINE OF
MEDIEVAL HISTORY

OUTLINE OF
MEDIEVAL HISTORY

BY

DANIEL D. MC GARRY, M.A., PH.D.
Professor of History

Curriculum of Medieval Studies

Saint Louis University
Saint Louis, Missouri
United States of America

AND

JAMES A. WAHL, C.R., M.A., PH.D.
Lecturer in History

Saint Jerome's College
University of Waterloo
Waterloo, Ontario
Canada

1968

LITTLEFIELD, ADAMS & CO.

TOTOWA, NEW JERSEY

Printed in the United States of America

Outline of Medieval History

Contents

MAPS

CORRELATION OF OUTLINE WITH MEDIEVAL HISTORY TEXTBOOKS

References are to Chapters (or Consecutively Numbered Sections)

a: Earlier part; b: Later part; c,d: Final parts (if further subdivided); x: passim (here and there)

Outline	Ault	Cantor	Collins	Hoyt	LaMonte	MacKinney	McGarry	O'Sullivan	Painter	Stephenson	Strayer	Thompson	Thorndike
I. FOUNDATIONS													
1. Roman Legacy	3a	1a, 2c	1		1a	1	1	1, 2, 4a	1a	1	1	1	1
2. Christian Heritage	4, 9a	1c, 2, 3	2b, 3, 5a, b	2, 3, 4x	2, 5x	3, 4a	2	10, 11, 12, 13, 14a	1c	2c, 4	1c	2, 3	3b, 8a
3. Decline of Western Empire	3b	1b, 2c	2		1b, 3x	2	4x	3, 4b	1b	2	1x	1	3a
4. Barbarians	5	4a	4a	4	3b	5a	3	5	2a	3a	2a	4a	2
II. EARLY MIDDLE AGES													
5. Barbarian Invasions	6	4b, c	4b	5	3c	5b	4	6, 7	2b	3c	2b	4b, 5a	4
6. New West: 500-700	7, 10	4c	6	6	9a	6	5	9	2x, 5a	3c, 7c	2c	5b, 8a	6
7. Byzantine Empire and Civilization	8	5a, 10a	7, 19x	13, 32	3, 4, 7, 8a, 18	7	6		3	5, 9a	3a, 6a	6	5, 11
8. Medieval Islam	14	5b, 10a, 16	8	14	6	8	7	27	3x	6, 9b	3b, c, 6b	7	9, 10
9. Carolingian Empire (700-877)	11	7b, c, 8a	9	15-20	9b	9	8	18a	5b	8	4	9	12
10. Decline and Collapse of Carolingian Empire	12, 13	8a	10	21	9c	10	9	18b	7	8c	5a	10	13
11. Feudalism	15a	8b	11	24, 25, 40, 41	12	11	10	21, 25	4, 9, 10	10, 11b	5b	11	15a
12. Economy and Society in Early Middle Ages	15b	9b, 10b	12, 20a	27, 28	13a	12	11	23, 25a	8, 10	11	5c	12	14a

Outline	Ault	Cantor	Collins	Hoyt	LaMonte	MacKinney	McGarry	O'Sullivan	Painter	Stephenson	Strayer	Thompson	Thorndike
13. Western Europe in Early Feudal Era	16, 17	9b	17a, 18a, 19a	18, 23, 25, 37	11	23a, 24a	12	19x	6, 15, 17a, 19a				15c
14. Central and Eastern Europe in Early Feudal Era	16	9c, d	13, 14a, 33x	22	8b, 10	19a	13	20a	4a, 16	12a	6c, d	13a	15b
15. Church in Early Middle Ages	9, 18a	6, 7c, 9a, d	5, 13a	9, 10, 26	2c	4b	14	8, 11x, 12x, 14	5x, 11, 12a	4x, 7a	2d, 5d, 6d	8b	7
16. Culture in Early Middle Ages	25a, 26a	3a, 7a, 8a	24a, 25a	11, 12, 19, 20	5, 13b	13, 14, 15, 16, 17	15	15a, 16x, 17x		7b		8c, 9b	8
III. HIGH MIDDLE AGES													
17. Economy and Society in High Middle Ages	20	11, 18a, 20c	20, 21	35, 36, 40, 41, 61-63	21, 22	18, 27a	16	24b, 25	22, 23, 24	13	7d, 11c	19, 20	14b, 17, 23x, 28, 29
18. Overseas Expansion and Crusades	19	14	19	33, 34	19, 20, 29	25, 26	17	28	21	12c, 18c	8b, 10c	18	18
19. Western Empire in High Middle Ages	18b, 21	12b, c, 18b, 20b	14, 15, 16b	29-31, 39, 70, 71	14, 25	19, 20	18	20	16c, 27	17b, 18a, 20	8a, 10b	13b, 14	16x, 19x, 20
20. England in High Middle Ages	17, 23	13, 18b, 20b	18	37a, 38, 64-66	16b, 17, 28	23	19	19	17b, 26	17a, 18a, 20b, 21a	7c, 9a, 11b, 12a	15, 25a	21
21. France in High Middle Ages	16, 22	18c, 20b	17	37b, 67-69	16a, 27	24b	20	19	15c, 25	17a, 18a, 20b, 21a	7b, 9b, 11a, 12b	16, 17	22
22. Other States in High Middle Ages	31		19x, 33x	33, 73-75	15, 26, 30, 31	24c	21		4b, 18, 19, 20	17b, c, 20b, c	7b, 10d		23
23. Church in High Middle Ages	18b, 24	12, 13b, 17, 19	14x, 15x, 16, 22, 23	30, 31x, 46-51	14a, 23, 24, 25a, 26x	19x, 20x, 21, 22	22	22b, 26	12, 13x, 14, 28, 29, 30	12b, 18b, 19, 20x	7a, 8a, c, 10a, b	13x, 14x, 21, 22	16, 19

	Ault	Cantor	Collins	Hoyt	LaMonte	MacKinney	McGarry	O'Sullivan	Painter	Stephenson	Strayer	Thompson	Thorndike
… in High Middle Ages	25	15, 16, 20a	24, 25	32, 33	43-45, 52-56	24, 25	23	15b, 16a, 17	13, 42, 43, 44, 45, 46a, 47a, 48, 49	14, 19c	8d, 10d	23	24, 25
25. Expression in High Middle Ages	26, 27	15d	26, 27	34	42, 57-60	26, 27	24	16c, 17b		11c, 15, 16	8d, 10d	24	26, 27
IV. LATER MIDDLE AGES													
26. Economy and Society in Later Middle Ages	32	21a, 22a	35x		84-86	27b	25	25c, 32	22c, 23a	24, 26c	13a	26a	36
27. France and England in Later Middle Ages	29	21c, 22a	28, 30	37, 38	76-78	29	26	31, 33a	31, 32, 33, 34, 35, 36, 37	22	13c	25, 26b, c	30, 35
28. Southern Europe in Later Middle Ages	31		32, 34	40		31	27	33b			13d, 14a	26d	32, 35c
29. Other States in Later Middle Ages	28, 31x		31, 33	35, 39	82, 83	30	28	30, 33c	38	23c	13d	27	33, 34
30. Church in Later Middle Ages	30	21c, 22a	29, 35x	36	72, 79, 80, 88, 89	28	29	29	39, 40, 41	21, 23	12	28	31
31. Culture in Later Middle Ages	33	21b, 22a	26x, 27x 35b	41	87-89	32b, 33b, 34b, 35b	30	17x	46b, 47b	25	13b, 14	29	37

Medieval History Textbooks:
Ault, Warren O., *Europe in the Middle Ages* (Boston, D. C. Heath and Company, 1937ff.)
Cantor, Norman F., *Medieval History* … (New York, The Macmillan Company, 1963)
Collins, Ross W., *History of Medieval Civilization in Europe* (Boston, Ginn and Company, 1936ff.)
Hoyt, Robert S., *Europe in the Middle Ages* (New York, Harcourt, Brace and Company, 1957ff.)
LaMonte, John L., *The World of the Middle Ages* (New York, Appleton-Century-Crofts, 1949ff.)
MacKinney, Loren C., *The Medieval World* (New York, Holt, Rinehart, and Winston, Inc. 1988ff.)
McGarry, Daniel D., *The Formative Middle Ages* (In preparation)
O'Sullivan, Jeremiah, and Burns, John F., *Medieval Europe* (New York, Appleton-Century-Crofts, 1943ff.)
Painter, Sidney, *History of the Middle Ages* (New York, Alfred A. Knopf, Inc. 1954ff.)
Stephenson, Carl, *Mediaeval History* ed. and rev. by Bryce Lyon (New York, Harper and Rowe, 1962ff.)
Strayer, Joseph R., and Munro, Dana C., *The Middle Ages* (New York, Appleton-Century-Crofts, 1921ff.)
Thompson, James W., and Johnson, Edgar N., *An Introduction to Medieval Europe, 300-1500* (New York, W. W. Norton & Co. Inc. 1931…)
Thorndike, Lynn, *History of Medieval Europe* (Boston, Houghton Mifflin Co., 1917ff.)

OUTLINE HISTORY OF
THE MIDDLE AGES

Introduction:
"The Middle Ages"

I. The "Middle Ages" (*c.* 400-1500 A.D.) comprise the interval from the close of classical antiquity to the dawn of modern history.

  A. The original term was derogatory, and was meant to designate a static unprogressive era.

    1. Depreciation of the Middle Ages resulted from a lack of historical knowledge concerning the period, as well as from certain prejudices.

    a. Leaders of the Renaissance, Reformation, and Age of Reason believed, respectively, in the superiority of classical Greco-Roman, early Christian, and Modern Civilization.

  B. Evaluation of the Middle Ages has been revised and greatly improved in the nineteenth and twentieth centuries.

    1. The importance of this era began to be recognized through the admiration of writers of the Age of Romanticism and the discoveries of researchers of the Age of Science.

    2. The Middle Ages are now recognized as dynamic, constructive, and formative for Western civilization.

II. Contributions of the Middle Ages include:

A. Territorial national states
B. Representative national assemblies
C. Concepts of limited and contractual government
   1. The contract theory of government and idea of popular sovereignty trace back to the Middle Ages.
   2. So does belief in limited governmental power.
D. Recognition of divinely sanctioned natural rights of individuals
E. Acceptance of the basic equality of all men and women
F. The emancipation of labor
G. Guarantees of trial by jury and freedom from arrest or punishment without due process of law
H. Romanesque, Gothic, and Renaissance architecture
I. Universities as cooperative centers of advanced studies and research
J. The conciliation of faith and reason
K. The beginnings of modern vernacular languages and literatures: French, German, English, Spanish, Italian, etc.
L. Inspired Romanesque, Gothic, and Renaissance sculptures, paintings, metalwork, woodwork, and stained glass
M. Written measured musical notation and complex polyphonic music, and simple, monodic "plain chant."

III. Subdivisions of the Middle Ages vary, but the following are common:

A. Transition from Classical Antiquity (*ca.* 300-500 A.D.)
B. Early Middle Ages (*ca.* 500-1050 A.D.)
   1. Sometimes subdivided at 843 into (a) Pre-Feudal and (b) Early Feudal.
C. High Middle Ages (*ca.* 1050-1300 A.D.)
   1. Sometimes subdivided at about 1200 into (a) Twelfth Century and (b) Thirteenth Century.
D. Later Middle Ages (*ca.* 1300-1500 A.D.)
   1. Also known as the Era of the Italian Renaissance.

IV. Readings on Medieval History include:

A. Basic Textbooks (For collation of their chapters, and ours, compare chart:)
   Ault, Warren O., *Europe in the Middle Ages* (Boston, D.C. Heath and Company, 1937ff.).

Cantor, Norman F., *Medieval History* (New York, The Macmillan Company, 1963).

Collins, Ross W., *History of Medieval Civilization in Europe* (Boston, Ginn & Co. 1936ff.).

Dahmus, Joseph H., *History of Medieval Civilization* (New York, Odyssey, 1964).

Hoyt, Robert S., *Europe in the Middle Ages* (New York, Harcourt, Brace Company, 1957ff.).

LaMonte, John L., *World of the Middle Ages* (New York, Appleton-Century-Crofts, 1949ff.).

MacKinney, Loren C., *The Medieval World* (New York, Holt, Rinehart and Winston, 1938ff.).

McGarry, Daniel D., *The Formative Middle Ages* (In preparation).

O'Sullivan, Jeremiah, and Burns, John F., *Medieval Europe* (New York, Appleton-Century-Crofts, 1943ff.).

Painter, Sidney, *History of the Middle Ages* (New York, Alfred A. Knopf, 1954ff.).

Stephenson, Carl, *Medieval History*, ed. and rev. by Bryce Lyon (New York, Harper and Row, 1962ff.).

Strayer, Joseph R., and Munro, Dana C., *The Middle Ages* (New York, Appleton-Century-Crofts, 1921ff.).

Thompson, James W., and Johnson, Edgar N., *An Introduction to Medieval Europe* (300-1500) (New York, W. W. Norton & Company, Inc. 1937ff.).

Thorndike, Lynn, *History of Medieval Europe*, (Boston, Houghton Mifflin Co., 1917ff.).

B. General Reference Works include:

Cambridge Medieval History

Catholic Encyclopedia

Encyclopedia Britannica

Encyclopedia of the Social Sciences

Paetow, Louis J. and others, *Guide to the Study of Medieval History* (New York, Crofts, 1931).

Speculum: A Journal of Medieval Studies

National Historical Reviews: American, English, French, German, etc.

PART I

ANCIENT FOUNDATIONS OF THE MIDDLE AGES

I. <u>Foundations</u> of the Middle Ages and pre-existing sources of Medieval Civilization were mainly three:
   A. <u>Roman</u>:
      Classical civilization developed by the Greeks culminated in and was transmitted by the Romans.
   B. <u>Christian</u>:
      Christianity with its New Testament evolved out of the ancient Jewish religion of the Old Testament.
   C. <u>Barbarian</u>:
      The Germans contributed the most important barbarian influence at this time. The Celts and Slavs also exerted minor influences, as did the peoples of Asia in more remote ways.
   D. <u>Medieval amalgamation</u> of these elements began with the decline of the Roman Empire and the advent of the new barbarian invasions and kingdoms.

Chapter 1

The Roman Legacy: The Roman Empire and Civilization (to 284 A.D.)

I. The Roman Legacy was one of the most important elements in Medieval (and Modern) Western civilization.

   A. Roman Territory at the height of the Empire included all the lands around the Mediterranean Sea and extended into the interior to the Rhine and beyond the Danube.

      1. Under the Republic the Romans established control of:

         a. Italy (366-264 B.C.)

         b. The Western Mediterranean after Rome defeated Carthage in the Punic Wars (264-146 B.C.):

            i. Sicily

            ii. Cisalpine Gaul (Po Valley)

            iii. Provence (Mediterranean France)

            iv. The Iberian Peninsula (whose conquest took some time more)

            v. North Africa and Egypt (another long struggle).

         c. The Eastern Mediterranean following the Punic Wars:

            i. The Balkans (Macedonia, Greece, etc.)

            ii. Most of Asia Minor

            iii. Syria and Palestine

        iv. Egypt.

    d. Gaul beyond the Alps was added by Julius Caesar.

  2. Under the Empire, (31 B.C. ff.) the Romans added:

    a. Britain

    b. Mauretania

    c. The rest of Asia Minor

    d. Dacia (temporarily)

    e. Even Arabia and Mesopotamia for a brief period.

B. <u>Government by Emperors</u> was a price the Romans paid for their far-flung dominion "over pine and palm."

  1. <u>Republican self-government</u> was inadequate for ruling Rome's vast Mediterranean and Western European Empire.

    a. Rome's senate-dominated, city-state republican constitution was unequal to the task of administration.

        i. Responsibility was indefinite and unfixed.

        ii. Terms of office were too short to provide experienced officials.

        iii. Inefficiency and extortion were common in provincial government.

        iv. Corruption and graft were rampant.

    b. Bitter class struggles plagued the Republic.

        i. While the rich became richer, the poor became poorer and more dissatisfied.

  2. <u>Transition</u> from republican to monarchical imperial government occurred in the final Pre-Christian century. (133-31 B.C.).

    a. Violent competition between Popular and Senatorial (aristocratic) parties encouraged the rise of demagogues and dictators.

        i. The Popular Party was led by the Gracchi Brothers (133-121 B.C.) and then by Marius (107-86 B.C.).

        ii. The Senatorial Party gained absolute power at the time of the dictator Sulla (82-78 B.C.).

    b. The First Triumvirate (60-49 B.C.) was a temporary compromise coalition of Pompey, Julius Caesar, and Crassus:

        i. After gaining both reputation and troops in Gaul, Caesar defeated Pompey.

    c. Julius Caesar became dictator for a time (48-44 B.C.).

        i. He initiated salutary reforms.

    d. The Second Triumvirate (43-42 B.C.) formed after Caesar's assassination, was another compromise coalition:

        i. Its members were Anthony (a lieutenant of Caesar), Octavian (Caesar's great-nephew and adopted son), and Lepidus (a wealthy general).

        ii. Anthony took the East, where he married Cleopatra and planned an independent Empire.

        iii. Octavian took the West and eventually forced a showdown in the name of the Senate.

3. Octavian became sole ruler as "Princeps" and later "Augustus," after defeating the forces of Anthony and Cleopatra at Actium (31 B.C.).

4. The Roman Empire, which succeeded the Republic, enjoyed a "Golden Age" for two centuries (27 B.C.-180 A.D.).

    a. As "Augustus" (27 B.C.-14 A.D.), Octavian enjoyed supreme executive and military powers and made his position hereditary.

    b. The remaining Julio-Claudian Emperors (14-68 A.D.) were a "motley crew" which included Tiberius, Caligula, Claudius, and Nero, with Claudius a relieving exception.

    c. Anarchy for a year (68-69 A.D.) followed Nero's assassination.

        i. The legions and their generals now learned that Emperors could be made elsewhere than in Rome, as Tacitus tells us.

    d. The Flavian line was installed by Flavius Vespasian (69-79), a former general who brought peace and quiet to Rome.

        i. He was followed by his sons: first the energetic Titus (79-81); then the unworthy Domitian (81-96).

    e. The "Good" or "Adoptive" Emperors, Nerva, Trajan, Hadrian, Antoninus Pius, and Marcus

Aurelius, ruled in relative tranquility and prosperity (96-180 A.D.).

    i. The apogee of the Empire came during this century.

  5. <u>A century of confusion</u> and decline (180-284 A.D.) followed.

    a. Much of this period was the "Era of the Barracks Emperors," when emperors were rapidly and arbitrarily made and unmade by the military.

      i. Most of the emperors in this era were ephemeral, holding only fleeting power and partial control.

      ii. The fall of the Roman Empire really began during this era.

        1) Civil war between contenders for power was the order of the day.

        2) Repeated barbarian invasions occurred.

        3) Commerce declined.

II. <u>Roman Civilization</u> was characterized by its genius for social organization, its assimilative capacity, and its practicality.

  A. Imperial government became more absolute, complex, and universal as time progressed.

    1. The Emperors became more autocratic.

      a. The Empire began as a "Dyarchy" in which Emperor and Senate theoretically shared supreme power.

      b. But the power of the Emperor grew steadily at the expense of that of the Senate.

        i. The single executive had an advantage over the plural legislative body.

        ii. Eventually the Emperor added legislative power to his supreme executive, military, and judicial authority.

      c. A large imperial bureaucracy developed.

      d. But there was a fatal flaw: The Romans never really regularized the manner of succession.

    2. Subdivisions of the Empire eventually included four great prefectures, composed of dioceses, divided into provinces, made up of *civitates*.

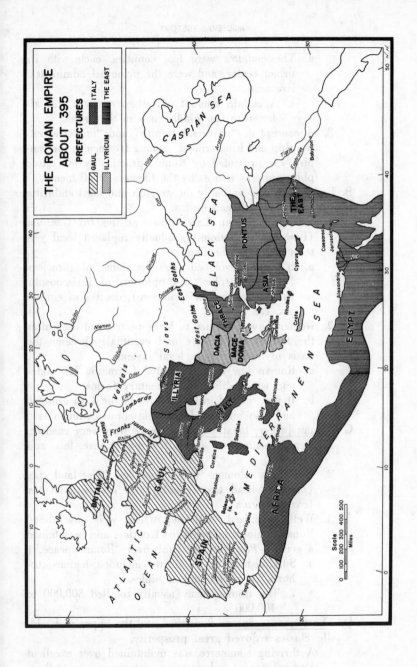

THE ROMAN EMPIRE
ABOUT 395

PREFECTURES

ITALY
THE EAST
GAUL
ILLYRICUM

Scale
0 100 200 300 400 500
Miles

        a. The *civitates* were like counties, each with its urban center, and were the principal administrative units.

           i. A certain amount of self-government was allowed to the middle class in the towns.

    3. A concept of "universal empire" and "universal citizenship and brotherhood" among freemen in the Empire was promoted by Roman practicality and Stoic philosophy as well as by the likeness of all men.

B. <u>Roman law</u> was probably the greatest and most enduring product of the Roman genius.

    1. Universal Roman Law known as the *Jus Gentium* (Law of the Nations) gradually replaced local systems of law in the Empire.

        a. It was developed by decisions of praetors (judges), replies and opinions of jurisconsults (authorities on jurisprudence), decrees of emperors, etc.

    2. Roman Law continued to be respected and used after the fall of the Empire and eventually became the basis of many modern legal systems.

        a. Roman law both infiltrated Germanic law codes and was codified in elementary forms.

        b. It was revived in fuller form in the 12th century, and also influenced canon law and common law.

C. <u>Roman justice, taxation, and defence</u> were very efficient.

    1. Roman justice was generally prompt, sure, fair, and efficient.

    2. Numerous Roman taxes included the land tax (*jugum*), head tax (*caput*), and occupational tax (*chrysargyrum*).

    3. Well organized, well equipped, well disciplined Roman legions defended the frontiers and maintained a general *Pax Romana* (universal "Roman peace.")

        a. Subdivisions of the army included legions, cohorts, centuries, and maniples.

           i. The Roman army usually totalled 300,000 to 400,000.

D. <u>The Roman economy</u> flourished and the upper and middle classes enjoyed great prosperity.

    1. A thriving commerce was maintained over excellent Roman roads and interior waterways, as well as

across the Mediterranean and its auxiliaries, such as the Black Sea.

2. The Roman Empire was "a world of cities."

    a. Great cities included Rome, Alexandria, Athens, Corinth, Carthage, and Marseilles.

        i. Rome's population may have been about a million at its greatest height.

3. The economy of the Western half of the Empire was more agricultural, whereas that of the Eastern part was more industrial and commercial.

E. Roman society was marred by much inequality and maldistribution.

  1. The greatest benefits were conferred on the upper classes, including the senatorial aristocracy along with a new class of capitalistic contractors, entrepreneurs, and financiers.

    a. Many members of the ordinary middle class enjoyed prosperity.

    b. The masses, however, in both town and country, tended to be reduced to dependence and insecurity.

  2. Roman society was also corrupted by excessive wealth and power on the one hand and extreme poverty and dependence on the other.

    a. Debauchery, drunkenness, divorce, and cruelty were common in the Empire.

    b. Garish display and lack of good taste flourished.

    c. The frivolous games and performances and the cruel encounters in the Colosseum reflected Roman debasement.

    d. The old religions had lost their hold, while Christianity was not yet securely established.

F. Roman literature, emulating the Greek, reflected a polished, lively, urbane society with cultivated sophisticated, tastes.

  1. It was passed on to the Middle Ages as the latter's literary heritage.

    a. Vergil was supreme in epic poetry with his *Aeneid*, which recounted the supposed wanderings of Aeneas and his establishment of the Roman people in Latium.

    b. In other fields of poetry the urbane Horace was

distinguished for his *Odes*; Ovid for his poems on loving and mythology; Juvenal for his cutting *Satires*; Martial for his witty *Epigrams*.

    c. In prose the grandiloquent Cicero was supreme with his *Orations* and *Essays*.

    d. Terence and Plautus composed entertaining comic drama.

    e. Roman historians included Livy whose *Decades* recounted the Roman story to the time of Augustus; Tacitus whose *Annales* and *Histories* covered the first century A.D.; and Suetonius who wrote the *Lives of the Caesars*.

  2. Latin became the learned and principal literary language of the Middle Ages in Western Europe.

G. <u>In philosophy</u>, the Romans preferred practical (applied) philosophy, or ethics.

  1. Epicureanism, with its belief in present pleasure, was favored by some, such as Epictetus.

  2. Stoicism, a preferred Roman philosophy, was advocated by such leaders as Seneca the Younger and Emperor Marcus Aurelius. It taught:

    a. The supremacy of virtue and need for unfailing constancy.

    b. The reign of reason and the sway of natural law.

    c. The universal Fatherhood of God and brotherhood of man.

H. <u>In the sciences</u> the Romans concentrated on *practical* application.

  1. The pure sciences were neglected.

    a. Uncritical dry compilations were made by such authors as Pliny the Elder.

  2. Practical sciences, such as engineering and sanitation, were stressed.

    a. Excellent construction-engineering was exemplified in Roman roads, bridges, and harbor facilities, as well as aqueducts.

    b. Public health and sanitation were promoted by governmental vigilance as well as by aqueducts and sewers, clinics and hospitals.

I. <u>In the arts</u> the Romans were more productive than original.

1. Roman architecture featured the structural use of cement and stone with arches, as well as the decorative use of Greek orders of columns and post and lintel construction.
2. Roman art was realistic and natural.

III. Readings on Roman History and Civilization include:

Boak, Arthur E., *A History of Rome to 565* A.D., (5th Edition, New York, Macmillan, 1964).

Trever, Albert A., *The Roman World* (in "History of Ancient Civilization," Vol. II) (New York, Harcourt Brace, 1939).

Chapot, Victor, *The Roman World* (New York, Knopf, 1928).

Frank, Tenney, *Economic History of Rome* (Baltimore, Johns Hopkins, 1927).

Duff, John W., *Literary History of Rome*, 2 vols. (New York, Scribner, 1927-1932).

Bailey, Cecil, ed., *Legacy of Rome* (Oxford, Clarendon, 1923).

Primary sources include the translated works of Livy, Tacitus, Suetonius, Julius Caesar, Dio Cassius, Vergil, Horace, Juvenal, Cicero, etc.

Can You Identify?

"First Triumvirate"	*chrysargyrum*
Julius Caesar	*"Pax Romana"*
"Second Triumvirate"	Vergil
Mark Anthony	Horace
Octavia	Ovid
"Augustus"	Cicero
"Adoptive Emperors"	Livy
"Barracks Emperors"	Tacitus
"Dyarchy"	Epicureanism
civitates	Stoicism
Jus Gentium	Marcus Aurelius
jugum	Seneca the Younger
caput	Pliny the Elder

Chapter 2

The Christian Heritage

I. Early Christianity arose in the Near East, spread rapidly, and eventually became dominant in the Roman Empire.
  A. The birth of Christianity occurred in Palestine in the 1st century A.D.
    1. Jesus Christ claimed to be the "Son of God," the "Messiah" or "Promised One."
      a. He preached with authority and worked miracles, the greatest of which was His Resurrection.
      b. He both preached and lived a "new law" and "new testament" of love.
      c. His message was sublime in its explanation of:
        i. God and God's concern for men
        ii. The social and individual virtues as ways of human salvation
        iii. The assurances of continued divine guidance for the Christian Church.
      d. Jesus manifested both human and divine goodness.
      e. After three years of public preaching, Jesus was convicted of blasphemy by the Jewish Sanhedrin, condemned to death for treason by the Roman Procurator, Pontius Pilate, and executed by crucifixion.
      f. According to the Apostles, Christ rose from the dead on the third day and subsequently ascended to heaven.
      g. The Gospels record Christ's life and work.
    2. The Apostles, chosen, instructed, and commissioned

by Christ, soon dispersed to "carry the good news to the ends of the earth."

a. After being persecuted in Jerusalem, the Apostles went to the major cities of the classical world.

    i. They first preached to the Jewish communities, then to the non-Jews (Gentiles) in the cities.

    ii. Peter, regarded as the head of the Apostles, went first to Antioch and later to Rome. He died as bishop of Rome.

    iii. Paul (Saul), a converted Pharisee, became the chief missionary and "Apostle of the Gentiles."

b. The Epistles and Acts record Apostolic teachings and activities.

B. The Expansion of Christianity, which grew "like a mustard seed," proceeded despite persecutions.

  1. A religious vacuum existed in the Roman world.

    a. Pagan beliefs and practices were crude, gross, confused, polytheistic, and incredible to the enlightened.

    b. Emperor worship was generally regarded as little more than a political symbol.

    c. Philosophical religions, such as Neoplatonism, lacked certainty, preciseness, and authority, as well as popular appeal.

    d. Judaism was too rigid in its requirements and too closely tied to a particular ethnic group.

    e. Eastern mystery religions, while attractive, were mythical and morally shallow.

  2. Christianity appeared to have the marks of a divinely revealed religion.

    a. Its doctrines concerning God were sublime and its moral ideals were high.

    b. It steadfastly claimed an authority handed down from its divine founder.

      i. Both Christ and the Apostles died to witness the sincerity and truth of their doctrines.

    c. Christianity assured its members of never-failing divine guidance.

d. It was certified by miracles, martyrs, and the good lives of its members.

3. <u>Persecutions</u> by the Roman government over a period of two and a half centuries failed to stop the spread of the Church.

a. It came to be an accepted principle of Roman law that "It is not permitted to be a Christian."

i. Nevertheless, governmental action against Christians was sporadic.

b. The Roman government periodically persecuted the Church.

i. There were at least nine major persecutions.

c. The first persecution was begun by Nero, who blamed the Christians for the great fire in Rome in 64 A.D.

d. The last persecutions (250 ff.) were the worst.

i. The persecution of Diocletian from 303 to 311 A.D. was the final and most severe persecution.

e. Tertullian said: "The blood of the martyrs is the seed of the Church."

C. <u>The Triumph of Christianity</u> in the Empire came in the 4th century.

1. Emperor Galerius issued an Edict of Toleration for Christians as he lay dying in 311.

a. The status of this edict became obscure after his death.

2. The Edict of Milan (313), a joint rescript of Constantine and Licinius granted definite toleration to the Christians.

3. Constantine the Great helped the Church in numerous ways.

a. He gave valuable properties to the Church, and granted exemptions and privileges to the clergy.

b. He was baptized on his deathbed (337) and had his sons raised as Christians.

4. Succeeding Emperors, including Gratian and Valentinian I, continued to favor the Christians.

5. Theodosius I the Great (d. 395) made orthodox Christianity the state religion.

a. Paganism was outlawed and pagan temples closed.

    i. Edicts of 391 and 392 sounded "the death-knell of paganism."

  b. The terms "Roman" and "Christian" were becoming synonymous by the end of the 4th century.

II. The Christian Church was an organized visible religious society.

 A. The Church was a visible society from its beginning.

  1. Initiation was by baptism and expulsion by excommunication.

  2. Christ and his Apostles referred to the Church as a living organism.

  3. The hierarchy in the Church was composed of:

   a. Bishops, who were regarded as the "Successors of the Apostles" with full power to teach, sanctify, and rule.

   b. The Bishop of Rome or "Pope," who enjoyed primacy among the other bishops as the successor of St. Peter.

   c. Presbyters—priests or elders—who held delegated and partial jurisdictional and sacramental powers as compared with the bishops.

    i. The exact meaning of "presbyters" in the New Testament is not clear: they are sometimes priests, sometimes elders, sometimes both.

   d. Deacons were chosen to supervise the social and charitable work of the church.

 B. Church and state were separate, autonomous societies.

  1. The Christian Church, as a forbidden institution, maintained a completely separate existence from the state until the 4th century.

  2. Several Popes repulsed governmental attempts to intimidate and coerce them to endorse heretical doctrines.

  3. St. Ambrose of Milan (339-397) insisted that the great Theodosius I do public penance, reminding him: "The Emperor is within, not above, the Church."

  4. Pope Gelasius I (492-96) declared to the Monophysite Emperor, Anastasius: "There are two powers ordained by God: the imperial and the priestly."

III. Christian doctrines were carefully defined and scrupulously transmitted.

    A. Doctrines and practices of the early Church included:
1. The Trinity of God: one divine nature but three persons.
2. The Divinity of Christ: a duality of natures (human and divine) in the unity of the person of the Son of God.
3. The Holy Eucharist as an offering and partaking of the body and blood of Christ, really present under the appearances of bread and wine.
    a. The Divine Liturgy or "Mass" in which the Sacrifice of Christ is mystically re-presented and the Last Supper repeated.
4. Sacraments, external signs instituted by Christ as instruments of His grace:
    a. Baptism by which one becomes a member of Christ's Mystical Body, the Church.
    b. Penance, or confession and forgiveness of sins.
    c. Reception of the Holy Eucharist (Communion).
    d. Holy Orders by which a man is given sacramental powers.
5. Faith, hope and charity: the fundamental "theological" virtues.
    a. They are called "theological" because they are directly concerned with God.
    b. Love (charity) of God and of one's fellow men in God are chief characteristics of believing, practising Christians.
6. The moral virtues: recognized as among the principal means of leading a life pleasing to God.
    a. Honesty, truthfulness, obedience, temperance, fortitude, humility, and purity were included.
7. Unity was insisted on and implemented by the sharing in the Eucharist.

    B. Heresies were doctrines contrary to those accepted by the Church at large.
1. Syncretic heresies resulted from confusing Christian doctrines with those of other religions.
    a. Manichaeism, derived from Zoroastrianism, was preached by a Persian named Manes.

            i. It taught an extreme dualism of inherently good and evil things and forces.

      b. Gnosticism was a religion whose adherents claimed a higher knowledge which revealed a dual principle of good and evil governing the world.

            i. It combined Jewish theology, oriental mysticism, and Greek philosophy.

  2. <u>Disciplinary heresies</u> differed from accepted Church practices.

      a. Novatianism denied readmission to the Church to the *lapsi* who had apostatized during persecutions.

      b. Donatism insisted that for valid sacraments it was necessary that their ministers be in the state of grace.

  3. <u>Doctrinal heresies</u> were usually Trinitarian or Christological.

      a. Monarchianism maintained that only the Father is true God.

      b. Arianism taught that Christ is only the adoptive son of God and not of one substance with the Father.

            i. Its founder was Arius, a priest of Alexandria.

      c. Nestorianism held that there are two persons as well as two natures in Christ.

            i. It was supported by the Patriarch Nestorius of Constantinople and the Syrian school.

      d. Monophysitism or Eutychianism taught that there is only one nature in Christ, the divine.

            i. Eutyches, an Alexandrian monk, was a leading early supporter, and its main strength was first in Egypt, secondly in Syria.

      e. Pelagianism, taught by the British monk Pelagius, denied original sin and the necessity of baptism and grace.

C. <u>The Fathers of the Church</u> were saintly, learned leaders who explained and defended orthodox doctrines.

  1. Orthodox doctrines were those held by the Church at large or the "universal Church" as opposed to particular sects.

      a. This orthodox Church came to be known as "Catholic" ("Ecumenical" or "Universal").

  2. The <u>Eastern Fathers</u> wrote in Greek:

    a. St. Athanasius, Archbishop of Alexandria, stoutly combatted Arianism despite great personal trials and hardships.

    b. The "Three Gregories," Saints Gregory of Nazianzen, Gregory Thaumaturgus (Miracle-worker) and Gregory of Nyssa, wrote spiritual and ascetical treatises and combatted heresy.

    c. St. John Chrysostom (the Golden-Tongued) vigorously promoted the cause of religion and virtue and opposed Arianism and Monophysitism.

    d. St. Basil the Great did likewise and prepared a Rule for Eastern monks.

3. The Western Fathers wrote in Latin, explaining orthodox doctrines, countering rising heresies, and preaching the way of Christian perfection.

    a. St. Ambrose of Milan (d. 397) composed beautiful hymns and homilies, wrote on Christian doctrines and virtues, and combatted Arianism.

    b. St. Augustine of Hippo (d. 430/31) wrote numerous works on the Trinity, Divine Grace, and other Christian beliefs.

       i. Augustine became the West's chief doctrinal authority besides the Bible.

    c. St. Jerome, a great scholar, translated the Bible from Hebrew and Greek into Latin and wrote many commentaries and letters as well.

       i. His Scriptural translation, the "Vulgate" or "Popular" one, was adopted as the official version by the Western Church.

    d. Pope St. Gregory I, the Great, wrote works of practical piety, such as his *Dialogues* (Lives of the Saints) and *Pastoral Care*.

D. Ecumenical (Universal) Councils were held from the 4th century on.

1. Ecumenical Councils condemned heresies, reaffirmed and clarified Church doctrines, and legislated to bring about further fulfillment of Christian life.

    a. They were held in the Eastern part of the Empire, where Christianity was older and stronger.

    b. They were attended by Bishops from the entire Christian world.

       c. Papal cooperation and approval was always sought and obtained.

  2. Early ecumenical councils included those of:
      a. Nicaea (325), which condemned Arianism.
      b. I Constantinople (381), which again condemned Arianism along with other heresies.
      c. Ephesus (431) which condemned Nestorianism.
      d. Chalcedon (451) which condemned Monophysitism.

IV. <u>Contributions</u> of the Christian Church to Western Society were numerous.

A. Greater meaning for life and uplifting of the human heart were supplied by Christian faith, hope, and charity.

B. Europe was one community with the Church as a nucleus, even after the barbarian "take-over."

C. Classical civilization was guarded and transmitted by the Church.

D. European society was made healthy, vigorous, and pleasant by the high moral code of Christianity.

  1. Christianity inculcated such beneficial virtues as monogamy, honesty, truthfulness, and charity.

  2. Ideological bases were provided for human dignity and rights, human equality and freedom.

V. <u>Readings</u> on Early Christianity include:

A. <u>Original Sources</u> such as:
  1. The *New Testament*, with the Gospels, the Acts of the Apostles, and the Epistles (Letters) of the Apostles.
  2. The *Patristic Writings* of both the Eastern (Greek) and Western (Latin) Fathers of the Church, available in various editions and translations.
  3. Eusebius of Caesarea, *Ecclesiastical History*, tr. C. F. Cruse (London, 1965).

B. <u>Secondary Works</u> such as:
    Hughes, Philip, *A History of the Church*, Vol. I (New York, Sheed and Ward, 1934).
    Schaff, Philip, *A History of the Christian Church*, Vols. I-III (Grand Rapids, Mich., Erdmans, 1949).
    Neill, Thomas P., and Schmandt, Raymond H., *A History of the Catholic Church* (Milwaukee, Bruce, 1957).
    Lebreton, Jules, and Zeiller, J., *History of the Primitive*

Church, 4 vols. (London, Burns, Oates, Washbourne, 1946-1948).

Hefele, Charles J., *A History of the Christian Councils From the Original Documents*, Vols. I, II, III, (Edinburgh, Clark, 1896).

Can You Identify?

Jesus Christ	Gnosticism
"Messiah"	Novatianism
Pontius Pilate	Donatism
"Gentiles"	Arianism
St. Peter	Nestorianism
St. Paul	Monophysitism
Neoplatonism	Eutyches
Tertullian	Pelagianism
Diocletian	"Fathers of the Church"
Galerius	"Catholic"
"Edict of Milan" (313)	St. Athanasius,
Constantine	The "Three Gregories"
Theodosius I	St. John Chrysostom
Bishop	St. Basil
Presbyter	St. Ambrose of Milan
Gelasius I	St. Augustine of Hippo
Holy Eucharist	St. Jerome
Sacrament	Gregory I
Holy Orders	Ecumenical Council
"heresy"	Council of Nicaea (325)
Manichaeism	Council of Chalcedon (451)

Chapter 3

Decline and Fall of
The Later Roman Empire in the West

I. <u>Factors in the decline and fall</u> of the Western Roman Empire (180-476) included:

A. <u>Political and military causes</u>:

   1. Growing absolutism made the government too dependent on the person of the emperor.

      a. Incompetent or mediocre emperors could cause great harm.

   2. Lack of popular participation in politics resulted in waning patriotism and passive indifference.

   3. The problem of the imperial succession, which was never solved, invited use of military force.

      a. No single established method for selecting the emperor existed.

      b. The Roman armies learned that they could make or unmake emperors by force.

      c. The emperor was usually a military leader, whose fortunes were closely associated with his army.

   4. Military domination of the government resulted.

      a. Roman expansion ceased and a defensive policy was inaugurated after the reign of Trajan (98-117).

      b. The frontier armies became largely autonomous under their own commanders.

      c. In times of doubt the armies often supported their own candidates for imperial office.

d. Previously the emperor ruled with the help of the army, but now the military ruled by means of the emperor.

5. A mercenary army mainly composed of barbarians developed:

   a. Barbarians were admitted into the army in increasing numbers from the time of Julius Caesar (48-44 B.C.)

   b. Both the soldiers and their commanders eventually came to be mainly foreign mercenaries.

      i. Most of them naturally lacked Roman patriotism.

   c. The soldiers who were settled on frontier lands developed more and more into "soldier-farmers."

      i. They became more interested in farming than soldiering.

   d. The army became spiritless, disorganized, and unreliable.

B. Economic Causes:

1. Poor distribution of economic profits contributed to economic decline.

   a. Wealth and profits came to be concentrated in the hands of a few.

   b. This restricted number of persons with funds cut down purchasing power and demand.

   c. It also stifled business initiative and deterred industry.

2. A stagnant economy resulted from slavery, bad distribution of profits, and unequal taxes.

   a. Large-scale industries failed to develop.

   b. Mechanization of industry was neglected.

   c. Industry and trade contracted rather than expanded.

3. The Western Roman economy, in particular, was unhealthy.

   a. It was excessively agricultural.

   b. Its industry lagged; its trade declined.

   c. The economy of many regions was self-contained.

4. Public finances became burdensome.

   a. The Roman government at first leaned heavily on spoils of war and tribute from subject peoples.

       b. But after the flow of spoils and tribute ceased, the government had to resort to heavy taxation.

5. The heavy taxation was poorly distributed.

       a. Taxation was arbitrary and tax collections followed the line of least resistance.

       b. Most of the burden fell on those least able to pay.

       c. The Senatorial class, which had the most money, failed to pay its share.

          i. The Senatorial class was largely exempt from taxation, as well as adverse to engaging in commerce.

       d. The rich escaped paying their share of taxes by the use of influence and bribery and by securing exemptions.

6. Eastward flow of gold and silver caused a shortage of coinage in the West.

       a. To obtain the products of Eastern industry, including luxury items, the West had to pay "hard cash" because of an unfavorable balance of trade.

       b. The Roman government tried to counter this drainage by fixing prices and debasing the currency.

       c. When inflation set in, people began to hoard what gold and silver they could get, further reducing the specie.

7. The latifundia system in agriculture (large estates) with slave and servile labor had paralyzing results.

       a. It forced more and more small farmers to drop out of competition.

          i. They gravitated into a position of dependency.

       b. This further aggravated poor economic distribution and diminished purchasing power and demand.

C. Social, Moral, and Cultural Causes:

1. Social maladies resulted from a class system with extremes of affluence and poverty, which tended to replace a relatively free, fluid society.

       a. As the rich acquired more wealth, the poor became poorer.

       b. Members of the Senatorial class, who frequently

possessed numerous large estates (*latifundia*), were often fabulously wealthy.

   c. Small farmers had to sell out or to seek the patronage of wealthy landholders.

      i. Only thus could they avoid mounting taxes and obtain security.

      ii. As a result they lost their freedom.

   d. The middle class declined in number and importance.

   e. Slaves and *coloni* (dependent agricultural workers) were at the bottom of the socio-economic structure.

      i. The number of such dependent workers steadily increased.

2. Moral decline resulted from many causes.

   a. The wealthy disregarded moral laws in the vain pursuit of pleasure.

   b. The very poor disregarded the same in an effort to make life bearable and escape from their destitution.

   c. The majority of the population was in a state of religious and moral transition.

      i. They no longer believed in the old pagan religious and moral codes, yet they were not fully converted to the new Christian religion and morality.

3. Cultural deterioration affected secular learning, literature, architecture, and art, which lapsed into an "iron age" of decadence.

   a. Literature became stilted, artificial, and undistinguished.

   b. Learning, like expression, was shallow.

   c. Art was uninspired.

   d. Secular architecture was also in decline.

   e. Some relief was provided by growing Christian culture.

II. The Decline and Fall of the Empire in the West occurred from 180 to 476 A.D.

   A. A chaotic century (180-284 A.D.) of violence, anarchy, and "Barracks Emperors" followed the death of Marcus Aurelius.

1. Commodus (180-193) unworthy son of the last of the "good" or "adoptive" Emperors was assassinated after a decade of misrule.
2. Various candidates for Emperor were now each supported by their own Roman armies.
   a. Stark militarism ensued.
   b. Meanwhile the Emperorship became weak and ephemeral.
      i. There were often several claimants at the same time, each holding out in a part of the Empire.
      ii. There was an average of one new imperial candidate a year.
         1) There were ninety such candidates in a hundred years.
3. The Empire seemed about to disintegrate.
   a. The barbarians overran the Rhine and Danube boundaries.
   b. Anarchy became commonplace, despite interludes of stronger rule under Emperors such as Septimus Severus (193-211) and Aurelian (270-75).
   c. Prolonged economic recession resulted.
      i. Trade, industry, and agriculture slumped.
B. The Absolute Emperors brought only partial and apparent recovery (284-395).
   1. Diocletian (284-305), a strong general, restored order and security.
      a. Diocletian used military concepts in his attempts to cure Rome's maladies.
         i. He divided the Empire into two parts, Eastern and Western, each ruled by an Augustus.
         ii. To provide for a regular succession, each Augustus had a younger Caesar appointed to rule over a part of his half and to succeed him.
         iii. Frontier armies were strengthened.
         iv. Prices and occupations were fixed.
         v. A larger bureaucracy developed.
         vi. The imperial office became absolute and was deified and surrounded by pomp and display.
   2. Constantine the Great (312-337) rose to sole supreme power.

      a. He became Augustus in the West (312) after a brief civil war.

      b. He became sole Emperor (324) by defeating Licinius.

      c. He moved his capital to Byzantium which became the "New Rome" as well as "Constantinople" (Constantine's City) (325).

      d. He tolerated, favored, and eventually joined the Christian Church.

          i. He raised his children as Christians.

      e. He continued and extended the reforms and control of Diocletian.

3. Constantius (336-361) eventually emerged as the sole supreme survivor among Constantine's sons.

      a. Constantius favored Arianism and exiled orthodox bishops.

4. Julian the Apostate (361-63) forsook Christianity and attempted to restore paganism.

      a. He did not meet with success.

5. Valentinian I (364-375) ruled the Western Empire while his brother Valens ruled in the East.

      a. He was succeeded by Gratian and Valentinian II.

6. Theodosius I the Great (379-395) established political and religious unity.

      a. He restored Roman rule in the Eastern Empire by quieting the Goths.

      b. Theodosius helped to restore unity and orthodoxy in the Church by sponsoring the ecumenical Council of (I) Constantinople (381).

      c. He outlawed public paganism in decrees of 391 and 392, which came to be known as "the Death-knell of paganism."

C. The Fall of the Roman Empire in the West now occurred (395-476).

  1. Weak Emperors shared power with their leading generals (395-455).

      a. Honorius who ruled in the West (395-423) retreated to the security of Ravenna.

          i. His Vandal general, Stilicho, restrained the Visigoths until he was killed at the command of the suspicious Honorius.

       ii. The Visigoths and other barbarians now overran most of the West.

    b. Valentinian III (423-455) also tried to rule from Ravenna.

       i. His mother, Honoria, managed most of the affairs of state.

       ii. His general, Aetius, defeated the Huns at Chalons (451).

       iii. The deluded Valentinian had Aetius killed (454), but was himself assassinated the following year.

  2. <u>Germanic generals</u> came to rule the Western Empire with ephemeral emperors as their puppets (455-476).

    a. Germanic generals and kings dominated the West (455-476).

       i. The Germanic nations outside of Italy now became independent.

       ii. Nominal Emperors in Italy were puppets of Germanic generals.

    b. Ricimer was ascendant in Italy and was followed by Orestes.

    c. Odoacer finally deposed the last Emperor, young Romulus Augustulus, and ended the Empire in the West (476).

       i. He sent the imperial insignia to the Eastern Emperor Zeno.

       ii. He pretended to rule as Zeno's lieutenant, but was actually independent.

III. <u>Readings</u> on the Later Roman Empire include:

Katz, Solomon, *The Decline of Rome and the Rise of Mediaeval Europe* (Ithaca, N.Y., Cornell, 1961) (paper).

Arragon, Reginald F., *The Transition From the Ancient to the Medieval World* (New York, Holt, 1936) (paper).

Lot, Ferdinand, *The End of the Ancient World and Beginnings of the Middle Ages*, tr. P. and M. Leon (New York, Harper, 1961) (paper).

Bury, John B., *History of the Later Roman Empire.* . . . (A.D. 395-565), 2 vols. (New York, Dover, 1958) (paper).

Salvian, *On the Government of God*, tr. Eva M. Sanford (New York, Columbia, 1930). A priest describes the moral ailments of the Later Empire.

Can You Identify?

Senatorial class	Theodosius I
coloni	Honorius
"Barracks Emperors"	Stilicho
Commodus	Valentinian III
"Absolute Emperors"	Honoria
Diocletian	Aetius
Constantine	Ricimer
Constantius	Odoacer (Odovacar)
Julian the Apostate	Zeno
Valentinian I	476
Valens	

Chapter 4

The Germanic Barbarians

I. <u>The Barbarians</u> contributed a third element to Medieval History.

A. <u>Barbarian territory</u> comprised all Europe beyond the Empire.

1. Germanic tribes held the lands between the Rhine and the Vistula, the Danube and the Don Rivers.

2. Slavic tribes were located beyond the Vistula and the Don Rivers.

3. A "Celtic fringe" remained free in Britanny and in the British Isles, except Britain (later England).

B. <u>Tacitus' "Germania"</u> is our principal source concerning the early Germans (written about 98 A.D.)

1. Tacitus stressed the good qualities of the Germans in opposition to what he felt were contemporary Roman defects.

2. He described the Germans as they were some three centuries before the great invasions.

3. Julius Caesar also provided information concerning the early Germans.

C. <u>The Germanic Barbarians</u> were the immediate neighbors of the Empire.

1. Physically the early Germans were a vigorous, hardy, warlike, Indo-European Aryan people.

a. They were apparently tall, dolichocephalic (long-headed), and fair.

2. Economically they were in a stage of barbarism transitional to civilization.

    a. They were partly pastoral, partly agricultural.
       i. They also engaged much in hunting and fishing.
    b. They were familiar with the use of iron, out of which they made tools and weapons.
    c. They had horses and often wagons.
    d. The coastal Germans, such as the Saxons and Danes, were daring, skilful seafarers.

3. Politically the early Germans were tribal, although they occasionally formed confederations for military purposes.
    a. The folk had two types of chiefs:
       i. Sacred hereditary chiefs had limited power.
       ii. Elected military chiefs led the folk during war with almost absolute power.
    b. Tribal assemblies, composed of the warriors, dealt with public affairs involving the tribe.
    c. The *comitatus* consisted of a sworn group of fellow warriors, bound by oath to their chief.
       i. Warfare was a favorite occupation.

4. Justice was administered by the tribal or village assembly.
    a. Compurgation (oaths in support of a person by "oath-helpers") and ordeals were resorted to in case of doubt.
    b. Fines were the most common form of punishment.
       i. In case of injury or death the *wergeld* (man-money) was shared by the offended or his survivors.

5. Polytheistic paganism was the religion of the early Germans.
    a. They worshipped natural forces and mythical deities.
    b. They had special reverence for white horses and the prophetical sense of women.

6. Their moral code was high in certain respects.
    a. They insisted on honesty.
    b. They were monogamous.
    c. They respected women and sexual purity.
    d. On the other hand, they had little restraint in gambling, drinking, anger, and fighting.

II. <u>Roman Influences</u> had modified the Germanic barbarians in many ways by the 4th century A.D.

   A. <u>Mutual contacts</u> of Germans and Romans prior to the great invasions were numerous.

      1. Incursions of Germanic barbarians into the Empire occurred several times prior to the great invasions (Volkerwanderung).

         a. Germans were probably among the invading Cimbri and Teutones of the 2nd century B.C.

         b. They competed unsuccessfully with Julius Caesar for Gaul in the 1st century B.C.

         c. They repelled Roman efforts to expand beyond the Rhine.

            i. In the great German victory of the Teutoberg Forest (9 A.D.) they destroyed three Roman legions.

         d. Whenever the Empire became weak in the 2nd, 3rd, and 4th centuries, the Germans invaded its provinces.

      2. Peaceful entry of Germanic barbarians into the Empire occurred in various ways.

         a. Germans were used in Roman armies in ever-increasing numbers.

         b. Whole tribes were accepted as *foederati* (allies) and given lands in return for their promise to help defend the frontiers.

         c. Germans also came into the Empire as laborers, *coloni* (serfs), and occasional slaves.

   B. <u>Roman influences</u> spurred German development in various ways.

      1. The Germans united into "nations" to resist the Romans as well as to compete with each other.

         a. They accepted permanent kings for similar reasons.

      2. They improved their military organization and discipline.

         a. They bettered their strategy.

         b. They increased their body armor.

      3. German trade and industry were expanded and improved.

      a. Roman coins came into common circulation among the Germans.

  4. The East Germans were converted to Christianity.

      a. But their Christianity was of the heretical Arian variety.

      b. The West Germans, however, remained pagan.

  5. The Christianized East Germans, such as the Goths, now began to become civilized.

      a. They acquired an alphabet and the beginnings of a literature.

III. <u>Other Barbarians in Europe</u> included the Indo-European Slavs, Balts, and Celtic fringe, together with occasional Mongoloid invaders.

  A. The Slavs were originally located in East-Central Europe.

    1. Their original home seems to have been in the vicinity of the Pripet Marshes (Southeast Poland and West Russia).

      a. Slavic expansion was persistent, if unspectacular.

      b. Three divisions of Slavs existed by the 6th Century A.D.:

        i. West Slavs (Poles, Czechs, Wends, etc.)

        ii. Southern Slavs (Serbs, Croats, etc.)

        iii. Eastern Slavs (Russians).

      c. The Eastern Slavs had settlements along the rivers of Russia, and carried on some trade with the Black Sea and Mediterranean peoples.

    2. The Slavic cultural level was below that of the early Germans and Celts.

      a. This was mainly because they were more peripheral and landlocked with respect to Mediterranean civilization.

      b. The language of the Slavs was Indo-European; they were agricultural and pastoral; and they had the use of iron.

  B. <u>The Celtic Fringe,</u> unruled by the Romans, was located in Ireland, Scotland, Wales, and parts of Brittany.

    1. The Celts were more advanced.

    2. They were politically disunited but one in their religion.

    3. They had bards and Druids and considerable lore.

   4. They respected knowledge and were fond of poetry and art.
   5. Their conversion to Christianity began in the 4th century with the missionary labors of Sts. Palladius and Patrick.
C. <u>Miscellaneous barbarians</u> included:
   1. The backward Balts, located along the eastern shores of the Baltic Sea.
      a. The Balts spoke an Indo-European language.
   2. Mongoloid immigrants who came into Europe from Asia through the Ural Gateway (to the south of the Urals), from time to time.
      a. Some settled in parts of Russia.
      b. Others moved westward.
         i. A common route was via the territory to the north of the Black Sea and then into Danubian lands.
            a) The Huns came by this route in the later 4th century A.D.
            b) So did the later Avars and Magyars.
      c. Mongoloid immigrants eventually were absorbed into Indo-European speaking Caucasoid peoples.

IV. <u>Readings</u> on the Barbarians include:

Coon, Carlton S., *The Races of Europe* (New York, Macmillan, 1939).

The Cambridge Medieval History, Volumes I and II (which have articles on various barbaric neighbors and invaders of the Empire).

Hodgkin, Thomas, *Italy and Her Invaders*, 8 vols. in 9 (Oxford, Clarendon, 1885-1899).

Tacitus, *Germania* (various translations and editions, including paperback).

Can You Identify?

Tacitus	*comitatus*
Germania	compurgation
Germanic Barbarians	*wergeld*
dolichocephalic	*foederati*

"nations" (early Germanic)   "Celtic fringe"
Slavs   Balts
Eastern Slavs   Mongoloid

PART II

THE EARLY MIDDLE AGES
(Ca. 400-1050)

I. The Early Middle Ages were an era of turbulence and readjustment.

   A. Political change and instability prevailed.
      1. Numerous Germanic and Slavic states replaced the old universal Roman Empire.
         a. Organization into territorial or "national" states prevailed.
         b. Most of these states were not permanent, as they were overthrown or absorbed in new combinations.
         c. Far-flung Byzantine, Moslem, and Carolingian Empires existed for a time.
      2. Warfare and violence became the order of the day.
         a. The barbarian invasions of the fifth and sixth centuries were succeeded by new invasions of Moslems, Magyars, Northmen, and others.
         b. Wars between states and civil wars were commonplace.
      3. Feudalism emerged as a compromise between Roman unity and Germanic particularism, whose chief service was military.

   B. Retrogression characterized most Western European institutions.
      1. The economy subsided to an agricultural, near subsistence level.

    2. Social dependence (serfdom) became widespread and town life waned.

    3. The Church became partly feudalized and the clergy partly secularized.

      a. Still the Church remained the main unifying civilizing force in Europe.

    4. Culturally, this was, to some extent, the "Dark Age."

  C. Ascendancy of the East was a feature of this period.

    1. The Eastern Mediterranean world of the Byzantines and the Moslems was much more advanced than the West.

    2. But the West began to recover towards the end of the period.

II. Readings on the Early Middle Ages include:

Burns, Cecil D., *The First Europe . . . 400-800* (New York, Norton, 1948).

Dawson, Christopher, *The Making of Europe* (New York, Macmillan, 1932).

Deanesly, Margaret, *History of Early Medieval Europe, 476-911*, (London, Methuen, 1956).

Lot, Ferdinand, *End of the Ancient World and Beginning of the Middle Ages*, (New York, Knopf, 1931).

Moss, Henry St. L. B., *Birth of the Middle Ages* (London, Oxford U., 1935).

Sullivan, Richard E., *Heirs of the Roman Empire* (Ithaca, New York, Cornel U., 1960).

Wallace-Hadrill, John M., *The Barbarian West, 400-1000* (London, Hutchinson, 1952).

Chapter 5

The Barbarian Invasions

I. <u>Barbarian invasions</u> of the Roman Empire, known as "the Great *Volkerwanderung*" took place from the 4th to the 6th centuries.

A. <u>Causes</u> of the Barbarian Invasions included:
   1. Attraction by the Roman Empire's fame, wealth, and luxuries.
   2. Prospects of being supported as defenders and rulers on Roman lands.
   3. Decline of the Roman Empire.
      a. Weakness of its defences and government.
      b. Military impotence of the Roman population.
   4. Pressures of other barbarians.
   5. Growing military strength and knowledge of the barbarians.

B. <u>General features</u> of the great invasions included:
   1. All invaders, except the Huns, were of the Germanic race.
   2. The number of invading barbarians was small as compared to that of native Roman subjects.
   3. Apathy of most of the Roman population toward the outcome.
   4. Desire of the Germans to "enjoy rather than destroy" the Empire.
      a. Their ambition was to be accepted as privileged *foederati* of the Empire.
         i. The latter were accepted allies, occupying, ruling, and defending critical territories.

     5. Composite nature of the invading peoples.
       a. They were coalitions of tribes who considered themselves one "nation."

C. <u>Peaceful penetration</u> occurred, as well as forcible occupation.
     1. Some barbarians entered the Empire as workers.
     2. The Roman army came to be composed mainly of Germanic barbarians.
     3. Entire German tribes were occasionally admitted as *foederati*. (See above).
       a. This was often after some show of force.

D. <u>The Huns</u> set in motion the Barbarian Invasions.
     1. The Huns were Mongoloid barbarians from Asia.
       a. They may have been descendants of the barbarians against whom the Chinese built their Great Wall.
     2. The Huns gradually moved westward, and appeared north of the Black Sea in the 370's.
       a. They overran the Ostrogoths who joined their horde.
     3. Pannonia (modern Hungary) on the upper middle Danube became the Hunnic base.
       a. The Huns dominated surrounding peoples and exacted tribute from the Roman Empire.

II. <u>The Visigoths</u>, who were the trailblazers of the great Invasions, fled before the Huns and obtained admittance to the Empire in 376.

A. <u>The Balkans</u> were the first stopping place of the Visigoths.
     1. The onslaught of the Huns set the Visigoths in motion.
       a. The Visigoths appealed to the Eastern Emperor Valens for admittance into the Balkans.
       b. They were allowed to settle south of the Danube as *foederati* (376).
       c. The Roman officials appointed to care for them treated the Visigoths so shabbily that they revolted.
     2. At Adrianople (378) the Visigoths badly defeated the Eastern Roman army.

      a. Emperor Valens was killed.

      b. The value of heavy cavalry as a striking force was demonstrated by the Goths.

      c. Adrianople marked:

         i. The beginning of the great Invasions.

         ii. The beginning of the end of Roman military superiority.

         iii. Transition to the ascendance of cavalry in warfare.

   3. Theodosius I, the Great, finally quieted the riotous Visigoths.

      a. He admitted many into the Roman army.

      b. He defeated some.

      c. He reestablished the rest as *foederati* in the Eastern Balkans.

B. The Visigothic westward movement began in the early 5th century.

   1. The Eastern Emperor Arcadius sent the restless Visigoths into Illyricum (399).

      a. Located in modern Yugoslavia, Illyricum was a jumping-off place for Italy.

      b. Alaric, the ambitious Visigothic leader, was made Master of Soldiers in Illyricum.

   2. Stilicho, able Vandal general in the West, repeatedly repelled the Visigoths from Italy.

      a. But the Western Emperor Honorius had Stilicho slain for supposed treason (408).

   3. Italy was now invaded by the Visigoths, who sacked Rome (410).

      a. Alaric died in southern Italy, (411), and was succeeded by his brother, Athaulf.

   4. Athaulf (411-415) led the Visigoths into Southwestern Gaul and then into Spain.

C. Southwestern Gaul and Spain became the Visigothic Kingdom.

   1. Southwestern Gaul was assigned to the Visigoths as *foederati* after they reconquered much of Spain for the Romans.

   2. Spain was taken by the Visigoths for themselves after 455.

3. Toulouse continued to be the Visigothic capital till 507.
   a. The Visigoths were then expelled from South-western Gaul by the Franks.
4. The Visigothic Kingdom was confined to Spain with minor exceptions after 507.

III. The Vandals established a Kingdom in North Africa and gained control of the Western Mediterranean Sea.

A. Gaul and Spain first experienced the Vandal scourge.
   1. Gaul was ravaged by the Vandals, accompanied by Alans and Suevi (407-409).
   2. Spain was next invaded by the Vandals, Alans, and Suevi (409ff.).
      a. Much of Spain was reconquered for the Romans by the Visigoths.
B. North Africa was invaded by the Vandals in 429.
   1. Gaiseric (Genseric) led the invasion of North Africa, apparently at the invitation of the disgruntled Roman governor, Boniface.
   2. North Africa was conquered by the Vandals on their own, after which they were accepted by the Roman government.
   3. The Western Mediterranean Sea came under Vandal naval control.
      a. Their fleet was based at Carthage.
      b. Several of the leading islands of the Western Mediterranean were taken.
      c. Rome was sacked by the Vandals in 455.
         i. The widowed Empress and her daughters were carried off to Africa.
      d. An Eastern Roman fleet together with Western naval elements was defeated by the Vandal navy in 468.

IV. The Huns made an unsuccessful bid for the Empire in the mid 5th century.

A. Gaul was invaded by the Huns led by Attila in 451.
   1. Attila claimed to be intervening on behalf of princess Honoria, who had foolishly appealed for his help.

2. At Chalons (451), the Huns were defeated by a composite army of Germans and Romans led by Aetius.

B. Italy was next invaded by the terrible Huns (452).

1. Rome was spared after the intervention of a Roman delegation headed by Pope Leo I.

   a. Attila was ill and his army plague ridden.

   b. Superstition played a part.

   c. Papal prestige was enhanced by the incident.

C. The end of the Huns as a power came after the death of Attila (453).

1. The Hunnic kingdom now disintegrated.

V. Italy was a magnet for many barbarian groups.

A. Germanic generals came into control of Italy after 455.

1. Ricimer was an Emperor-maker (456-472).

2. Odovacar (Odoacer) ruled Italy as a nominal lieutenant of the Eastern Emperor Zeno (476-490).

B. The Ostrogoths obtained control of Italy in the early 490's.

1. Earlier locations of the Ostrogoths had been, successively: Southern Russia, North of the Black Sea, Pannonia, and the Eastern Balkans.

2. The Eastern Emperor Zeno sent the Ostrogoths westward under their leader Theodoric (488).

3. Italy was taken by the Goths (489-493) through conquest, diplomacy, and treachery.

4. Theodoric the Great (493-526) ruled Italy wisely.

   a. He respected Roman civilization and the Catholic Church although he was a German and Arian.

C. The Lombards took much of Italy from the recently victorious Byzantines (568ff.).

1. The Lombard invasion came in 568, only 14 years after the Byzantines had completed their conquest of Italy (534-554).

2. Lombard conquests in Italy included most of Northern Italy and much of the interior of central Italy.

   a. Lombard holdings included the Po Valley,

which came to be known as "Lombardy," in
addition to the Marches of Friuii, Verona, and
Tuscany, and the Duchies of Spoleto and Bene-
ventum.

b. The Lombards had little respect for Roman
civilization and religion.

    i. They were called "Unspeakables" by the Ro-
mans.

3. The Byzantines retained possession of coastal
strongholds and Southern Italy and Sicily.

a. They could do this because they had control of
the sea.

b. Byzantine holdings included Naples, Rome,
Genoa, Venice, Ravenna, and the Pentapolis.
with adjacent territories as well as southern
Italy and Sicily.

VI. Gaul was invaded by several barbarian groups.

A. Various barbarians first parcelled out Gaul among
themselves.

1. The Visigoths took over Southwestern Gaul as *foederati* of the Romans.

2. The Ostrogoths came into temporary control of
coastal Mediterranean Gaul east of the Rhone
River.

3. The Burgundians were settled in the Savoy region
as *foederati* by Aetius.

a. They took over most of the Rhone-Saône Valley
above Provence after 455.

4. The Alemanni expanded across the Upper Rhine
into former Roman territories.

B. The Franks settled in northern Gaul and eventually
conquered the whole of Gaul.

1. The Salian Franks from across the Lower (Northern) Rhine River were settled in Northwestern
Gaul as *foederati* by Emperor Julian (361-3).

a. They further expanded their holdings during
the confusion of the 5th century.

2. The Ripuarian Franks from across the Middle
Rhine invaded the territory around Cologne (407).

3. Clovis (481-511), a strong Salian King, united the
Franks and conquered most of Gaul.

VII. <u>Britain</u> was attacked and eventually overrun by barbarians in the 5th century.

    A. <u>Celts and Picts,</u> warlike barbarians, along insular frontiers, first invaded after the withdrawal of the Roman legions.

    B. <u>Germanic Angles, Saxons, and Jutes</u> eventually conquered Britain.

        1. They seem to have been first invited in as helpers against the Picts and Scots.

        2. Roman civilization was almost completely wiped out in Britain.

VIII. <u>Readings</u> on the Barbarian Invasions include:

Hodgkin, Thomas, *Italy and Her Invaders*, 8 vols. in 9 (Oxford, Clarendon, 1885-1899).

Villari, Pasquale, *The Barbarian Invasions* of Italy, 2 vols. (London, T. Unwin, 1913).

Hayes, Carlton, *Introduction to the Sources Relating to the Germanic Invasions* (New York, Columbia University, 1909).

Pertinent chapters in *The Cambridge Medieval History*, Volumes I and II, and in (already) recommended books on the Early Middle Ages, including those by Margaret Deansley, Cecil D. Burns, H. S. L. Moss, J. M. Wallace-Hadrill, and Ferdinand Lot.

Can You Identify

Volkerwanderung	Huns
Pannonia	Attila
Visigoths	Chalons (451)
Adrianople (378)	Theodoric
Arcadius	Lombards
Illyricum	Burgundians
Alaric	Alemanni
Athaulf	Franks
Toulouse	Salian Franks
Vandals	Clovis
Gaiseric	Picts
455	Angles

Chapter 6

The Early Germanic Kingdoms (c. 500-700) Especially Merovingian Frankland

I. <u>Germanic Kingdoms</u> replaced the old Roman Empire in the West (*ca.* 500-700).

   A. <u>The Vandal Kingdom</u> in North Africa lasted for a century (*ca.* 429-533).
      1. Gaiseric (Genseric), its founder (428-477), was a strong ruler.
         a. For some time the Vandal navy controlled the Western Mediterranean.
      2. The Kingdom was soon torn by internal strife, aggravated by the religious question.
         a. The Vandals were Arians amidst a predominantly Catholic population.
      3. The Vandal Kingdom was overthrown in 533 by the Byzantine general Belisarius.

   B. <u>The Visigothic Kingdom</u> in Spain lasted for two and a half centuries.
      1. At first it included Southwestern Gaul and had its capital at Toulouse.
         a. Spain was acquired after 455.
         b. The Visigoths were expelled from Aquitaine by the Franks in 507.
      2. The Visigothic Kingdom in Spain was loosely organized and turbulent.
         a. A few strong rulers provided temporary periods of brilliance.

        b. Church influence was strong after the conversion of the Visigoths to Catholicism (587 ff.).

           i. The Councils of Toledo were both ecclesiastical and secular.

    3. Visigothic rule was eventually overthrown by the Moslems (711-718).

C. The Burgundians built up a short-lived kingdom in Southeastern Gaul in the Rhone-Saône Valley in the fifth century.

    1. It was absorbed by the Franks in 532.

D. The Ostrogoths ruled Italy for half a century (490-554).

    1. Theodoric the Great (490-526) gave the Italians a respite of comparative peace, prosperity, and security.

        a. Romans and Goths lived side by side in harmony during most of his reign.

           i. The Romans retained their own laws, courts. and administrative offices.

           ii. Goths were tried by their own courts under their own laws.

           iii. Suits involving Goths and Romans were tried in mixed courts.

           iv. Similar duality and reciprocity existed in other fields.

        b. Theodoric was friendly to Roman institutions and tried to restore Italy to its former glory.

           i. He fostered agriculture and helped to bring more land under cultivation.

           ii. He kept up the roads and maintained the aqueducts.

           iii. Cities were ornamented by the preservation of old monuments and the erection of new ones.

    2. After Theodoric (526 ff.) the Ostrogothic kingdom became weak, and divided.

        a. Theodoric's daughter, Amalsantha, was overthrown by her ungrateful cousin Theodahad.

        b. Civil conflict ensued.

    3. Classical culture was preserved and, to some extent, transmitted under Theodoric.

        a. Cassiodorus was a great intellectual leader.

           i. He was a leading minister for successive Ostrogothic kings.

          ii. He cultivated the art of letter writing.

         iii. He wrote a great "History of the Goths," which has been lost.

         iv. After his retirement from public life, Cassiodorus founded monasteries wherein he encouraged learning.

             1) His *Institutes of Divine and Secular Learning* provided a program of educational readings, religious and classical, for his monks.

             2) Cassiodorus also fostered the copying of manuscripts as a regular occupation of his monks.

    b. Boethius, another of Theodoric's ministers, also promoted learning and undertook to translate all of Aristotle and Plato.

           i. Boethius actually translated and commented on most of Aristotle's *Organon*, and so made available Aristotle's logic in Latin.

          ii. Boethius also composed various treatises on the liberal arts.

         iii. While in prison, he composed his famous work, *On the Consolation of Philosophy*.

  4. The Byzantines now conquered Italy.

    a. Belisarius invaded Italy in 534 to restore it to the Byzantine Empire.

           i. The Goths now deposed the weak Theodahad and replaced him with the able Witigis.

    b. When Witigis was taken prisoner, the daring Totila was elected and resumed resistance.

    c. The strenuous struggle known as the "Gothic Wars" lasted twenty years (until 554).

           i. The Goths were finally subdued.

          ii. The peninsula was left in a state of exhaustion.

E. The Lombards entered Italy in 568, filling a partial void left by the overthrow of the Ostrogothic kingdom and growing Byzantine weakness.

  1. Lombard conquests included most of Northern Italy (the Po Valley: "Lombardy") and parts of central Italy.

       a. The Lombards were the least civilized, cruelest people Italy had experienced since the Huns.

  2. The Lombard Kingdom in Italy was loosely organized.

       a. Shortly after the Lombards invaded Italy, their King, Alboin, was murdered.

       b. For a short while (574-584) the kingship was suspended.

       c. The kingship was revived by Authari.

       d. Strong kings such as Agilulf, Liutprand, Aistulf, and Desiderius, appeared from time to time.

       e. Lombard holdings were divided into numerous, often virtually independent, dukedoms.

  3. The Byzantines retained possession of much of Italy.

       a. Included were the heel and toe of the peninsula, together with Naples, Rome, Genoa, Venice, Ravenna, and surrounding territories.

       b. The Byzantine fleet supplied and defended these areas.

       c. Italy was to remain a divided country until the 19th century.

  4. Papal political power grew partly as a result of the hostility of the Lombards and the weakness of the Byzantines.

       a. The Byzantine exarch at Ravenna was unable to protect imperial holdings in Italy.

       b. Solicitude for Rome and the native Italians devolved upon the Pope.

       c. Papal leadership led to growth of the notion of a papal state.

          i. Political independence was very suitable for Papal leadership in the universal Church.

       d. Charlemagne overthrew Lombard rule in Italy in 774 in response to a Papal plea.

II. The Kingdom of the Franks became the leading Germanic Kingdom.

  A. The Merovingian Franks established the strongest, most permanent Germanic state.

    1. Before Clovis (prior to 481) the Franks were still divided into two groups, Salian and Ripuarian, each composed of smaller states ruled by kinglets.

      a. The Franks were originally located beyond the Rhine from the North Seas to the region south of Cologne.

      b. With the collapse of imperial defences (406 ff.) the Franks also occupied adjoining imperial territories.

         i. The Salians occupied what is now the Low Countries and northern France.

        ii. The Ripuarians occupied both sides of the Rhine around Cologne.

      c. The Non-Frankish Alemanni were farther to the south, up river.

         i. They, too, came to straddle the Rhine.

2. <u>Clovis</u> (481-511) succeeded in obtaining control of much of Western Europe, including most of Gaul and Western Germany.

      a. Clovis was the strong, unscrupulous kinglet of the Tournai Franks.

      b. By various means, including warfare, deception, and diplomacy, Clovis united all the Franks under his sole rule.

      c. He took the valley of the Seine from the Romano-Gauls.

         i. In 486 he defeated Syagrius, the Roman general who held the area around Paris and Soissons.

      d. In 496 Clovis obtained much territory and secured his flank by defeating the Alemanni in the Rhine Valley south of Cologne.

3. <u>Conversion</u> of the Franks to orthodox Christianity followed the conversion of Clovis (496).

      a. Clovis' wife Clothilda, a Catholic Christian, prayed persistently for him.

      b. The conversion of Clovis was partly the result of a vow made during the crucial battle of Tolbiac (496) with the Alemanni.

      c. The conversion was also a wise political move calculated to win the loyalty of the Romano-Gauls.

      d. Some 3,000 Frankish warriors were baptized with Clovis at Reims in 496.

4. <u>Southwestern Gaul</u> was now annexed by Clovis.
   a. He used his Catholicism to muster general support for a "crusade" against the Arian Visigoths.
   b. Clovis drove the Visigoths out of southwestern Gaul in 507.
   c. In Gaul, only the Mediterranean coastal territories of Septimania and Provence, together with Burgundy, now remained outside Frankish control.
5. <u>The Sons of Clovis</u> (511-561) rounded out Frankish realms.
   a. When Clovis died in 511 he divided his realms among his four sons.
   b. The sons of Clovis continued Frankish expansion by taking Burgundy, Provence, Thuringia, and Bavaria.
   c. Chlotar I succeeded in reuniting the kingdom briefly (558-561).
6. Civil conflict, led by rival queens Fredegonda and Brunehilda, ensued after 561.
7. The last strong Merovingians were Clothar II and Dagobert (d. 639).
8. "Do-Nothing Kings" (*Rois-Faineants*) is a name given to the final Merovingians (639-751).
   a. They lived in idleness and dissipation.
   b. The real power was held by shrewd Mayors of the Palace.

III. <u>Merovingian Civilization</u> exemplified civilization in the Early Germanic Kingdoms, wherein diverse elements co-existed.

   A. <u>Government</u> was composed of both Roman and Germanic elements.
      1. <u>The Merovingian Monarchy</u> was a contrast of opposites.
         a. The king claimed autocratic power but was checked by the fear of his more powerful nobles.
         b. The office of the monarch was partly hereditary, partly elective; the magnates elected the king, but their choice was limited to the royal family and usually to the eldest son.

2. <u>Administration</u> of the central government was carried out by officials of the royal household.
   a. Among these were the Seneschal, Marshall, and Constable.
   b. The Mayor of the Palace was the most important personage.
      i. The mayor, an adaptation from late Roman times, was virtual prime minister.
   c. The popular Assemblies lapsed, except as means of military mobilization.
3. <u>Local authority</u> was vested in counts, dukes, and bishops.
   a. The count ruled over an area formerly designated by the Romans as a *civitas*.
      i. The *civitas* was usually a territory previously inhabited by a tribe.
      ii. The count had full governmental power in his area.
      iii. He presided over courts, administered justice, collected fines, and mustered and led military forces.
   b. The duke was military leader of a region composed of several counties grouped together for purposes of warfare.
   c. Counts and dukes received no salaries, but supported themselves from part of the revenues of government and from the great estates which they possessed and administered.
   d. The bishop was often chief officer in the town.
      i. Major cities had become episcopal sees during the Empire.
         1) This helped keep them from almost complete abandonment.
   e. Local lords became more and more powerful.
      i. The central government found it difficult to cope with them.
      ii. The power of the magnates seriously rivalled that of the king.
4. <u>Governmental finance</u> was mainly agrarian.
   a. It became a principle that the king should "live off his own" rather than rely on taxes.

   i. Royal estates, known as the *fisc*, were the chief source of royal revenue.

   ii. Direct taxes, such as the Roman *capitatio* and *iugum*, fell by the wayside.

   iii. A few indirect taxes remained.

  5. <u>Law</u> was originally personal and multiple.

   a. Different systems of law originally governed the native Romans and the Germans.

    i. The Romans followed Roman law as found in simple codes such as those of Theodosius II and Alaric II.

    ii. The Germanic groups each followed their own customary national or tribal laws.

     1) These were codified at early dates.

     2) Eventually the personal systems coalesced into territorial systems such as the *Fuero Juzgo* of the Visigoths.

B. <u>Merovingian life</u> was simple.

  1. <u>Germanic justice</u> was crude.

   a. It was ordinarily administered by courts consisting of fellows of the accused.

   b. In cases of doubt, oaths, compurgation, duels, and ordeals were invoked.

    i. These relied on a divine judgment in favor of the innocent.

   c. Fines including blood money (*wergelds* or man-money) were commonly used as a way of obtaining satisfaction for injuries, including manslaughter.

  2. <u>The economy</u> declined to an agrarian, subsistence level.

   a. Commercial decline was promoted by civil wars, Byzantine decline, and growing Moslem ascendance in the Mediterranean.

   b. Industry was at a low ebb.

    i. Craftsmanship deteriorated.

   c. Agriculture was the chief occupation.

  3. <u>Society</u> was becoming stratified into three classes:

   (1) Wealthy, governing, landholding aristocracy

   (2) Dependent serfs, whose number was increasing

   (3) Clergy who were a privileged class apart.

4. The Church was very important and influential.
   a. Bishops were the chief spokesmen and officials of
      the native Roman population.
   b. After the conversion of the Germans to orthodox
      Christianity, the Bishops became leading advisers,
      representatives of rulers.
   c. The German kings often controlled episcopal ap-
      pointments.
5. Culture also declined.
   a. Illiteracy became the rule among the laity.
   b. The clergy, in general, were poorly educated.
   c. Literature generally lapsed.
   d. Art and architecture became crude.

IV. Readings on the Early Germanic Kingdoms include:
   A. General:
      Wallace-Hadrill, John M., *The Barbarian West* (London,
         Hutchinsons, 1952).
      Articles in *The Cambridge Medieval History*, Volume II,
         and in general works on the *Early Middle Ages*.
   B. Merovingian Gaul:
      Dill, Samuel, *Roman Society in Gaul in the Merovingian
         Age* (London, Macmillan, 1926).
      Gregory of Tours, *History of the Franks*, 2 vols. Tr. O. M.
         Dalton (Oxford, Clarendon, (Volume I is a general in-
         troduction to the era; Volume II is a translation of
         Gregory's *History*).
   C. Other Germanic Kingdoms:
      Paul the Deacon, *History of the Langobards*, tr. W. D.
         Foalks (New York, Longmans, 1907).
      Villari, Pasquale, *The Barbarian Invasions of Italy* 2 vols.
         (London, T. F. Unwin, 1913).
      Ziegler, Aloysius, *Church and State in Visigothic Spain*
         (Washington, Catholic University of America 1930).

Can You Identify?

Vandal Kingdom (5th-6th cen-   Ostrogothic Kingdom (6th century)   tury)
Visigothic Kingdom (5th-8th   Lombard Kingdom (6th to 8th
   century)   century)

Byzantine Italy (7th century)
Cassiodorus
Boethius
Witigis
Totila
Alboin
Ravenna
Merovingian
Alemanni
Clovis
Clothilda

496
Clothar I
Clothar II
"Do-Nothing Kings"
Mayor of the Palace
civitas
Count
Duke
fisc
wergeld

Chapter 7

Byzantine History and Civilization

I. The Eastern Roman or Byzantine Empire survived the Western Roman Empire for a thousand eventful years (476-1453).

  A. Reasons for survival of the Eastern Empire included:
  1. A more advanced and balanced economy.
  2. Greater governmental revenues.
  3. Less extended, less vulnerable frontiers, making invasions by the Germanic barbarians more difficult.
  4. A dual heartland: in both the Balkans and Asia Minor—if one failed the other continued.
  5. Large, strongly fortified cities, of which the mightiest, most impregnable was Constantinople.

  B. The survival of the Eastern Empire (395-518) contrasted with the fall of the Western Empire.
  1. Some emperors sent troublesome barbarians Westward:
      a. Arcadius (395-491) assigned the Visigoths to Illyricum.
      b. Zeno (474-491) dispatched the Ostrogoths to Italy.
  2. Other emperors overcame the internal barbarian menace by other means:
      a. Leo I (457-474) had the Gothic "Kingmaker" Aspar and his sons slain and counterbalanced the Goths in the army with Isaurians.
      b. Anastasius (491-518) ousted the Isaurians from the army and forcibly suppressed them in their homeland.

3. Heresies were a leading cause of division in the early Byzantine Empire.

    a. The Nestorians were strong in Syria, but their leaders were expelled from the Empire.

    b. The Monophysites were strong in Egypt and later also in Syria.

        i. The movement was partly nationalistic and racist.

        ii. Imperial efforts to reconcile the heretics were fruitless.

C. The "Justinian Renaissance" was the "First Golden Age" of the Byzantine Empire (518-610).

1. Justin (518-527) was a simple, honest soldier who rose to the throne through luck.

    a. He prepared the way for his nephew, Justinian.

2. <u>Justinian</u> the Great (527-565) was an intelligent, dynamic executive.

    a. He skillfully utilized able helpers such as:

        i. Theodora, his faithful wife

        ii. The eunuch Narses, his devoted minister

        iii. John of Cappodocia, his grasping tax-collector

        iv. Tribonian, his learned jurist

        v. Belisarius, his brilliant general.

    b. Justinian's "grand plan" was to restore both the political and religious unity and the prosperity of the Roman Empire.

        i. This required:

           1) Reconquest of the West

           2) Reconciliation of the Monophysites.

3. Western territories recovered by Justinian included:

    a. North Africa, swiftly conquered by Belisarius (532-4).

    b. Sicily, used as a stepping stone to Italy.

    c. Italy, reconquered after a long and difficult war of 20 years (534-554).

        i. Ostrogothic resistance was dogged.

        ii. The Franks became uncertain allies in the hope of territorial gains.

        iii. Justinian was afraid to give Belisarius too many troops.

        iv. Eventually Narses conquered Italy with a large army and diplomatic craft.

    d. Southern Spain was occupied while helping a Visigothic usurper retain the throne (554ff.).

4. Buildings and public works were constructed by Justinian on a large scale:

    a. *Sancta Sophia* cathedral in Constantinople was one of the "seven wonders of the world."

    b. Fortifications were built along the frontiers.

    c. Various churches and public buildings were constructed.

5. Codification of Roman law was probably Justinian's most lasting contribution.

    a. A commission of jurists headed by Tribonian was appointed to codify Roman law.

    b. The resultant *Corpus Juris Civilis* (Body of Civil Law) consisted of:

        i. The *Code*—the codified laws themselves.

        ii. The *Digest*—summaries of pertinent authoritative legal opinions.

        iii. The *Institutes*—concise legal principles.

        iv. The *Novels*—supplemental new laws established by Justinian.

6. The Monophysites would not be reconciled by anything short of acceptance of their doctrines.

    a. Justinian's efforts to win them over by compromise failed.

        i. Condemnation of semi-Nestorian writings in the "Affair of the Three Chapters" was wasted effort.

    b. The Monophysites remained dominant in Egypt and strong in Syria.

7. <u>Justinian's successors</u> (565-610) experienced decline and disintegration.

    a. Avars and Slavs overran the Balkans.

    b. The Persians gained the offensive in the Near East.

    c. The last Byzantine Emperor in the period, Phocas, was a madman.

C. <u>The Heraclian Era</u> (610-717) was the Empire's "darkest hour" during the Early Middle Ages.

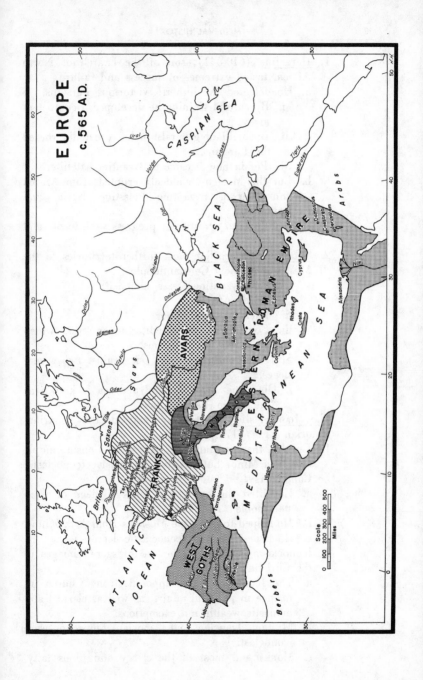

EUROPE
c. 565 A.D.

1. <u>Heraclius</u> (610-641), son of the Exarch of North Africa, tasted extremes of success and failure.
   a. He defeated the hitherto victorious Persians.
      i. By careful training he developed a competent army.
      ii. By brilliant generalship he repeatedly routed the Persians.
      iii. Persia now became a Byzantine satellite.
   b. But the Moslems suddenly erupted from Arabia and overran Byzantine Palestine, Syria, and Egypt.
      i. Efforts to arrest their progress were feeble and futile.
2. <u>Subsequent Heraclians</u> lost further territories to the Moslems but held Constantinople.
   a. Further Byzantine losses included:
      i. North Africa
      ii. Parts of Asia Minor
      iii. Control of the Mediterranean Sea, which passed to the Moslems.
   b. Still Constantinople held out against two severe sieges.
      i. One long siege by land and sea is known as "the Seven Years' Siege."
D. <u>The Iconoclastic Controversy</u> marred the Isaurian-Amorian Era (717-867).
   1. *Leo III*, the Isaurian (717-41) saved Constantinople and Asia Minor but initiated the divisive Iconoclastic Controversy.
      a. He lifted the oppressive land-sea siege of Constantinople (717-718).
      b. He helped to drive the Moslems from Asia Minor.
      c. He issued the first Iconoclastic decrees.
   2. Iconoclasm condemned the use of sacred images in the Christian religion.
      a. The Iconoclasts also opposed strong Church influence in political affairs, as well as clerical and monastic wealth and exemptions.
      b. Militant Isaurian and Amorian Emperors were iconoclastic.
      c. Monks and most of the clergy and pious laity,

especially women, were called "iconodules" (sacred image-reverers).

3. Controversy raged intermittently until 843.
    a. Subsequent Isaurian Emperors stepped up the persecution of "iconodules."
    b. The VII Ecumenical Council of Nicaea II (787) condemned Iconoclasm.
    c. However, the Amorian Emperors resumed Iconoclasm.
    d. The end of Iconoclasm came with a Council held in 843, during the regency of Empress Theodora.
4. Byzantine recovery resumed under Caesar Bardas.
    a. Bardas ruled in the name of his nephew, Michael III, the Drunkard, (842-867).
    b. The offensive was gained against the Moslems.
    c. Basil, "the Groom," from Macedonia brought about the murders of both Bardas and Michael, and seized the throne (867).

E. The "Macedonian Renaissance" gave Byzantium its "Second Golden Age" (867-1056).
1. The Macedonian emperors restored Byzantium to a position of dominance in the Eastern Mediterranean.
    a. Basil I (867-886), founder of the line, restored strong rule, initiated reforms, and recovered territory in Italy.
    b. Leo VI, the Wise, (886-892) completed the new law code, the *Basilics*.
    c. Constantine VII, Porpyrogenitus, (912-957) was a patron of learning, and was served well by his ministers.
        i. Admiral Romanus Lecapenus, Constantine's father-in-law, regained Byzantine control of the seas.
        ii. Meanwhile, Byzantine generals were successful on land.
    d. Nicephorus II, Phocas, (963-969) and John Tzmisces (969-976) conducted a "crusade" against the Moslems in the Near East.
        i. They won Syria, Northern Palestine, and Eastern Mediterranean islands.

e. Basil II, the "Bulgar Slayer" (976-1025) obtained control of the Balkans and Armenia.

2. Territorial gains in the Macedonian Era included:
   a. Much territory in the Near East
   b. Most of the Balkans
   c. Parts of Southern Italy
   d. Command of the seas.

3. Government became more absolute.

4. Decline began under the aged empresses Zoe and Theodora, last of the Macedonians (1025-1056).

F. Recurrent decline, punctuated by partial recovery, marked the final four centuries of history (1056-1453).

1. The "Time of Troubles" (1056-1081) was a dismal era when ephemeral emperors were unable to hold off foreign invaders.
   a. The Seljuk Turks overran Palestine, Syria, and Armenia.
      i. Their victory at Manzikert (1071) secured Armenia and opened up Asia Minor, where they established the "Sultanate of Rum" (Rome).
   b. Petchenegs invaded and ravaged the Balkans.
   c. The Normans conquered remaining Byzantine possessions in Southern Italy and then turned to the Balkans.

2. The Comneni (1081-1185) led a Byzantine rally.
   a. Alexius Comnenus (1081-1118) recouped Byzantine fortunes.
      i. He stopped the advances of the Seljuk Turks in far northwestern Asia Minor where he recovered some territory.
      ii. He foiled the Normans and Petchenegs in the Balkans.
      iii. He encouraged the First Crusade by his appeal to the West for auxiliaries.
   b. Manuel Comnenus (1143-1180) invited disaster by overextending himself.
      i. He was too pro-western and too involved in Italian affairs according to the standards of most Byzantines.

      ii. At Myriocephalon, (1176) the surprised By-zantines were defeated by the Seljuk Sultan of Iconium.

3. The Angeli (1185-1204) presented a sorry spectacle.
   a. Civil war developed between members of this fratricidal family.
   b. Isaac was overthrown by his brother Alexius III who was overthrown by Isaac's son Alexius IV with Crusader assistance.

4. The Latin Empire of Constantinople (1204-1261) was established by members of the Fourth Crusade who seized the Byzantine capital.
   a. The Latin Crusaders took Constantinople when Alexius IV failed to keep his promises.
   b. The weak, disunited Latin Empire included only parts of the Byzantine Empire.
   c. Byzantine resistance-centers held out at Nicaea, Epirus, and Trebizond.
   d. The Bulgarians became temporarily ascendant in the Balkans.

5. The Paleologi (1261-1453) were the final Byzantine dynasty.
   a. The shrewd Michael VII, Paleologus, who suc-ceeded to the rule of Nicaea and Thessalonica, re-covered Constantinople (1261).
      i. He reconstituted the Byzantine Empire.
      ii. He helped foil the ambitious Charles of An-jou, King of Sicily, by the "Sicilian Vespers" (1282).
   b. Subsequent Paleologi indulged excessively in ru-inous civil wars and religious controversy.

6. The Ottoman Turks eventually overthrew the Byzan-tine Empire.
   a. They occupied Northwestern Asia Minor in the 13th century.
   b. They overran much of the Balkans in the 14th century.
   c. They took Constantinople (1453) with the help of a large fleet and a great army whose numerical superiority was 10 to 1.

II. <u>Byzantine civilization</u> was advanced and sophisticated, but relatively static and uncreative.

  A. <u>Component elements</u> in Byzantine civilization included:

    1. The Greek element, influencing language, literature, learning, etc.

    2. The Roman element, prevailing in government, law, military traditions, etc.

    3. The Christian element, dominant in religion, morals, expression, etc.

    4. The Eastern element, strong in the arts and other aspects of life.

  B. <u>Byzantine government</u> was autocratic, bureaucratic, efficient, and highly regulatory.

    1. The Emperor was known as "Autokrator."

      a. He was considered the source of Byzantine law and above all secular law.

      b. He was regarded as the father of the Eastern Christian people.

    2. The central Byzantine government consisted of several well constituted, comparatively competent departments.

    3. The government regulated many aspects of Byzantine life, such as trade, interest on loans, foreign travel, etc.

    4. Themes (provinces) ruled by *strategoi* were the main local subdivisions of the Empire.

      a. The *strategoi* had both military and civil authority.

  C. <u>Security</u> was provided by craft and diplomacy as well as by force.

    1. The old Roman policy of "divide and rule" was followed.

    2. Bribes, gifts, and tribute were copiously used in diplomacy.

    3. The Byzantine army was well organized, well disciplined, and well equipped.

      a. Byzantine generals studied warfare as a science.

      b. "Greek fire," a combustible compound that burned on contact, was extensively used by both navy and army.

D. Byzantine law and justice were essentially Roman.
   1. Roman law was codified in Latin by Justinian.
   2. Subsequent codes in Greek were made by the Isaurians (the *Ecloga*) and the Macedonians (the *Basilics*).
   3. Byzantine law became progressively more Christian.
E. The Byzantine economy was highly commercial and industrialized.
   1. Constantinople was a crossroads of world trade.
   2. Luxury goods were produced in large quantities and sold at high profits.
   3. Society had three classes: aristocracy, middle class, and laborers.
      a. The middle class was considerable.
      b. Literacy was widespread among the upper classes.
F. The Byzantine Church broke off communion with Rome in the 11th century.
   1. Preliminaries to full Schism included:
      a. Pretensions of Byzantine patriarchs.
      b. Eastern heresies.
      c. The so-called "Photian Schism" (9th century) a partial break with Rome.
   2. Contributing to the Schism were:
      a. Differences in language, traditions, and interests.
      b. International rivalries.
      c. Disputes over organization and control of the Church.
         i. Disputed fields included the Balkans, Southern Italy and Sicily, and Palestine.
      d. Papal claims to primacy and supremacy throughout the Church.
   3. The Eastern Schism began when envoys of Pope Leo IX and Patriarch Cerularius angrily excommunicated each other in 1054.
   4. The Eastern Church eventually became a loose association of national churches.
      a. Each Church had its own patriarch and often its own liturgical language.
      b. The Eastern Church was more mystical and rigid in discipline than the Western Chucrh.
      c. The last ecumenical council recognized by the Byzantines was that of Nicaea II held in 787.

G. Byzantine culture, with some exceptions, was more re-
productive than creative.
1. Study of its classical Greek heritage was a major
preoccupation.
2. Literature, with the exception of religious literature
and poetry, was largely imitative and second-rate.
3. Philosophy and the sciences (natural and social)
made little new progress.
4. Historiography was cultivated with success.
   a. Representative historians included: Procopius
   (6th century). Anna Comnena (11th century),
   and John Cantacuzene (14th century).
5. Architecture and art were also exceptional for their
excellence.
   a. Byzantine architecture featured domes, penden-
   tives, and mosaics or (later) frescoes.
      i. Greek cross churches were common.
      ii. The later Macedonian style was more ornate
      and lighter than the earlier Justinian style.
H. The Byzantine legacy to posterity was important and included:
1. Greek literature, learning, and culture.
2. Eastern Christianity.
3. Roman law and other Roman institutions and traditions.
4. Near Eastern technology and art forms.
5. Beneficiaries included:
   a. Eastern and Southeastern Europe.
   b. The Moslems.
   c. Western Europe.

III. Readings on Byzantine history and civilization include:
1. Vasiliev, Alexander A., *History of the Byzantine Empire*
(Madison, University of Wisconsin, 1952).
2. Runciman, Steven, *Byzantine Civilization* (London, Longmans, 1948).
3. Diehl, Charles, *Byzantium: Greatness and Decline* (New
Brunswick, N. J., Rutgers, 1957).
4. Procopius, *Works: Wars, Secret History*, and *Buildings*, tr.
H. B. Dewing, 7 vols. (London, Heinemann, 1914-1940).
5. Comnena, Anna, *The Alexiad*. . . , tr. E. A. Dawes (London, K. Paul, 1926).

Can You Identify?

Aspar
Anastasius
"Justinian Renaissance"
Justin
Justinian
Theodora
Belisarius
Narses
Sancta Sophia
Corpus Juris Civilis
Code
Digest
Institutes
Novels
"Affair of the Three Chapters"
Heraclius
Leo III, Emperor
Iconoclasm
"iconodules"
Nicaea II (787)
Caesar Bardas
"Macedonian Renaissance"
Basil I

Constantine VII
Romanus Lecapenus
Nicephorus II, Phocas
Basil II
"Time of Troubles" (1056-1081)
Manzikert (1071)
Alexius Comnenus
Manuel Comnenus
Myriocephalon (1176)
Angeli (1185-1204)
Latin Empire of Constantinople
Paleologi
Michael VII
1453
autokrator
themes
strategoi
"Greek fire"
"Photian Schism"
"Eastern Schism"
Procopius
Anna Comnena

Chapter 8

Medieval Islam

I. <u>Islam</u> appropriated a large share of the Mediterranean and Asiatic worlds and became the leading competitor of Christianity.

  A. <u>The Moslem Church-State</u> founded in the early 7th century, soon spread over the Near Eastern, North African, and Southern Asiatic worlds.

    1. Arabia was a peripheral and backward peninsula.

      a. Most Arabs were nomadic, warlike Bedouins.

    2. <u>Mohammed</u>, the "Prophet of Islam," was an orphan who rose to become a caravan leader, trader, capitalist, and religious leader.

      a. He married Khadijah, a caravan owner, and lived in Mecca.

      b. His meditations led him to the conviction that he was divinely called to preach a new religion to his fellows.

    3. The survival of Islam defied the attacks of its opponents and the lethargy of many Arabs.

      a. The "Hegira" (622) or forced flight from Mecca to Medina gave the religion a new start.

      b. It came to be accepted as the foundation of Islam and the first year of the Islamic calendar.

    4. A theocratic state developed at Medina.

      a. Various pressures contributed:

        i. An internal contest with the Medinese Jews.

        ii. External war against the Meccans.

      b. Much of Midwestern Arabia was Moslem by Mohammed's death in 632.

B. <u>The Islamic Religion</u> became one of the world's leading religions.
   1. Sources of Islam included elements of Judaism, Christianity, and Zoroastrianism, as well as Mohammed's reported revelations.
   2. The Koran (Reading, Recitation), which contains the revelations accorded to Mohammed, is the Islamic Bible.
   3. Key doctrines include:
      a. Strict monotheism: the unequivocal oneness of God
      b. God's transcendent, purely spiritual nature and perfection
      c. God's providence and concern for men
      d. The Divine commission of Old Testament Prophets, Christ, and Mohammed, the last of the Prophets.
      e. Further important doctrines include:
         i. Permissability of polygamy for those able to "afford" it.
         ii. Prohibition of intoxicating drinks
         iii. The Holy War (*jihad*) for the promotion of Islam
      d. Prohibition of lifelike images of men or animals.
   4. Key obligations of the Moslems (five pillars of Islam) include:
      a. Prayer five times daily, facing Mecca
      b. Acceptance of the Moslem creed: "There is no God but Allah, and Mohammed is his prophet"
      c. Fasting from sunrise to sunset during the month of Ramadan
      d. Almsgiving (about 2½ to 10% of one's income)
      e. Pilgrimage to Mecca at least once (if possible).
C. <u>The Caliphate</u> became the political system of Islam after Mohammed's death in 632.
   1. The Caliphs were the "successors" of Mohammed.
      a. They did not, however, inherit his prophetic office.
      b. They became political heads of the theocratic Moslem state.

2. Islamic expansion was rapid during the first century of the Caliphate.
   a. Reasons for this phenomenal expansion included:
      i. Limited and simple obligations of Moslems, well suited to nomadic peoples.
      ii. The military superiority of the Arabs, united by a new religion and fired by the concept of the "holy war."
      iii. The principle of "conversion or the sword."
      iv. Capable leadership of early Caliphs.
3. Assimilation of the civilizations of conquered peoples was fairly rapid.

D. The Orthodox Caliphs (632-61) were elected from the early "companions" of the Prophet.
   1. They were four: Abu Bakr, Omar, Othman, and Ali.
   2. Features of the Orthodox Caliphate included:
      a. Gradual acceptance of certain aspects of the governments and ways of conquered peoples.
      b. Great expansion into: Arabia outside the Hijaz, Palestine, Syria, Iraq, some of Iran, and Egypt.
      c. Formation of the "Islamic constitution" and important Islamic traditions.

E. The Umayyad Caliphs (661-750) further expanded and organized the Islamic State.
   1. Aspects of the Umayyad Caliphate included:
      a. A "Byzantine Successor-State" with many institutions modeled on those of the Byzantines.
      b. Hereditary Caliphate in the Umayyad family.
      c. Damascus in Syria as the Caliphal capital.
   2. Expansion under the Umayyads included:
      a. Iran and territories to its north and east, such as Transoxiana and Afghanistan.
      b. North Africa, Spain, and several Mediterranean islands.
      c. Although subjected to two severe sieges, one of which was known as "The Seven Years Siege," Constantinople did not capitulate.
         i. Byzantine naval strength, "Greek fire," the great walls of the city, and barbarian assistance helped to ward off the Moslems.

F. The Abbasid Caliphs (750 ff.) contrasted with the Umayyads in many ways.

1. Accession of the Abbasids (750) followed a revolt against the Umayyads.
   a. The Abbasids, who traced their origins to an uncle of the Prophet, seized the reigns of power.
2. Features of the Abbasid Caliphate include:
   a. A more cosmopolitan outlook and greater Persian influence.
      i. Bagdad became the capital.
   b. Diminished concern with the Mediterranean.
   c. The religious office of the Caliph was emphasized more.
3. Control of the Caliphate was exercised in succession by Turkish bodyguards, the Persian Buwayhids, the Seljuk Turks, and the Khwarizm Shahs.

G. Disintegration of the Caliphate occurred under the nominal rule of the Abbasids.
   1. Causes of disintegration were both internal and external:
      a. Conflicting views regarding the proper manner of Caliphal succession
      b. Doctrinal differences
      c. Ambitions and pretensions of local governors and generals
      d. Rivalries among component peoples and areas
      e. Periodic incursions of warlike Asiatics, such as Turks or Mongols.
   2. Autonomous states which emerged in the Moslem world included Spain, Morocco, Tunisia, Egypt, Syria, Persia, Khorosan, etc.
      a. Rival Caliphates had capitals at Bagdad (Abbasids), Cairo (Fatimids), and Cordova (Umayyads) in the 10th century.

II. Moslem civilization was temporarily (*ca.* 800-1100) the most advanced and progressive in the Mediterranean world.

A. Elements of Byzantine, Persian, Greek, Roman, Indian, and Arabian cultures influenced the Moslems.
   1. Unifying factors were the Islamic cult and its Arabic language.
B. Islamic government was theocratic and autocratic.
   1. The Moslem State was a community of believers under a successor or delegate of the Prophet.

a. It lacked a sharp distinction between religious and political elements.

2. Central government was presided over by a Caliph, who was an absolute ruler.

    a. Emirs, Sultans, and Khans (etc.) subsequently assumed sovereign power over various parts of the Moslem world.

    b. A departmentalized bureaucracy developed.

       i. *Diwans* or bureaus were headed by *vizirs* or superintendents, under a grand *vizir* or prime minister.

3. Local government was run by Emirs (governors) assisted by *Amils* (lieutenant governors) and *Walis* (judges).

4. Law was derived from the Koran, (primary and principle source), Roman law, precedents, customs, traditions, and common sense.

5. Taxes, in imitation of those of conquered peoples, were numerous.

    a. Poll taxes, land taxes, and tariffs were included.

    b. Moslems were exempt from poll taxes (head taxes).

6. Armies were usually heterogeneous both in composition and methods.

    a. Numbers rather than strategy were their strong point.

    b. Mobility was emphasized.

       i. Camels provided "desert power."

       ii. Light cavalry with mounted archers was the principal striking force.

    c. Naval power, built up with indigenous "know how," enabled the Moslems to control the Mediterranean.

C. <u>Moslem economy and society</u> were advanced.

1. Commerce was stimulated and encouraged by a far-flung Islamic community.

2. Industry flourished in its old Near Eastern haunts.

3. Agriculture was promoted by improved methods.

D. <u>Islamic Religion</u> experienced both development and division.

1. Elaboration of the faith was promoted by holy men and students of the Koran.
2. Sects of various types arose.
   a. *Sunnites* or traditionalists were the orthodox majority.
   b. Many became *Shiites* believing in the descent of divinely illumined *imams* from the Prophet through Ali and Fatima.
      i. The Shiites subdivided into numerous varieties.
   c. *Sufis* were religious ascetics.
E. <u>Islamic Culture</u> was a mixture of various elements.
   1. Alien cultures were gradually accepted and adapted.
      a. The Arabs at first stayed aloof from foreign cultures.
      b. Under the Umayyads they began to taste and assimilate foreign cultural elements.
      c. Under the Abbasids they enthusiastically embraced foreign cultures.
   2. Translations of Greek and Persian scientific, philosophical, and literary works were made, (750-950) first via other languages such as Aramaic, then directly from the originals.
   3. Education was fostered in mosque schools (*kuttabs*), seminaries (*madrasahs*), and institutes of higher learning such as the *Bait-al-Hikmah* at Bagdad.
F. Arabic literature blossomed in several forms such as love poetry (human and divine), fiction (short stories featuring men and animals), and historiography.
G. <u>Theology and philosophy</u> were jointly cultivated.
   1. Philosophers, such as Alfarabi and Avicenna, sought to reconcile Plato and Aristotle, faith and reason.
   2. Theologians, such as Al-Ghazzali, sought to find the relation between religion, philosophy, and Sufi mysticism.
H. <u>Mathematics and the natural sciences</u> progressed.
   1. Mathematical advances were numerous, and included Arabic numbers, algebra, analytical geometry, and trigonometry.
   2. Sciences in which important progress was made in-

cluded physics, optics, astronomy, chemistry (originally alchemy), and medicine.

    a. Latin translations of Arabic scientific and medical works became textbooks in high medieval universities in the West.

I. Islamic Arts and Music had a special cosmopolitan and Eastern flavor.

    1. Architecture was ornate and complex, using convoluted arches, fretted capitals, stalactite vaulting, bulbous domes, etc.

    2. Art was decorative rather than representational.

        a. Lifelike representations of men and animals were thought to contribute to idolatry.

        b. Geometric forms, conventionalized figures, and ornate Arabic letters were featured.

    3. Music and poetry were widely composed.

        a. Many musical instruments were introduced into the West by the Arabs.

        b. Arabic music and poetry influenced that of Southern Europe.

III. Influences of Islam on Western Europe were numerous and included:

    1. Containment (restriction) of Christianity, now largely cut off from Asia and Africa

    2. The crusading impulse—both as a reaction and in imitation

    3. Temporary feudalism and manorialism

    4. Eventual industrial and commercial expansion

    5. Overseas exploration and conquests

    6. Mathematical advances—such as Arabic numerals, algebra, etc.

    7. Scientific progress—especially in optics, astronomy, chemistry, and medicine

    8. Philosophical revival and scholasticism

    9. Poetical and musical forms.

IV. Readings on Medieval Islam include:

Hitti, Philip K., *History of the Arabs*, (New York, Macmillan, 1951).

Muir, William, *Life of Mahomet* (London, Smith, Elder, 1878).

Muir, William, *The Caliphate* . . . (Edinburgh, Grant, 1915).
Lewis, Bernard, *The Arabs in History* (London, Hutchinsons, 1950).
The Koran (in various editions and translations).

Can You Identify?

Islam	Bagdad
Mohammed	*diwan*
Khadijah	*vizir*
Hegira	*emir*
622	*wali*
Mecca	Sunnites
Medina	Shiites
Koran	*imam*
jihad	*sufis*
Ramadan	*kuttab*
Caliph	*madrasah*
"Orthodox caliphs"	Avicenna
Umayyad Caliphs	Al-Ghazzali
Abbasid Caliphs	

Chapter 9

The Carolingian Revival and Empire

I. The Carolingians replaced the Merovingians and built up a Western Empire.

A. The Carolingian Mayors of the Palace in Austrasia rose to supreme power over all Frankland (613-687).

1. The Mayor of the Palace was a sort of Prime Minister representing the King and acting as spokesman for the aristocracy.

2. Pepin I, a wealthy Austrasian landowner who had helped overthrow Queen Brunehilda, became the first Carolingian Mayor of the Palace in Austrasia (613-29 and 39-40).

3. The Carolingian Grimoald (643-6), as Mayor, attempted to seize the crown for his son, but failed, and both he and his son were tortured and executed.

4. Ebroin, a strong Neustrian mayor (656-81), was ascendant throughout Frankland for a while, but was assassinated in 681.

5. Pepin II defeated the Neustrian mayor (Ebroin's successor) at Tertry and united all Frankland under the Carolingian mayoralty (687).

B. Charles Martel (711-741), illegitimate son of Pepin II, became strong enough to rule for a while without appointing a King.

1. The cavalry was built up by Martel.

a. He confiscated church properties and distributed them as benefices in return for mounted military service.

2. The battle of Tours (732) resulted in a Frankish victory over Moslem invaders from Spain.

3. St. Boniface promoted Church expansion and reform with Charles' patronage.

   a. Martel supported the missionary labors of St. Boniface in Germany.

   b. Boniface reorganized the Frankish Church.

      i. The German bishops took an oath of submission to Rome.

      ii. Church Councils were held more often.

      iii. Independent Irish monks were replaced by Benedictine monks.

         1) The latter brought with them a more uniform and more suitable form of monastic observance.

4. Martel finally ruled as a practically independent prince.

C. Pepin III (Mayor since 741) ascended the throne of Frankland in 751.

   1. Pepin III and Carloman first ruled jointly as Mayors (741-747) after Martel's death.

   2. Pepin's accession to the throne (751) made him king in name as he had been ruler in fact.

      a. Pepin first obtained the approval of the Pope.

      b. He was duly elected by the Frankish nobility.

      c. Pepin was consecrated and installed by Boniface and his fellow bishops.

         i. The new dynasty, inaugurated by religious consecration, enjoyed a special advantage which the Merovingians never had.

         ii. The last Merovingian was tonsured and retired to a monastery.

   3. The rule of Pepin III was efficient and beneficial.

      a. He expanded Frankland.

      b. He cooperated in Church reform and educational improvement.

      c. He supported missionary activities.

   4. Pope Stephen II appealed to Pepin for aid and personally consecrated him in 754.

      a. The Pope was being threatened by the Lombards under King Aistulf (749-56).

        i. Anxious to unify Italy, Aistulf was at the gates of Rome.

        ii. Pope Stephen crossed the Alps to seek Pepin's help.

    b. When Pepin agreed to help him, the Pope repeated the rite of consecration.

        i. The Pope forbade the Franks to choose a king from any other family.

        ii. Pepin was given the title of "Patrician of Rome."

5. The "Donations of Pepin" constituting the Papal States resulted when Pepin III overcame the Lombard King Aistulf.

    a. Pepin intervened in Italy in 754 and 756.

        i. He forced the Lombards to submit and desist.

        ii. In the "Donations of Pepin" (754 and 756), he granted to the Pope territories in central Italy which constituted the "Papal States."

D. Charlemagne (768-814) reconstituted an empire in the West.

1. He soon consolidated his power and strengthened his kingdom.

    a. He assumed sole rule of Frankland on the early death of his brother Carloman (771).

    b. He maintained close ties with the Church and papacy.

2. His intervention in Italy won for Charlemagne control of the greater part of that peninsula.

    a. He aided the Papacy against the Lombards in 774.

        i. Charlemagne defeated and deposed the Lombard King Desiderius.

        ii. He took the title of "King of the Lombards" and the direct rule of northern Italy.

        iii. He renewed and expanded the Donations of Pepin.

3. The Saxons were conquered and converted after about thirty-seven years of warfare.

    a. Numerous campaigns and laws, and the use of both force and persuasion were needed.

4. The "Spanish March" was established in Catalonia at the expense of the Moors.
   a. Northeastern Spain was conquered by the Franks and became the "Spanish March."
   b. Charlemagne's rearguard under Count Roland was ambushed by the Gascons during an early retreat from Spain.
      i. This gave rise to the famous poem, *The Song of Roland*.
5. The Slavs and Avars along the Eastern frontier were subdued and forced to pay tribute.
   a. But these territories were not incorporated into Frankland.
6. Coronation as Emperor (800) was one of the most significant events in Charlemagne's reign.
   a. Charlemagne's conquests doubled his territory.
   b. Pope Leo III was in need of help.
      i. Previous cooperation induced the Pope to turn to Charlemagne.
   c. At Rome, Charles quieted disturbances and backed the Pope against his enemies.
   d. The coronation of Charles as Emperor by Pope Leo III occurred on Christmas Day, 800.
      i. The coronation regularized relations between Emperor and Pope.
      ii. Charlemagne replaced the Eastern Emperor as nominal overlord in the West.
      iii. In theory, the Roman Empire in the West was revived.

II. Carolingian Renovations provided a foundation for European progress.
   A. Government was improved and strengthened.
      1. Consecration made the ruler a religious as well as a political leader.
      2. National Assemblies were revived, largely to obtain support for important projects.
      3. New laws (capitularies) regulated many aspects of Frankish life, both secular and religious.
      4. *Scabini* or professional judges replaced the declining

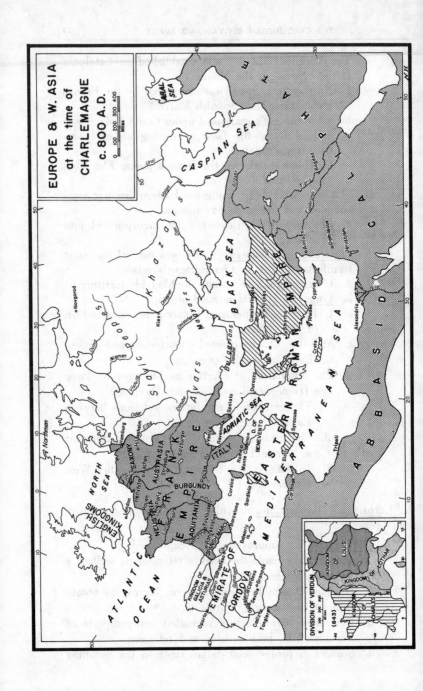

EUROPE & W. ASIA
at the time of
CHARLEMAGNE
c. 800 A.D.

0 100 200 300 400
Miles

CASPIAN SEA

ARAL
SEA

Ural

Volga

BLACK SEA

CONSTANTINOPLE

MEDITERRANEAN SEA

EASTERN ROMAN EMPIRE

Crete

Rhodes

Cyprus

Alexandria

ABBASIDS

Baghdad

Tigris

Euphrates

Damascus

Antioch

Tripoli

CASPIAN

Khazars

Slavic Peoples

Magyars

Bulgarians

Avars

Niemen

Dnieper

Dniester

Danube

Kiev

oNovgorod

Oder

Vistula

Elbe

Hamburg

FRANK EMPIRE

SAXONY

AUSTRASIA

NEUSTRIA

BURGUNDY

AQUITAINE

ITALY

ADRIATIC SEA

Venice

Ravenna

Rome

D. OF SPOLETO

D. OF BENEVENTO

Monte Cassino

Durazzo

Spalato

Salona

Naples

Sicily

Syracuse

Corsica

Sardinia

Carthage

Balearic Is.

NORTH SEA

ATLANTIC OCEAN

ENGLISH KINGDOMS

Northmen

KINGDOM OF GALICIA & ASTURIAS

EMIRATE OF CORDOVA

Cordova

Seville

Toledo

Cadiz

Tangier

DIVISION OF VERDUN
(843)

KINGDOM OF LOUIS

KINGDOM OF LOTHAR

KINGDOM OF CHARLES

moot courts, thus regularizing the administration of justice.

5. *Missi Dominici* kept a close watch on local administration.

   a. These traveling agents of the central government investigated and supervised the administration of the counts.

   b. They heard complaints, provided justice, and saw to the implementation of imperial decrees.

6. The county system was spread in Germany, Italy, etc.

7. Feudalism was foreshadowed.

   a. Lands (benefices, fiefs) were distributed on condition of mounted military service.

   b. Charlemagne insisted on oaths of personal loyalty from his subjects.

8. Required military service was reassessed.

   a. Military service was related to property.

      i. Those who possessed insufficient land to support one knight were grouped into sets of four.

      ii. Each of the four persons in such a group took turns in fighting.

B. Carolingian society attained a certain maturity.

1. Roman, Christian, and German elements were extensively blended.

2. Church and State cooperation was increased.

   a. The anointed, sacrosanct monarch was a spiritual as well as temporal leader.

   b. Charlemagne legislated on church affairs and appointed bishops and abbots.

   c. He assisted missionary efforts and supported church reform.

3. The economy became more agrarian and society more stratified.

   a. Agriculture on royal estates was made more efficient by detailed directives and closer supervision.

C. The Carolingian "Renaissance" utilized the cultural heritage of the past.

1. Factors aiding this endeavor included:
    a. The relative peace and security of the times
    b. The power and wealth of the monarchy
    c. The vision of men like Charlemagne and Alcuin.
2. Education was stressed in order to provide capable leaders.
    a. Monastic and cathedral schools maintained and expanded educational facilities.
    b. The palace school gained renown as a rendezvous of scholars.
        i. Along with the Emperor himself, the school included:
            1) Alcuin of York, educator and liturgist.
            2) Paul the Deacon, poet and historian.
            3) Paulinus of Nola, theological and literary scholar.
            4) Theodulph of Orleans, author, savant, and poet.
            5) Einhard, minister and biographer of Charlemagne.
            6) Peter of Pisa, classical scholar and teacher of Latin.
    c. The Carolingian "miniscule" resulted from a reformation of handwriting.
        i. This was a clear, beautiful handwriting in small letters, from which we derive our lower-case print.
    d. Copying of manuscripts was encouraged in the monasteries.
3. The Vulgate translation of the Bible was restored and emended.
4. Further renaissance was also fostered in architecture, the arts, literature, and other fields.
    a. A fine cathedral at Aachen was reared in quasi-Byzantine style.
    b. Manuscript illumination became more expressive.
    c. Lively Latin poetry was composed by Alcuin, Theodulf, and others.
    d. Disputes concerning the Eucharist, predestination, the Trinity (*Filioque*) and sacred images developed.

e. Little original thinking was done.
   i. The only notable speculative thinker of the 9th century was John Scotus Erigena, "born out of due time."
D. Carolingian contributions included:
   1. Religious consecration of monarchs and close cooperation of Church and State.
   2. The restored imperial office.
   3. Use of national assemblies.
   4. Legislation and professional judges.
   5. Feudalism and mounted warfare.
   6. Educational revival and general cultural renaissance.

III. Readings on Carolingian history include:

Hodgkin, Thomas, *Charles the Great* (London, Macmillan, 1921).
Davis, Henry W. C., *Charlemagne* (London, Putnams, 1925).
Easton, Stewart, and Wieruszowski, Helene, *The Era of Charlemagne* (Princeton, N. J., Van Nostrand, 1961).
Fichtenau, Henry, *The Carolingian Empire* (Oxford, Blackwell, 1957).
Mullinger, Charles B., *Schools of Charles the Great* (New York, Stechert, 1904).
Hinks, Roger P., *Carolingian Art* (London, Sidgwick, 1935).
Einhard and the Monk of St. Gall, *Early Lives of Charlemagne* (London, Chatto, 1926). (There are various translations of Einhard.)

Can You Identify?

Carolingian	Carloman
Mayor of the Palace	Stephen II
Pepin I	Aistulf
Grimoald	"Donations of Pepin"
Ebroin	Charlemagne
Pepin II	Desiderius
Tertry (687)	"Spanish March"
Charles Martel	Roland
Tours (732)	800 A.D.
St. Boniface	Leo III, Pope
Pepin III	assemblies (Carolingian)

capitularies

scabini

Missi Dominici

"Carolingian Renaissance"

Alcuin

Paul the Deacon

Filioque

Theodulf

Einhard

"Carolingian minuscule"

Aachen

John Scotus Erigena

Chapter 10

Dissolution of the Carolingian Empire

I. Factors for decline and disintegration after Charlemagne (814 ff.) were internal and external.

  A. Internal political factors included:

    1. Weaker rulers, with nicknames such as "the Pious," "the Fat," "the Simple," "the Child."

    2. The "fatal Frankish custom" of dividing the realm among surviving legitimate sons.

    3. Rivalries: regional, racial, factional, and personal.

    4. Alienation of the *fisc* (giving away of royal estates) to obtain supporters.

    5. The growing power of local lords due to:

      a. The new hereditary nature of local offices.

      b. The spread of vassalage.

      c. The necessity of local defences against sudden hostile attacks.

  B. Internal economic and social factors included:

    1. The decline of long-range Mediterranean commerce.

      a. The Mediterranean became a "Moslem lake," largely controlled by Moslem sea power.

    2. The decrease of local and inter-regional trade.

      a. Local barons levied heavy taxes on trade.

      b. Brigands harassed and robbed traders on land.

      c. Pirates robbed traders on water.

    3. The predominately agrarian nature of the economy.

      a. The economy relapsed to an agricultural subsistence level.

      b. Serfdom became more common.

       c. Towns became shadows of their former selves, as trade and industry lapsed.

C. <u>External factors</u> were even more influential.

  1. <u>Viking incursions</u> were a leading cause.

     a. Many Northmen erupted from Scandinavia during the late 8th to early 10th centuries.

        i. These Vikings were typical Nordics: tall, fair, blond, and blue-eyed.

        ii. They were in the iron age technologically, but in the late stone age culturally.

        iii. They came in turn as:

          1) traders,

          2) raiders, and

          3) conquering settlers.

        iv. They travelled in long, swift, racing-type boats, propelled by oar and sail.

        v. Their ships were capable of making their way up the rivers into the interior.

     b. The Vikings attacked suddenly and unexpectedly.

        i. Monasteries and coastal towns were their favorite targets.

     c. The Northmen inspired great fear.

        i. The invocation, "From the fury of the Northmen, oh Lord, deliver us," was added to the litany.

     d. The British Isles were a favorite early target.

        i. English monasteries were attacked (793 ff.).

        ii. A large-scale Danish invasion of England took place during the mid-ninth century.

        iii. The Danish inundation of England was not checked until Alfred the Great won the Treaty of Wedmore (878), limiting the Danes to Northeast England ("the Danelaw").

        iv. Much of Ireland came under Norse control, temporarily, while Scotland and outlying islands were also invaded.

     e. The Low Countries were a favorite and rewarding target until the Northmen were defeated there by Arnulf in the Battle of the Dyle (891).

     f. France bore much of the brunt of the Norse onslaught.

  i. Its wealth and exposed coast and numerous rivers made France a prime target.
  ii. Most leading French coastal and river cities had been sacked by mid century.
  iii. Eventually, Northmen led by Rollo obtained the Dukedom of Normandy as a pay-off to stop their attacks and serve as a buffer.
g. In Russia, Northmen established the first large Russian state: the principality of Kiev.
h. Other places were also invaded by the Northmen:
  i. Iceland, Greenland, and North America (*c.* 1000) were reached.
  ii. The Northmen also invaded the Mediterranean and Black Seas and attacked Constantinople.
  iii. Norman descendents of Vikings conquered England, Southern Italy, and Sicily, and participated in the Crusades, in the 11th century.
2. <u>Magyars and Slavs</u> along the Eastern frontiers invaded Germany and even Italy.
  a. The Magyars were Asiatic invaders who moved into Hungary in the late 9th century.
  b. The Magyars invaded Germany regularly and Italy, repeatedly, plundering and exacting tributes.
    i. Their pressures contributed to the rise of defensive Dukedoms in Germany.
    ii. They further perturbed already troubled and divided Italy.
    iii. The Magyar threat, though at first divisive, eventually contributed to the unification of Germany.
  c. The Slavs also raided frontier territories.
3. <u>Moslem raiders</u> harassed Mediterranean France as well as Italy.
  a. The Moslems conquered strategic islands of the Mediterranean (Sicily, the Belearics, etc.)
  b. They invaded Italy and southern France, where they maintained bases.
D. <u>Disintegration</u> resulted from the raids by Northmen, Magyars, and Moslems.

1. It became necessary to provide for autonomous local defence and security.
2. Government soon followed suit and became mainly local.

II. Charlemagne's successors (814 ff.) saw Western Europe break up into several kingdoms subdivided into feudal principalities.

A. Louis the Pious (814-40), Charlemagne's sole surviving son, was weak and indecisive.

1. He was overly susceptible to the influence of churchmen, family, and friends.
2. In his Partition of 817, Louis tried to will an intact Empire to his eldest son, Lothair, with his two younger sons as sub-kings.
3. His proposal to abandon the custom of division was strongly opposed by:
   a. His "dispossessed," less-favored sons, Louis and Pepin (later Charles), and their adherents.
   b. His new young wife, Judith, who was looking out for the interests of her son, Charles the Bald.
   c. Local "patriots" and selfish lords.
4. Louis wavered and changed the plan of succession several times.
   a. The question of succession disturbed his entire reign.
   b. Several plans were announced and changed.
   c. These served to confuse the situation and sharpen rivalries.

B. The War of the Three Brothers (840-843) eventually settled the issue.

1. Civil War between Lothair, who favored unity, and his two brothers, Louis and Charles, who wanted to be independent, followed the death of Louis Pious (840).
   a. The bloody Battle of Fontenay (841) was indecisive.
   b. The mutual Strassburg Oaths (841) pledged Louis and Charles and their followers to fight together against Lothair until victorious.
2. The Treaty of Verdun (843), negotiated through intermediaries to avoid further civil war, arranged that:

        a. Frankland was to be divided into three sovereign parts:

           i. The West, French-speaking part was to go to Charles the Bald.

          ii. The East, German-speaking portion was to fall to Louis the German.

         iii. The middle, mixed portion, consisting of the Rhineland, the Rhoneland, and Italy, was to go to Lothair.

        b. Lothair retained the title (but not the real power) of "Emperor."

    3. The "System of Concord" of amicable conferences for settlement of differences, attempted by the brothers after Verdun, did not last long.

C. The middle portion (843 ff.) although the richest, was also the weakest part.

    1. The middle portion was heterogeneous geographically, historically, linguistically, and culturally.

        a. It soon broke into fragments and became prey to stronger, more homogenous neighbors.

        b. Emperor Lothair ruled over the entire Middle portion 843-855.

    2. Division of the middle portion into three kingdoms (Italy, Burgundy, and Lotharingia,) took place after Lothair's death (855).

        a. The French and German monarchs struggled untiringly to win this area.

        b. Italy was the scene of division, contesting factions, and foreign interference.

        c. Burgundy soon split into two unstable kingdoms: Burgundy and Provence (or Arles).

        d. Lotharingia or the Rhineland was ruled by Lothair II until his death without heir (869).

           i. Lothair was kept from remarrying and producing a direct heir by his ambitious uncles and a conscientious Papacy.

          ii. The Treaty of Mersen (870) subsequently divided Lotharingia between Charles the Bald and Louis the German.

         iii. After a period of oscillation, the Rhineland became a part of the German Empire (925).

D. <u>West Frankland</u> (France) was richer than East Frankland, but more divided and weaker.

   1. Charles the Bald (843-877) was an able, intelligent ruler.

      a. He patronized scholars such as John Scotus Erigena.

      b. Feudalization in West Frankland was promoted by repeated raids of the Northmen, which rapidly increased.

   2. The Robertian-Carolingian feud (887-987), which followed the deposition of Charles the Fat, hastened disintegration and feudalization.

      a. The Robertians were counts of Paris who bravely withstood the Northmen.

         i. They were made dukes of Francia as a result.

      b. Robertian kings alternated with Carolingian kings (887-987).

E. <u>East Frankland</u> (Germany), although less developed and more exposed, was more aggressive and successful.

   1. Difficulties served as healthy stimuli.

   2. Louis the German (843-876) competently held his own.

      a. After his death Germany was divided among his three sons.

   3. Charles the Fat (876-887) became Emperor and sole ruler of all Frankland (by 884).

   4. Arnulf, an illegitimate but able Carolingian, ruled East Frankland (887-899).

      a. Arnulf invaded Italy and was crowned Emperor (896), though to little avail.

   5. Louis the Child (900-911), the last Carolingian ruler of Germany died prematurely.

      a. He had failed to restrain either the Magyars or the Dukes.

III. <u>Readings</u> on the Disintegration of Frankland as well as the Northmen and Magyars include:

   The Cambridge Medieval History, Vol. III.

   Thompson, James W., *The Dissolution of the Carolingian Fisc* (Berkeley, University of California, 1935) and *The De-*

cline *of the Missi Dominici in Frankish Gaul* (Chicago,
University of Chicago, 1903).

Kendrick, Thomas D., *History of the Vikings* (New York,
Scribners, 1930).

Macartney, Carlile A., *The Magyars in the Ninth Century* (Cambridge, Eng., University, 1930).

Books cited elsewhere on: The Early Middle Ages, The Franks,
France, Germany, and Feudalism.

Can You Identify?

"The fatal Frankish custom"
fisc
Vikings
"Danelaw"
Dyle (891)
Rollo
Normandy
Kiev
Magyars
Louis the Pious
Lothair
Judith
Charles the Bald

"War of the Three Brothers"
Fontenay (841)
Strassburg Oaths (842)
Treaty of Verdun (843)
System of Concord (843 ff.)
Lotharingia
Lothair II
Mersen (870)
Robertians
Louis the German
Charles the Fat
Arnulf
Louis the Child

Chapter 11

Feudalism

I. <u>Feudalism</u> was the political, military, economic, and social system which prevailed in medieval Western Europe, especially from the 9th to the 12th centuries.

  A. <u>The feudal system</u> combined governmental functions, military responsibilities, and landholding.

    1. Full feudalism developed on the continent by the 9th century and continued for a few centuries.

      a. It was slow in coming and slow in going.

      b. Differences were marked from locale to locale and period to period.

        i. Classic feudalism was found in France from the 9th to the 11th centuries.

        ii. Feudalism did not prevail in England until the 11th century nor in Germany until the 12th century.

    2. Essential features of feudalism, which existed simultaneously, were:

      a. Personal: vassalage, involving personal dependence and allegiance.

        i. The "man" or "vassal" paid homage and swore fidelity to his lord.

      b. Territorial: a fief or conditional landholding was granted to the vassal in return for his pledge of various services (military and political).

      c. Military: military service consisted of mounted service in the field.

        i. Aggressive service was usually limited to

about forty days a year, while defensive service was unlimited.

   ii. This service was at the vassal's own expense.

d. Governmental: governmental responsibilities and divided sovereignty characterized feudalism.

   i. Government was associated with landholding, and vice versa.

   ii. Attendance of the vassal at the lord's court was required to help render justice and give advice.

   iii. Among public rights exercised independently by many lords were:

   a) Minting coins

   b) Waging private war

   c) Exercising high and final justice.

   iv. The feudal king was a *suzerain* rather than a sovereign.

B. Origins of feudalism may be traced back to German and Roman antecedents.

1. The comitatus was a German antecedent.

   a. The *comitatus* was a body of warriors bound to their chief by oaths of fidelity.

   b. The feudal vassal likewise took an oath of fealty to his feudal lord.

2. The *precarium* of the Romans was another antecedent.

   a. The practice of *precarium* (*precarious tenure*) appeared in late Roman times.

   i. Under this system, land was held on condition of some service or payment.

3. The *patrocinium* was still another Roman antecedent.

   a. This was the relation between a wealthy, powerful patron and his dependent client.

4. The Carolingians promoted feudalism by giving out benefices on condition of mounted military service, and by requiring oaths of fidelity from their free subjects.

   a. A beneficed retainer was called a *vassus, vassalus, homo,* or *fidelis*.

C. Obligations of vassals, besides military and governmental services, included:

1. Reliefs, which were payments made when fiefs passed to new holders.
    a. Since originally the fief was not hereditary and had reverted back to the lord, the relief was a "buying back" of the land.
    b. The price included, in addition to promises of vassalage, a payment of money, frequently amounting to a year's income ("annate") from the fief.
2. Aids, which were customary "donations" regularly made to the lord when he was faced with heavy expense, such as:
    a. The knighting of the lord's eldest son.
    b. The marriage of his eldest daughter.
    c. Ransom for a captured lord.
    d. Extraordinary or "voluntary" aids were voted for exigencies not determined by custom, such as an overseas expedition.
3. Hospitality (*droit de gite*), which obliged the vassal to provide board and lodging for the lord and his retinue.
    a. The lord's right to demand hospitality (right of purveyance) was at first unlimited.
    b. Eventually it was restricted and was often commuted to a money payment.
D. Rights of Feudal lords included:
1. Forfeiture which could be invoked when the vassal failed to live up to his essential obligations.
    a. The fief could then revert to the lord.
    b. This right was often neglected by lords for practical reasons.
    c. Rulers, however, could and did invoke forfeiture to bring back fiefs to the direct holdings of the crown.
2. Escheat which applied whenever a vassal died without direct heir.
    a. The lord could then reclaim the fief.
    b. Escheat prevented the fief from falling into the hands of someone of doubtful loyalty.
3. Wardship which applied when a vassal died leaving a minor heir.

a. The lord could now exercise wardship and administer the fief during the ward's years as a minor.

b. Since the ward could not perform the customary services, the lord received the income of the fief during this time.

4. Foremarriage which was the lord's right to control the marriages of feudal heiresses.

a. The lord could insist that his consent be obtained, before the marriage of a female heiress.

b. In this way the lord could prevent a female vassal from marrying an incompetent or allying through marriage with a family hostile to him.

c. Since husbands assumed full power over fiefs, the right of foremarriage was very important.

E. Feudal relations applied only to the upper aristocratic and military element of medieval society (about 10%).

1. Manorial terms and relations applied only to ordinary, rural, and work-a-day elements of medieval society (about 90%).

II. Various Aspects of life became "feudalized."

A. Feudal law and justice were determined by customs.

1. Feudal law was not statute law but customary law.

a. Law was "found" when the judiciary discovered the true custom and applied it.

2. Feudal justice was administered on each level of society from the royal council to the village court.

a. This justice was usually pronounced by a judge or a panel of "peers" (equals).

i. The "peers" represented the community in which the crime had been committed.

ii. The judge was often an official such as a count, one of whose many functions was administering justice.

b. Oaths and co-swearing, invoking God as a witness, were used in trials.

c. Ordeals, calling on God to manifest the innocence or guilt of a man, were also used.

B. Feudal warfare contributed to the rise of knighthood, castles, and chivalry.

1. Warfare was endemic in feudalism.
   a. Each lord of any consequence had the right to wage private war.
   b. Lack of precision in boundaries and relationships provoked much conflict.
   c. The Church attempted to curb bellicose activities.
      i. She promoted the *Truce of God* which forbade fighting on certain days and in certain periods.
         a) Periods included under the *Truce of God* were week ends, Lent, and holy days.
      ii. The Church also sponsored the *Peace of God* which exempted certain persons from attack.
         a) Clerics, tradesmen, women, and children were declared exempt.
2. The knight was a professional mounted warrior of upper-class status.
   a. The prevalence of war assured the knight's importance.
   b. The knight's training included periods as a page and a squire.
   c. Valor and prowess, loyalty and fidelity were knightly virtues.
3. The castle was both the home and fortress of the feudal lord.
   a. Before the military use of gunpowder, the castle was a most important instrument of warfare.
   b. Originally built of wood, castles were constructed of stone from the 12th century on.
      i. Knowledge gained in the Crusades was used to improve castles.
   c. Early forms of castles were the so-called "motte and bailey" castles, which were structures atop hills (mottes) with courtyards (bailies) surrounded by palisades or walls and ditches.
   d. Subsequent castles became concentric with various refinements such as moats, drawbridges, crenelations, parapets, etc.
   e. Castles were not remarkable for comfort or cleanliness, but they were superior as abodes to the cottages of peasants.

4. Chivalry was the feudal code of behavior.
   a. At first only military virtues were required of a man.
   b. The cult of courtly love and other refinements were added under the influence of poets and troubadours.
   c. The Church attempted to Christianize chivalry by stressing fair play, defense of the weak, devotion to the Church, and respect for womanhood.

5. Heraldry consisted of identifying and descriptive devices or designs known as "coats of arms."
   a. Heraldry served to identify knights, largely hidden under their armor.
   b. It was also a partial record of family history and a source of family pride.

C. The Church both influenced and was influenced by feudalism.
   1. It succeeded in tempering feudal relationships with Christian attitudes and principles.
      a. It moderated the rigors of feudal warfare.
      b. It exempted certain persons (Peace of God) and periods (Truce of God) from warfare.
   2. Since churchmen held extensive lands and offices, they participated in the feudal system.
      a. Churchmen often were responsible for providing feudal services and military assistance.
   3. Many Church offices were controlled by lay lords and kings who appointed priests and bishops.
   4. Many prelates became intimately involved in secular and political affairs.
      a. Divided loyalty resulted.

D. An Evaluation of feudalism shows both advantages and disadvantages.
   1. Advantages include:
      a. Feudalism held society together in relative safety.
         i. It prevented a complete collapse of orderly society in Western Europe.
      b. With capable rulers, feudalism could make for strong government.
      c. Agriculture was encouraged and land cleared.

    d. Feudalism may be seen as a compromise between Christian ideals and military exigencies.
  2. Disadvantages include:
    a. Feudalism fostered localism.
    b. Continuous petty feudal warfare caused disorder and violence.
    c. Decline of inter-regional trade hampered the economy.
    d. Central governments were often weak.
    e. Justice was unequal and there was no organized police system.
    f. Social castes were promoted.
    g. Education and learning suffered.

III. <u>Readings</u> on Feudalism include:

  Stephenson, Carl, *Mediaeval Feudalism* (Ithaca, Cornell, 1942).
  Ganshof, Francois L., *Feudalism* (tr.) (New York, Harper, 1961).
  Bloch, Marc, *Feudal Society*, (tr.) (Chicago, University of Chicago, 1961).
  Prestage, Edgar, ed., *Chivalry* (London, K. Paul, 1928).
  Painter, Sidney, *Rise of the Feudal Monarchies* (Ithaca, Cornell, 1951).

Can You Identify?

feudalism	forfeiture
vassal	escheat
fief	wardship
sovereignty	foremarriage
suzerain	peers
comitatus	ordeals
precarium	Truce of God
patrocinium	Peace of God
annate	knight
"aid" (feudal)	*motte* and *bailey* castle
"relief" (feudal)	chivalry
hospitality (*droit de gite*)	heraldry

Chapter 12

Economic and Social Bases
of the Early Middle Ages

I. <u>Economic decline and readjustment</u> occurred during the Early Middle Ages.

    A. <u>The decline of commerce and industry</u> was precipitated by many factors.

        1. <u>Commerce</u> suffered a series of crippling shocks.

            a. Decline began during the violent, confused period of the Barracks Emperors (to 284).

            b. Remedies attempted by the Absolute Emperors (284-395) proved inadequate.

            c. Barbarian invasions (5th-6th centuries) accelerated the decline.

            d. Deterioration continued in the turbulent and warring early Germanic kingdoms (6th-8th centuries).

            e. Moslem control of the Mediterranean Sea restricted Carolingian contributions to peace, order, and unity.

                i. The Carolingian economy was primarily agrarian.

            f. The disintegration and trials of Western Europe after Charlemagne (814 ff.) further promoted decline.

                i. The renewed invasions by Northmen, Magyars, Slavs and African Moslems brought the economy to its lowest point.

2. Obstacles to commerce were numerous and increased after the collapse of the Carolingian Empire (814 ff.).
   a. Roads and bridges fell into disrepair.
   b. Travel was unsafe because of pirates and bandits.
   c. Frequent wars and civil disturbances also hindered trade.
   d. Numerous tolls and duties made traffic difficult and costly.
   e. Attacks of Northmen and Magyars turned many trading towns into military strongholds.
   f. Gold coins ceased to be minted and silver coins became standard.
   g. Interest was banned as usurious.
   h. Agrarianism and the prevalence of self-sufficient large estates contributed to commercial decline.
3. Industry, along with towns and the middle class, declined with the decline of commerce.
   a. Industry was largely manorial, domestic, and monastic.
   b. The main industries were associated with worship and warfare.
   c. Towns ceased to be important commercial and industrial centers.
      i. Urban populations were reduced to a fraction of what they had been.
   d. Craftsmen were inferior.
   e. Retailers and merchants largely disappeared.
      i. Jews and Syrians took over much of what was left of trade.
B. Agriculture was the primary economic occupation in the Early Middle Ages.
   1. Manorialism was the chief form of agricultural organization.
      a. Agriculture was the occupation of the vast majority.
      b. Most manorial workers were serfs or quasi-serfs who passed their entire lives on the manor.
   2. The manor was originally the lord's dwelling.
      a. The term was extended to include all his lands and the people who worked and lived on them.
      b. The Roman *latifundium* or villa, where slaves or

coloni bound to the soil worked for the owner and themselves, was an antecedent.

3. <u>Government of the manor,</u> like the manor itself, was partly seigniorial, partly communal (cooperative).

    a. The master (seignior) or his steward, aided by the bailiff, supervised the operation of the manor.

    b. To some extent the peasants were left to themselves, and the unit ran itself.

        i. A set of regulatory customs was acquired over the years.

        ii. The peasants were headed by a reeve and enforced their own laws in their own courts.

4. The village was the characteristic dwelling place.

    a. In the village lived the peasants, free and serf, who worked their own land and the lord's.

    b. If the village was completely owned by one lord, village and manor coincided.

        i. Sometimes one village was divided between two or more manors.

        ii. A single manor could also contain more than one village.

5. <u>Manorial buildings</u> included:

    a. The manor house: residence of the lord.

        i. It was usually a "big house" situated a little distance from the village.

        ii. Many manor houses were three-room structures containing a dining hall, parlor and bedroom.

        iii. If the lord lived elsewhere, as in a castle, the steward might occupy the manor house.

    b. The church generally was located near the main thoroughfare, with its own enclosure, and the rectory, churchyard, and cemetery were nearby.

    c. Peasants usually lived in crude one-room huts, which sometimes had cellars or attics.

    d. Each manor usually had a smithy, mill, and bake-oven.

6. <u>Officials</u> of the manor included:

    a. The steward, who represented the lord when he was absent.

    b. The bailiff, who was the steward's right-hand man and had direct charge of the peasants.

    c. The reeve, who was the official representative and head of the peasants.

7. <u>Manorial lands</u> were subdivided into various parts.

    a. Arable land was divided into two or three "open" (non-fenced) fields.

       i. The two-field system, in which one half the arable was kept fallow each year, was continued in the drier Mediterranean lands.

       ii. The more productive three-field system, in which only a third of the arable remained fallow, was generally used north of the Mediterranean.

    b. In the three-field system:

       i. One field was planted with winter grain.

       ii. The second was planted with spring grain.

       iii. The third field was allowed to remain fallow to recover its fertility.

       iv. The fields were rotated so that each field was fallow once every three years.

       v. Production was thus increased and plowing labor cut (since fallow lands had to be plowed twice a year), while labor was better distributed.

    c. The peasants' lands were scattered through the fields in strips of about an acre each. (This amount could be plowed in a long morning.)

    d. The lord's holdings (*demesne*) were either scattered throughout the fields or located in one continuous place.

       i. They were worked by the peasants along with their own holdings.

       ii. The lord's demesne often amounted to about a third of the arable land.

    e. Common meadows and pastures were used to feed the animals.

8. <u>Duties of the peasants</u> included labor and payments.

    a. "Week work" consisted of about three days a week of working for the lord.

    b. "Boon-work" obliged the peasants to harvest the lord's crops before their own.

       c. *Corvées* were special services for the maintenance of roads, bridges, and other public works.

       d. Payments in money or kind included:

          i. The *heriot*: an inheritance tax ordinarily consisting of the best animal.

          ii. *Pannage*: a payment required for the privilege of keeping pigs in the lord's forest.

          iii. *Banalities*: fees or a percentage demanded for use of the lord's ovens, mill, wine-press, etc.

          iv. The *merchet*: payment for permission to marry outside the manor.

          v. The *taille* (tax): In general, peasants were *taillable à merci*—taxable at the lord's wish.

          vi. A tithe: 10% or so of all produce was theoretically given to the church.

    9. <u>Some agricultural progress</u> occurred.

       a. The heavy wheeled plow was introduced.

       b. Horse-collars, horseshoes, and tandem-harnesses made it possible to use horses for plowing, making plowing much more rapid.

       c. Water mills provided power to grind grain.

       d. The three-field system was a big improvement over the two-field system.

II. <u>Early Medieval Society</u> was both static and fluid.

  A. <u>Three classes</u> were distinguished in medieval society.

    1. The clergy formed the first class, whose principal role was to pray.

    2. The nobles, who were the warriors and rulers, constituted the second class, whose principal role was to fight.

    3. The laborers were the third class, who supported the clergy and nobles as well as themselves.

       a. The majority of laborers were peasants, who constituted the greater part of medieval society.

       b. Most of them were serfs and villeins.

          i. Only partly free, they were bound to the soil and owed all the duties which could be exacted.

       c. Other types of rural workers were also found.

          i. Freeholders were men who held their own land of which they could freely dispose.

        ii. Cottagers (cottars) and borders (bordars) possessed only a hut and a small amount of land and depended on hired work for subsistence.

        iii. Slaves were found but in decreasing numbers.

B. <u>The life of the peasants</u> was rough, hard, and simple.

  1. They lived in close contiguity in villages.

  2. Small huts made of local material (wood or mud) provided their shelter.

  3. Their regular work day lasted from sunrise to sunset.

  4. Their diet was simple but substantial.

    a. Black (brown) bread from grain was their staff of life.

    b. Butter in the north and olive oil in the south provided fat.

    c. Beer in the north and wine in the south were their common beverages.

    d. Pork from their half-wild pigs supplied the bulk of their meat.

    e. Mutton and beef were rarely had except when animals had to be killed.

    f. Vegetables were grown in the plots around each hut.

    e. Numerous holy days provided occasions for feasting and merrymaking.

C. <u>The life of the aristocracy</u> was largely devoted to fighting, governing, managing, and recreating.

  1. Tournaments and single combats such as duels simulated warfare in times of peace.

  2. Hunting and hawking were favorite male pastimes.

  3. Gaming, drinking, feasting, and listening to minstrels were common forms of recreation.

  4. Illicit affairs resulting in illegitimate children were common.

  5. The aristocracy was generally uneducated and frequently coarse, rude, boorish and violent.

  6. Women, though often influential, had a somewhat inferior status.

    a. Their main task was to bear children and see to domestic duties.

D. <u>The life of the clergy</u> was a good one by contemporary standards.
   1. Their primary functions were spiritual and religious.
   2. They were involved to some extent in the feudal system.
      a. Prelates held fiefs and exercised governmental and administrative offices.
      b. Local clergy were subject in part to local lords and were closely associated with the peasants to whom they ministered.
   3. Priests and monks rendered important social services as teachers, authors, historians, and copyists.

III. <u>Readings</u> on Early Medieval Economy and Society include:

Boissonade, Prosper, *Life and Work in Medieval Europe* (New York, Knopf, 1927).

Hone, Nathaniel, *The Manor and Manorial Records* (London, Methuen, 1906).

Cambridge Economic History, Vols. I, II, and III (New York, Cambridge U., 1941 ff.)

White, Lyon, *Medieval Technology and Social Change*, (Oxford, Clarendon, 1962).

Davis, William S., *Life on a Mediaeval Barony*, (New York, Harper, 1923).

Can You Identify?

agrarianism	*corvées*
manorialism	*heriot*
manor	banalities
latifundium	*merchet*
seignior	*taille*
steward	tithe
bailiff	serf
reeve	villein
demesne	cottar
"week-work"	bordar
"boon-work"	tournament

Chapter 13

Western Europe in the
Early Feudal Age (to ca. 1100)

I. <u>In Feudal France</u> (888-1106) the power of the king waned and multiple divisions prevailed, but the institution of the monarchy continued.

A. <u>Factors of weakness</u> were both external and internal.

    1. Numerous Viking and Moslem raids caused responsibility for defence and government to devolve on local lords.

    2. Alternating Robertians and Carolingians "held" and competed for the throne for a hundred years (888-987).

        a. The Robertians were supported by recent achievements, the Carolingians by tradition.

        b. Odo (Eudes), son of Robert the Strong, was elected by the magnates to replace the deposed Charles the Fat in 888.

        c. The Robertian Odo was succeeded by a Carolingian, Charles the Simple, who was in turn succeeded by a Robertian, etc.

        d. To gain support, the contestants distributed lands and allowed the great lords to become more powerful and independent.

        e. This internal strife, which weakened France, was encouraged by German rulers.

    3. Sectionalism was supported by ethnology, geography, historical traditions, and personal ambitions.

B. Capetian continuity and persistence helped stabilize the French monarchy (987 ff).

1. Capetian accession was a turning point in French history.

   a. The election of Hugh Capet in 987 inaugurated the Capetian dynasty.

      i. The direct line of the Carolingians had died out.

   b. Each Capetian king produced a male heir. for three and a half centuries.

   c. The concept of an hereditary kingship came to be entrenched.

2. The early Capetians (987-1106) did little more than establish their line securely on the throne.

   a. The four early Capetians were: Hugh (Capet), Robert II (the Pious), Henry I, and Philip I.

   b. Each had his son crowned during his own lifetime.

   c. Effective Capetian control was limited to the Ile de France.

   d. As long as the kings had little real power, the magnates accorded them nominal recognition.

   e. Hugh Capet had been elected with the help of Archbishop Adalbert of Reims, and the Capetians continued to receive Church support.

   f. Little increase in royal possessions and power occurred.

      i. The first three Capetians concentrated on holding the Ile de France, in which Paris and Orleans were the two important centers.

      ii. Philip I succeeded in acquiring a small amount of land.

   g. Dukes and Counts as powerful or more powerful than the French King included:

      i. The Dukes of Normandy, Brittany, Aquitaine, and Burgundy.

      ii. The Counts of Toulouse, Anjou, Flanders, Champagne and Blois.

C. The office of monarch included certain actual and potential rights and duties:

1. Defense of the kingdom against foreign attack.

    2. Defense of the Church against internal and external enemies.

    3. Protection of towns.

    4. Aid to the helpless, such as orphans, widows and the needy.

II. The Iberian Peninsula (*ca.* 711-1085) was mainly under Moslem control, but with beginnings of the Christian Reconquest.

    A. The Moslems overthrew the Visigothic kingdom (711-718) and ruled most of the peninsula.

        1. The Visigothic kingdom collapsed rapidly.

           a. It had been weakened by rivalries and internecine strife.

        2. Moslem Spain prospered for some time.

           a. Abd-al-Rahman, of the deposed Umayyad dynasty, fled to Spain where he founded an independent Emirate (756).

           b. In 931 Umayyad Spain became a Caliphate which lasted until 1031.

           c. An era of *taifas* (petty states) with temporary Moroccan overlords ensued.

        3. Internal divisions characterized Moslem Spain.

           a. The Moslems were divided into Arab, Berber, and Syrian factions.

           b. There was also division between the ruling Moslem minority and subject Christian majority.

        4. Moslem Spain was prosperous and cultured.

    B. The Christian "Reconquest" was well under way in Spain by the 11th century.

        1. The "*Reconquista*" was encouraged by Church support and by French assistance.

        2. Asturias, a small area in the northern mountains became a focal point of resistance.

        3. The Christian states of Galicia, Leon, Castile, and Portugal appeared in the north and west.

        4. Those of Navarre, Aragon, and Barcelona arose in the northeast.

        5. Christian expansion increased as the Umayyad Caliphate broke up into petty *taifas*.

           a. The Christians now took the offensive.

      b. With the fall of Toledo (1085) about one-third of the peninsula was in Christian hands.

III. <u>Anglo-Saxon England</u> was a product of Germanic, Christian, Italian, and Scandinavian influences.

  A. <u>Angles, Saxons, and Jutes</u> invaded Britain after the withdrawal of the Roman legions in the early 5th century.

    1. They seem originally to have been invited to aid the Britons against the Picts and Scots.

    2. They eventually took over Britain, exterminating, expelling or subjecting the native Celts.

  B. <u>Christianity</u> came to England in an organized way with the mission of St. Augustine (597 ff).

    1. Irish monks had spread the faith in the north and west of England.

      a. But the Celtic Church lacked organization.

    2. St. Augustine was sent to England by Pope Gregory I.

      a. He began his work in Kent with Canterbury as his base.

    3. The Council of Whitby (664) decided that the Roman dicipline and calendar should replace Celtic practices in England.

      a. Roman influences and organization gave the Church new life and strength.

    4. Archbishop Theodore of Tarsus improved the organization of the English Church.

      a. In 673 he held a synod which promulgated canons to be observed throughout all of England.

      b. He reorganized dioceses and promoted education.

  C. <u>Political fragmentation</u>, however, long prevailed.

    1. The "Heptarchy" of seven kingdoms (*ca.* 613-828) emerged from the original tribal settlements.

      a. The Heptarchy consisted of: Northumbria, Mercia, East Anglia, Wessex, Sussex, Essex, and Kent.

    2. Bretwaldas, or more powerful rulers, achieved hegemony one after another.

      a. Northumbria was dominant in the 7th century.

      b. Mercia rose to power in the 8th century.

        i. Ethelbald assumed the title "British King" and

    Offa claimed the title "King of all the land of
    the English."
  c. Wessex took the lead in the 9th century.
    i. Egbert (802-39) overthrew the Mercian yoke
    and became Bretwalda.
D. Unification developed as a result of English resistance to
 Danish invasions.
  1. The Danes won control of large parts of England in
   the 870's.
   a. Northumbria, East Anglia and Mercia were over-
    run.
  2. Alfred the Great of Wessex (871-99) succeeded in
   "containing the Danes."
   a. For seven years Alfred was on the defensive, yet
    refused to give up.
    i. The Danes captured Chippenham in 878, scat-
    tering the West Saxons.
   b. Alfred reorganized and defeated the Danes at
    Eddington (878).
   c. The Treaty of Wedmore (878) limited the Danes
    to the northeastern part of England "the Dane-
    law."
  3. Reforms of various types were introduced by Alfred.
   a. The *fyrd*, a militia composed of freemen, was re-
    organized.
   b. Alfred fortified towns and other strategic places,
    detailing a garrison for each district.
   c. A navy was also developed.
   d. Education and learning were promoted by Al-
    fred.
    i. For this purpose Alfred translated important
    Latin works into English.
  4. Alfred's earlier successors continued his policy of unification.
   a. The Danelaw was gradually incorporated.
  5. Ethelred the Unready (979-1016) was inept and im-
   prudent.
   a. He paid tribute to the Danes to keep them from
    attacking.
   b. For this purpose he levied a tax which came to
    be called the "Danegeld."

E. <u>Danish rule</u> in England lasted from 1016-1042.
   1. King Swein of Denmark and his son Canute con-
      quered England in 1013.
      a. After King Ethelred and Edmund Ironside both
         died in 1016, England became a part of the Danish
         Empire.
   2. <u>Canute</u> (Cnut) The Great succeeded his father in
      1016, and ruled Denmark, Norway and England until
      his death in 1035.
      a. A wise ruler, Canute brought peace and prosperity
         to England.
      b. He promoted the spread of the Latin, Christian
         culture.
      c. He was an ally of the Church.
      d. He collected the only national tax in Western Eu-
         rope: the Danegeld, which remained in force.
   3. Canute's sons, Harold and Harthecanute (d. 1042)
      lost control of England.
F. <u>Edward the Confessor</u> was restored to his English patri-
   mony in 1042 and ruled until 1066.
   1. The Witan elected Edward as king.
   2. Norman advisers and ecclesiastical officials accom-
      panied Edward.
      a. This angered the Anglo-Danish Earls.
   3. Edward was weak although pious and popular.
      a. Earl Godwin of Wessex and his son Harold God-
         winson held the real power.

IV. <u>Anglo-Saxon institutions</u> were strongly influenced by Ger-
    manic customs as well as by Christian concepts.

   A. <u>Government</u> was carried on by the king, the Witan and
      local officials and moots.
      1. The kingship was partly hereditary, partly elective.
      2. The Witan or *Witangemot* was the council of wise
         men or magnates.
         a. It discussed important questions.
         b. It judged cases of major importance.
         c. It issued "dooms" or laws which were clarifica-
            tions of custom.
      3. The shire (share: county) was the largest political
         division.

    a. Each shire had its own assembly or "shire-moot."

        i. This was originally presided over by the "ealdorman," who also led the shire forces in battle.

        ii. Later, the shire-reeve or "sheriff," the king's local representative, was in charge of each shire.

        iii. Eventually, sheriff, earl and bishop jointly presided over the shire-moot.

4. Subdivisions of shires included: hundreds, *tuns* or vills, and boroughs.

    a. Hundreds were called *"Wapentakes"* in Danish sections.

        i. Hundreds originally seem to have been composed of one hundred families or to have provided one hundred fighting men.

        ii. The hundred-moots were attended by representatives from the vills.

    b. The vill or *tun* (town) was the smallest unit and had its own village-moot or tun-moot.

    c. Boroughs were organized urban communities.

        i. Some self-government and political organization appeared in the boroughs.

5. Special features of the English state included:

    a. The "Danegeld," a direct tax

    b. The Earls, who appeared during the Danish occupation and ruled over several shires

    c. *"Thegns"* (thanes) or lesser nobles and *"cnights"* who were similar to knights on the continent

    d. Housecarls who were the king's personal bodyguard.

B. <u>Anglo-Saxon civilization,</u> though vital, generally lagged behind that on the continent.

1. The Church gave England its closest ties to the continent and its greatest force for unity.

    a. The Danish Wars disrupted the ecclesiastical life organized by Archbishop Theodore of Tarsus in the 7th century.

    b. A 10th century reform led by Dunstan, Archbishop of Canterbury (960-88), revived the Church, but was disrupted by new invasions.

      c. The English church was generally loyal to the Pope but was also dominated by the king.

  2. Vernacular literature developed early.

      a. *Beowulf*, the *Anglo-Saxon Chronicle*, the translations of Alfred the Great, and the works of Aelfric are examples of Old English literature.

  3. Learning flourished for a while in the 7th-8th centuries, but then declined.

      a. Aldhelm of Malmesbury, Venerable Bede, and Alcuin were eminent English scholars of the early period.

      b. Cathedral schools, such as York and Canterbury, as well as monastic schools, such as Wearmouth, Jarrow, and Malmesbury, were centers of learning.

V. Readings on Western Europe in the Early Feudal Era:

A. General:

    Petit-Dutaillis, Charles, *The Feudal Monarchy in France and England From the Tenth to the Thirteenth Centuries*, (trans.) London, Routledge, 1949).

    Painter, Sidney, *Rise of the Feudal Monarchies*, (Ithaca, Cornell, 1951).

B. On France:

    Funck-Brentano, Jacques C., *The Earliest Times*, (trans.) (New York, Putnam, 1927).

    Guignebert, Charles, *History of the French People*, 2 vols, Vol. I (New York, Macmillan, 1930).

C. On Spain:

    Altamira, Rafael, *History of Spain*, (trans.) (New York, Van Nostrand, 1949).

D. On England:

    Stenton, Frank, *Anglo Saxon England*, (Oxford, Clarendon Press, 1947).

    Bede the Venerable, St., *Ecclesiastical History of the English People* (in various editions).

Can You Identify?

Robertians	Hugh Capet
Odo	Adalbert of Reims
Capetians	Ile de France

Adb al Rahman
taifas
Reconquista
Asturias
Angles
Jutes
St. Augustine (of Canterbury)
Council of Whitby (664)
Theodore of Tarsus
Heptarchy
Bretwalda
Wessex
Egbert
Alfred
Eddington (Ethandune) (878)
Treaty of Wedmore (878)
fyrd
"Danelaw"
Ethelred

Canute (Cnut)
Edward the Confessor
Godwin
Harold Godwinson
Witangemot
dooms
shire
moot
ealdorman
shire-reeve
hundred
Wapentake
tun
borough
Danegeld
thegn (thane)
cnight
housecarl
Dunstan of Canterbury

Chapter 14

Central and Eastern Europe
in the Early Middle Ages

I. The German Empire arose in the Early Middle Ages (888-1056).

A. Factors of strength and weakness competed in German history.

1. Strengthening factors included:
   a. The Carolingian monarchical tradition
   b. Germany's exposed position, which kept the Germans a hardy, warlike race
   c. A common culture and language (despite differences of dialect)
   d. Common enemies, including the French to the West and the Slavs to the East.

2. Weakening factors included:
   a. Indefinite boundaries
   b. Large "stem" (tribal) duchies of Franconia, Swabia, Saxony and Bavaria, which vied for control
   c. Independent allodial holdings of the aristocracy, never fully subjected to the monarchy
   d. Regional differences of various sorts
   e. A partly elective monarchy which made succession dependent on the favor of the great lords
   f. Possessions in Italy which distracted rulers and entailed straddling the Alps.

             i. Kings often gave insufficient attention to problems in Germany.

             ii. Papal opposition in Italy often foiled German rulers.

3. The Last Carolingians (888-911) in Germany were harassed by foreign incursions and the rise of the Dukes.

    a. Arnulf (888-899) was a strong leader, who countered the Slavic thrusts on the East and dealt the Northmen a major defeat at the Dyle River (891).

        i. He invaded Italy where he was crowned Emperor (896).

    b. Louis the Child, the last Carolingian King in Germany, (900-911) was too young to be effective.

        i. Magyar incursions (ca. 900 ff) necessitated local organization for defense by regional Dukes.

    c. Conrad of Franconia (911-918), elected by the magnates to succeed Louis, was related to the Carolingian house.

        i. He, too, was powerless before the Magyars and unable to control the Dukes.

B. The Earlier Saxon (Ottonian) Emperors (918-973) unified Germany to a considerable extent and raised it to the status of an Empire.

1. Henry I (the Fowler) (918-36) gave the Saxon line a good start.

    a. Henry I controlled the Dukes in external matters but left them free as to internal affairs.

    b. He bought a temporary peace with the Magyars by annual tribute.

    c. He encouraged colonization along the frontiers, established fortified burgs, and trained local militia to defend them.

    d. He defeated the Magyars at the Unstrutt River in 933.

    e. Henry also occupied Lorraine and began the German eastward advance beyond the Elbe.

2. <u>Otto I, the Great</u> (936-73) sought to imitate Charlemagne.
   a. Otto overcame several ducal rebellions.
   b. He inflicted a decisive defeat on the Magyars at Lechfeld (955).
   c. Otto first tried to strengthen his position by putting members of his family in charge of the duchies, but this "family policy" failed.
   d. Otto then adopted an "ecclesiastical policy" of using bishops as political agents.
      i. He could name his own appointees who, as celibates, had no dynastic or familial ambitions.
   e. Otto made significant territorial gains.
      i. He organized "marches" or strong border counties in territory taken from the Slavs.
      ii. Burgundy was made a vassal state.
      iii. Otto intervened in Italy where he assumed the title of King (951), at first with an Italian as vicar.
   f. Otto was crowned Emperor in 962, reviving the Roman Empire in the West.
   g. Cultural progress adorned the Ottonian era.
      i. Otto patronized the arts, which were influenced by Byzantine forms.
      ii. Education was promoted by men of learning such as Bruno, Archbishop of Cologne.

C. <u>The Later Saxon Emperors</u> (973-1024) profited from the work of their predecessors with varying success.
   1. <u>Otto II</u> (973-983) encountered several difficulties.
      a. He was confronted by rebellions at home, which he overcame.
      b. He invaded Italy, where he was defeated in 982 and died the following year.
      c. The Slavs in German-held territory beyond the Elbe revolted during the confusion and regained their independence.
   2. <u>Otto III</u> (983-1002) embarked on a new imperial policy, which granted autonomy in internal affairs to component parts of the Empire.

      a. His preoccupation with Italy allowed the German nobles to grow unruly.
        i. The Slavs, too, made substantial gains.
        ii. Otto tried to move his capital to Rome but the Romans revolted.
      b. One of Otto's accomplishments was to have non-Romans elected to the Holy See, emphasizing its universality.
   3. Henry II of Bavaria (1002-1024) was a prudent ruler.
      a. Henry restored monarchical control in Germany and security along the frontiers.
      b. Although primarily concerned with Germany, he defended imperial rights in Italy, where he was crowned Emperor in 1014.
      c. Henry II and his wife promoted reform in the church and monasteries, and both attained sainthood.

D. Under the Earlier Franconians (1024-1056) the Empire reached its apogee.
   1. Monarchical power was at its fullest extent.
      a. The dukes and the Church were controlled.
      b. States along the eastern frontier became tributaries.
      c. The Emperor ruled much of Italy and appointed Popes.
   2. Conrad II (1024-39) was a strong ruler.
      a. He restrained the dukes by overcoming their rebellions and supporting the rights of lesser lords.
      b. He transferred administrative control to *ministeriales* or ex-serfs.
      c. He installed his son Henry as duke of most of the duchies.
      d. Conrad controlled Burgundy and Italy and claimed the overlordship of Poland and Hungary.
      e. He was cool, though respectful, to the Church.
   3. Henry III (1039-56) was a powerful ruler who carried to completion many of his father's policies.
      a. He continued the use of *ministeriales*.
      b. He returned to the "ecclesiastical policy" of appointing and using bishops and abbots as secular officials.

   c. A royal domain was being built up in S. Saxony
      and Thuringia.
   d. Henry furthered the eastern expansion of German
      influence.
      i. Poland, Hungary, and Bohemia all became
         fiefs of the Empire.
   e. Henry intervened in papal affairs and nominated
      four successive popes.
      i. Leo IX (1049-54), the Emperor's saintly uncle,
         who had been Bishop of Toul introduced the
         Cluniac-Gregorian reform.

II. The Slavs in the Early Middle Ages were incorporated into
    the Christian and civilized worlds of the Eastern and West-
    ern Empires.

   A. Their favorable situation enabled the Slavs to absorb
      Christian European civilization and to expand at the ex-
      pense of barbaric neighbors.
      1. Their initial base seems to have been in the vicinity
         of the Pripet Marshes and Dnieper River (Eastern
         Poland and Western Russia).
      2. Christianization and civilization of the Slavs occurred
         in the 9th and 10th centuries.
         a. Sts. Cyril and Methodius brought Christianity
            from Constantinople to the Moravians and ad-
            jacent Slavs in the 9th century.
            i. They formulated the Slavonic alphabet and
               translated parts of the Bible as well as the
               liturgy.
         b. The Western Slavs were subsequently incorporated
            into the Western Church.
         c. Eastern Christianity was carried to the Bulgarians,
            Croats, and Serbs in the 9th century, and to the
            Russians in the 10th.
   B. Division of the expanding Slavic peoples resulted in three
      groups.
      1. The Western Slavs occupied Eastern Central Europe.
         a. Poles, Czechs, Moravians, Polabians, Slovaks, and
            Wends were included in this group.
         b. The far Western Slavs were eventually subjected
            by the Germans.

        i. There was a temporary Moravian Empire in the 9th century, but it was overthrown by the Magyars.

        ii. Bohemia was subjected by the Germans despite its repeated attempts to gain independence.

    c. Hungary was occupied by the Magyars in the 10th century.

        i. Much of its population continued to be Slavic.

        ii. It was Christianized and made into a kingdom around the year 1000.

    d. Poland was Christianized and incorporated into the Western Church by the 11th century.

  2. The Southern Slavs moved into the Bulkans in the 6th to 7th centuries.

    a. The Bulgarians were a combination of Slavonized Mongoloids (Bulgars) and Slavs proper.

        i. The Bulgars united with the Slavs north and south of the Danube mouth area (7th century).

        ii. The Bulgarians were converted to Christianity in the 9th century.

        iii. The "First Bulgarian Empire" was dominant over much of the Balkans from about 893 to 1018.

    b. The Serbs and Croats founded kingdoms in the 11th century.

  3. The Eastern Slavs eventually expanded over Russia.

    a. The first large state in Russia was established by the Scandinavians, when they founded the principality of Kiev as their leading center (9th century).

        i. They had access to Byzantium by water, and besieged Constantinople several times.

    b. In the late 10th century, Prince Vladimir of Kiev was converted by Byzantine missionaries.

        i. He led the conversion of Russia to the Eastern Church.

    c. The Kievan state reached its height under Yaroslav the Wise (1019-1054).

III. Readings on Central and Eastern Europe in the Early Middle Ages include:

A. On the Germans and the Empire:

Thompson, James W., *Feudal Germany* (Chicago, U. Press, 1928).

Barraclough, Geoffrey, *Origins of Modern Germany* (Oxford, U. Press, 1947).

Reinhardt, Kurt, *Germany: Two Thousand Years* (Milwaukee, Bruce, 1950) and paper, 2 vols. (New York, Ungar, 1961).

Fisher, Herbert A. L., *The Medieval Empire*, 2 vols. (London, Macmillan, 1896).

B. On the Slavs in general:

Cross, Samuel H., *Slavic Civilization Through the Ages* (Cambridge, Harvard U. Press, 1948).

Dvornik, Frantisek, *Making of Central and Eastern Europe* (London, Polish Research Center, 1949).

Halecki, Oskar, *Borderlands of Western Civilization* (New York, Ronald Press Co., 1952).

C. On Russia and the Balkans:

Vernadsky, George, *A History of Russia*, 3 vols. to 1500 (New Haven, Yale U. Press, 1943ff.).

Pares, Bernard, *History of Russia* (New York, Knopf, 1944).

Schevill, Ferdinand, *History of the Balkan Peninsula* (New York, Harcourt, Brace, 1922).

Can You Identify?

stem duchies	Henry II
Conrad of Franconia	Franconian Emperors
Ottonian (Saxon) Emperors	Conrad II
Henry I (Fowler)	Henry III
burgs	*ministeriales*
Unstrutt River (933)	Leo IX
Otto I, Great	Sts. Cyril and Methodius
Lechfeld (955)	Western Slavs
"Family policy" (of Otto I)	Southern Slavs
"Ecclesiastical policy" (Otto I)	Bulgars
962	Bulgarians
Bruno	Eastern Slavs
Otto II	Kiev
Otto III	Vladimir

Chapter 15

The Church in the Early Middle Ages

I. The Papacy was a guiding, unifying, strengthening force in the Western world during the Early Middle Ages.

A. Papal prestige increased following toleration and transfer of the imperial capital to Constantinople (4th century ff.).

1. The Bishop of Rome became the temporal as well as spiritual leader of the Romans.

2. The Popes were recognized as the successors of St. Peter and the chief officers of the Christian Church.

3. They maintained unblemished orthodoxy and successfully asserted their primacy in the Church.

B. Three great Popes in the 4th to 6th centuries were influential in the consolidation of Papal power.

1. Leo I (440-461) spoke out for Papal primacy.

a. He asserted that "Peter speaks through Leo."

b. He secured an edict from Valentinian III recognizing his superior jurisdiction.

c. He successfully quashed the "Robber Council" of Ephesus (449).

d. He brought the ecumenical Council of Chalcedon (451) to accept his formula of faith condemning Monophysitism.

2. Gelasius I (492-496) enunciated the "two swords" theory, recognizing two independent powers—secular and spiritual—each sovereign in its own sphere.

a. The spiritual power is eventually superior, however, because temporal interests are secondary to the spiritual, said Gelasius.

3. <u>Gregory I</u> (the Great) (590-604) strengthened both the spiritual and temporal authority of the Papacy.

   a. He improved Papal government and increased Papal revenues.

   b. He organized a militia to defend Rome and negotiated a treaty with the Lombards.

   c. Gregory asserted Papal primacy and reproved John the Faster of Constantinople for assuming the title of "Ecumenical Patriarch."

   d. He took the lead in administrative and liturgical reforms.

      i. The worship service was organized and Gregorian plain chant was promoted.

   e. Gregory I also promoted missionary expansion, as in England.

C. <u>Papal independence</u> was preserved in the 7th and earlier 8th centuries by maintaining a balance of power between Lombards and Byzantines in Italy.

1. In the 8th century a Lombard revival posed a threat to Rome.

   a. The Lombard Kings began to expand into Byzantine and Papal territories.

   b. Byzantine help was not forthcoming due to preoccupation with the Moslems.

   c. The rift became pronounced when the Byzantine Emperors espoused heretical Iconoclasm.

D. <u>The era of the great Carolingians</u> (751-814) saw increased Papal-Frankish cooperation and the rise of Carolingian leanings to Caesaro-papism.

1. The Papal-Frankish alliance began when Pope Stephen II approved Pepin's right to ascend the Frankish throne (751) and obtained in return Pepin's pledge of protection against the Lombards.

   a. Stephen personally re-crowned Pepin (754).

   b. Pepin III restrained the Lombards, and ceded central Italy to the Papacy in the "Donations of Pepin" (754-756).

   c. Charlemagne ended Lombard power in 774, con-

firming and expanding Papal territories (Donation of Charlemagne).

  2. A somewhat theocratic Empire was inaugurated by
     Charlemagne.
     a. Although Leo III crowned Charlemagne Emperor
        on Christmas Day, 800, Charlemagne considered
        the Pope a purely spiritual leader.
        i. Charlemagne assumed much of the external
           administration of the Church.
     b. He appointed Church prelates, summoned Church
        councils, instituted ecclesiastical reforms, and dis-
        posed of Church lands.

E. Under the Later Carolingians of the 9th century the
   strength of the Papacy grew as that of the monarchs
   declined.

  1. The Papacy emerged as the main leader and nucleus
     of unity in the West.
  2. Nicholas I (858-67) asserted strong papal leader-
     ship.
     a. Nicholas interceded in a struggle over the Patri-
        archate of Constantinople and deposed Photius as
        a usurper.
     b. He also prevented Lothair II of Lotharingia from
        putting aside his wife and marrying his mistress.
     c. He overruled and reprimanded Archbishop Hinc-
        mar of Reims.
  3. The Pseudo-Isidorean Decretals ("False Decretals")
     strengthened the Papacy's position.
     a. They stressed freedom of the Church from lay
        control, and supremacy of the Papacy over the
        episcopate.
     b. These spurious decretals were evidently forged in
        France in the 9th century by opponents of arch-
        episcopal domination.

F. Feudal involvement enmeshed the Church and the Papacy
   (10th-11th centuries).

  1. The disposal of ecclesiastical offices and benefices be-
     came the prize of ambitious rulers and feudal lords.
     a. Many ecclesiastical offices came under lay control
        and simony spread.

       b. Increased secularization and decreased spirituality of Church personnel ensued.

  2. Control of Papal elections fluctuated between Italian factions and the Emperor.

       a. The prestige of the Papacy declined, although it did not disappear.

       b. The Italian houses of Spoleto and Theophylact controlled nominations for the Papal office (867-963).

       c. The German Emperors nominated Popes (963-1003).

       d. Italian houses (first that of Tusculum and then that of Crescentii) dominated the Papacy 1003-1046.

       e. Emperor Henry III reasserted imperial control by 1046, but by 1049 the Gregorian reform movement was under way.

  3. The Papal record of maintaining orthodoxy and papal primacy was unblemished even in this "Age of Iron."

II. Monasticism was both a pillar of strength and a fountain of spiritual rejuvenation in the early medieval Church.

  A. Monasticism is a way of life in which persons live apart from the world in order to achieve sanctity and to glorify God.

    1. Inspired by ideals of closer union with God and greater perfection, monks seek a life of prayer, asceticism, and concentration on Christian virtues.

    2. There were previous examples of monasticism in Judaism, Buddhism, and Hinduism.

  B. Eastern Christian Monasticism arose in desolate, unpopulated areas ("deserts") of Syria, Palestine, and Egypt in the 3rd to 4th centuries.

    1. Solitary forms were at first practiced by hermits such as St. Anthony of Egypt (280-356).

    2. Communal forms arose with the introduction of cenobitical monasticism by St. Pachomius in the Nile Valley (ca. 320).

    3. St. Basil of Caesarea moderated the severity of the Pachomian rule and his Ascetica or "Rule" came to be accepted throughout the East.

C. <u>Western Christian Monasticism</u> arose in the 4th and 5th centuries.
  1. Western monasticism at first slavishly imitated Eastern practices.
  2. Monastic rules were eventually authored by leaders like Honoratus of Lerins, John Cassian, Martin of Tours, St. Columban, etc.
  3. Irish monks followed Celtic forms, stressing great austerities, assiduous scholarship, and missionary zeal.

D. <u>Benedictine Monasticism</u> won ascendance throughout the West by about 800 A.D.
  1. St. Benedict of Nursia (480-542) drew up the Benedictine Rule and established several monasteries, including the Abbey of Monte Cassino.
  2. Benedict's Rule was marked by moderation, balance, and a sympathetic understanding of human nature.
     a. Adequate food, clothing, relaxation, and sleep were provided, and extreme mortifications discouraged.
     b. Prayer, work, and "refection" (sleep, recreation, and meals) each occupied about eight hours of the 24-hour day.
     c. Each Benedictine monastery was autonomous and self-supporting under an abbot elected by the monks.

E. <u>Contributions of monasticism</u> in Western Europe were many:
  1. The monks promoted religion both by teaching and by example.
  2. Great missionaries such as Saints Patrick, Columban, Boniface, and Augustine of Canterbury were monks.
  3. Charity and social work formed part of the Benedictine way of life.
     a. The monasteries provided schools, both academic and technical, as well as libraries, old age homes, hospitals, orphanages, hostels, and relief agencies.
  4. The monks improved agriculture and promoted the manual arts.
  5. Leading scholars, writers, and educators (such as Bede and Alcuin) were produced by monastic schools.

III. Church Reform and Expansion were promoted by monks and Popes, as well as by other influences.

A. Reform emanated from the monasteries.

   1. St. Benedict of Aniane attempted to reform and unify Benedictine monasteries in Gaul during the early 9th century.

      a. However, his reforms were too formal and particular to be continued beyond a limited time.

   2: The Cluniac Reform (10th century) was originally monastic.

      a. In 910 Duke William of Burgundy, to atone for his sins, allowed the new monastery of Cluny to be free from secular control.

      b. The Cluniac Rule stressed the liturgical aspect of Benedictine monasticism (*Lectio divina*) over manual labor.

      c. In the Cluniac Congregation, all monasteries were under priors subject to the Abbot of Cluny.

      d. Rapid spread of the Cluniac Reform occurred under the direction of five long-lived, saintly abbots.

      e. By 1100 there were over 300 Cluniac houses.

   3. The Gregorian Reform was the Cluniac reform as extended in modified form to the Episcopacy and Papacy.

      a. Bishops were soon being chosen from among the members of Cluny.

      b. The Cluniac reform came to the Papacy in the person of Leo IX in 1049.

      c. Gregory VII, greatest of all the Cluniac Popes, was formerly the monk Hildebrand, and from him the expanded movement took the name of "Gregorian" or "Hildebrandine."

      d. The Papacy now sought to free itself and the Episcopacy from all secular control.

B. Expansion of Christianity throughout Europe beyond the old Roman Empire was effected in the Early Middle Ages.

   1. Chief agents of expansion were the monks and the Popes, assisted by bishops, and monarchs.

    a. Communities of monks mutually supported each other in arduous missionary activities.

    b. The Papacy encouraged and commissioned missionaries to organize the Church in various countries.

    c. Conversion was accomplished by marriage, concentration on rulers, the sword, prayer, perseverance, and martyrdom.

2. Western and Central European barbarians converted in the early Middle Ages by dynamic organizing missionaries or "Apostles" included the people of:

    a. Ireland—St. Patrick (5th century)

    b. Scotland—St. Columbanus (6th century)

    c. England—St. Augustine (6th century)

    d. Netherlands—St. Willibrod (8th century)

    e. Germany—St. Boniface (8th century)

    f. Denmark and Sweden—St. Ansgar (9th century)

    g. Hungary—St. Stephen (about 1000).

3. The conversion of the Slavs mainly proceeded from Constantinople.

    a. Sts. Cyril and Methodius (9th century) were the initial "Apostles of the Slavs."

      i. They began the conversion of Greater Moravia and Bulgaria (9th century).

    b. The Serbs and other Southern Slavs became Eastern Christians (9th century ff.).

    c. The Kievan Russians were converted in the 10th century.

    d. The Western Slavs in Poland, Bohemia, Hungary, etc., were absorbed by the Western Church about 1000 A.D.

IV. Miscellaneous developments included the Eastern Schism and progress in faith and morals.

    A. The Eastern Schism resulted from a widening rift between Eastern and Western Churches.

    1. The "Photian Schism" (9th century) originated over the intrusion of Photius into the See of Constantinople.

      a. Appointed by Caesar Bardas to replace "deposed" Patriarch Ignatius, Photius was declared a usurper by Nicholas I.

        b. Photius replied by accusing the Western Church of various "errors," such as inclusion of the "*filioque*" in the creed and the use of unleavened bread in the Eucharist.

        c. The break was later healed.

    2. The definitive Schism came in 1054.

        a. The Cluniacs were attempting to assert Papal supremacy.

        b. Michael Cerularius, the Byzantine Patriarch, was excommunicated by Papal envoys when he refused to submit to Papal authority.

        c. Cerularius "returned the compliment" by removing the Pope's name from the diptychs.

B. Progress of Christian faith and morality continued despite difficulties and limitations.

    1. The clergy, although imperfect, usually did a good job.

    2. Lay Christians, also imperfect, usually had faith and sought after virtue.

    3. Feudal influences adversely affected the clergy, since the laity usually controlled appointments to clerical offices.

        a. Many prelates were worldly.

        b. Many of the lower clergy were lax.

        c. The clergy were often poorly educated.

V. Readings on the Church in the Early Middle Ages include:

Hughes, Philips, *History of the Church, II* (New York, Sheed and Ward, 1932 ff.).

Flick, Alexander C., *Rise of the Mediaeval Church* (New York, Putnam's, 1909).

Mourett, Fernand, and Thompson, Newton, *History of the Catholic Church*, III (St. Louis, Herder, 1941).

Mann, Horace K., *Lives of the Popes in the Early Middle Ages*, 18 vols. (London, K. Paul, 1925-1932).

Workman, Herbert B., *Evolution of the Monastic Ideal* (London, Kelly, 1913).

Butler, Cuthbert, *Benedictine Monachism* . . . (New York, Longmans, 1924).

Daly, L. J., *Benedictine Monasticism* (New York, Sheed, 1964).

Benedict of Nursia, St., *The Benedictine Rule* (various translations and editions).

Can You Identify?

Leo I, Pope

Gelasius I

Gregory I

Leo III, Pope

Nicholas I

Theophylact

Tusculum

monasticism

St. Anthony of Egypt

St. Pachomius

St. Basil

St. Benedict of Nursia

St. Benedict of Aniane

Cluniac Reform

Gregorian Reform

Hildebrand

St. Patrick

St. Columbanus

St. Willibrod

St. Stephen of Hungary

Eastern Schism

Photian Schism

Photius

Michael Cerularius

Chapter 16

Early Medieval Culture

I. <u>Early Medieval Culture</u> was derived from various sources and preserved by the Church.

   A. <u>Various elements</u> were combined in Early Medieval culture.

      1. Classical (Greco-Roman), barbarian (Teutonic and Celtic), and Christian influences all contributed.

   B. <u>The Church</u> was the chief guardian and nurse of Early Medieval culture.

      1. The monasteries were its main custodians and adapters.

II. <u>Education and learning</u> in the Early Middle Ages were primarily in the care of the Church.

   A. <u>The chief purpose</u> of education in this era was the training of priests and monks, although outsiders were also included.

   B. <u>Schools</u> were mainly of two types:

      1. Cathedral schools were connected with episcopal seats.

         a. Education of secular priests was their chief aim.

         b. Orleans, Reims, Chartres, Cologne, and York were examples of good cathedral schools.

      2. Monastic schools were connected with monasteries.

         a. The training of monks was their primary goal.

         b. Schools at Reichenau, Tours, Fulda, Jarrow, and Malmesbury were in this category.

      3. Other schools of lesser importance included occa-

sional parish schools, song schools, and lay schools (in Italy).

C. The curriculum comprised the seven liberal arts and Christian doctrine.

   1. The "seven liberal arts" consisted of the *trivium* and *quadrivium*.

      a. The *trivium* taught the use of words and reason and was basic for a general education.

         i. The *trivium* (triple course) included grammar (with literature), rhetoric (including law generally), and logic.

      b. The *quadrivium* was the medieval training in science and mathematics.

         i. This (quadruple course) was composed of arithmetic, geometry, astronomy, and music (theory).

         ii. The *quadrivium* was less well known and its study was largely confined to the more learned.

   2. "Divine Learning," or the study of Christian doctrine, was the crowning part of early medieval learning.

      a. Church doctrines, laws, and traditions were studied.

      b. Sacred Scriptures, the Fathers, liturgical works, and various ecclesiastical writings, such as scriptural commentaries, were used as sources.

   3. Monastic learning was more advanced at first.

      a. Monasteries had *scriptoria* for copying manuscripts.

      b. Many monasteries had good libraries containing fine assortments of both Christian and classical works.

      c. Literary learning often was considerable.

      d. The philosophical consideration of religion was undertaken to a small degree.

      e. Lay literacy gradually spread, particularly among the nobility.

D. Educational leaders in the Early Middle Ages included:

   1. Boethius (6th century), a minister of Theodoric, translated and commented on Aristotle's logical

works, and wrote the *Consolation of Philosophy*, as well as treatises on arithmetic and music.

2. Cassiodorus (6th century), another of Theodoric's ministers, composed a guide for monastic studies, known as *The Institutes of Divine and Secular Learning*, and various other works to promote learning.

3. Isidore of Seville (7th century), bishop and teacher, was the author of famous encyclopedias: the *Etymologies* and *Differences*, as well as other pedagogical treatises.

4. Venerable Bede (8th century), an English monk, who wrote several textbooks, is most famous for his *Ecclesiastical History of the English People*.

5. Charlemagne promoted the Carolingian Renaissance in education.

6. Alcuin (8th-9th centuries), who had been educated and had taught for a time at York, headed the Palace School of Charlemagne and sparked the Carolingian Renaissance.

7. Rhabanus Maurus (9th century), known as "The Schoolmaster of Germany," was a famous teacher at Fulda, who contributed a work "On Education of Clerics."

8. John Scotus Erigena (9th century) was a brilliant Irish scholar and proto-scholastic, who wrote a philosophical discourse, "On the Division of Nature."

9. Walafrid Strabo (9th century), Abbot of Reichenau, composed the *Glossa Ordinaria*, an abridgement of patristic commentaries on the Scriptures and a standard reference.

10. Lupus of Ferrières (9th century), assiduously copied and collated classical manuscripts in an effort to improve existing texts.

11. Alfred the Great (10th century) promoted translations and learning in England.
   a. Key works of Boethius, Orosius, Gregory the Great, Augustine, and Bede were translated by Alfred and his helpers.

12. Gerbert of Aurillac, a master at Reims who became

Pope Sylvester II, (999-1003), promoted science and mathematics as well as the liberal arts.

III. <u>Literature</u> was composed in Latin, for the most part, though sometimes in the vernacular.

    A. <u>Latin poetry</u> was a favorite literary form.

        1. New devices in Latin poetry included the use of accentuated rhythm and rhyme.

        2. Latin poets of the 4th-6th centuries with examples of their works include:

            a. Ambrose of Milan: "Hymn at Cockcrow"

            b. Augustine of Hippo: "Yearning for Eternal Love"

            c. Paulinus of Nola: "To Ausonius"

            d. Prudentius of Spain: "Hymn for the Burial of the Dead"

            e. Boethius: "On the Consolation of Philosophy"

            f. Fortunatus (an Italian, working in France): "Vexilla Regis."

        3. Latin poets of the 8th-9th century ("Carolingian Renaissance" Era) and examples of their work include:

            a. Alcuin: "Lament for a Cuckoo"

            b. Rhabanus Maurus: "Veni Creator Spiritus"

            c. Walafrid Strabo: "On Gardening"

            d. Angilbert: "Battle of Fontenoy"

            e. Also written were many anonymous poems such as: "The Monk of Angers," a drinking song, and "The Philosopher and his Cat," an Irish satire.

    B. <u>Vernacular literature</u> began to be cultivated.

        1. Anglo-Saxon and Irish compositions were the main examples of vernacular literature.

        2. Anglo-Saxon literature included such works as:

            a. Narrative poems like *Beowulf* and *The Battle of Brunanburgh*

            b. Caedmon's *Master of the World*

            c. The anonymous *Ruined City*.

        3. Irish literature contributed works such as:

            a. The *Cuchulain's Cycle*, adventure stories combining prose and poetry

            b. Lyrical pieces such as the *Deer's Cry, Hermit's Song,* and *Winter Song.*

C. History writing received an early impetus because of Christian interests and classical examples.

1. General Church history was an initial interest.

   a. Eusebius of Caesarea (4th century) has been called the "Father of Church History" because of his *Church History* and *Chronography*.

   b. Augustine's *City of God* was a profound philosophy of history and a defense of Christianity.

   c. Orosius (5-6th centuries) essayed an elementary *History of the World*.

2. "National" histories followed the barbarian invasions.

   a. Cassiodorus composed a *History of the Goths*, which has been lost except for its dim reflection in Jordanes' *History of the Goths*.

   b. Gregory of Tours (6th century) wrote a *History of the Franks*.

   c. Paul the Deacon composed a *History of the Lombards* (8th century).

   d. Venerable Bede authored the excellent *Ecclesiastical History of the English People*.

3. Biographies of saints, bishops, and national leaders were popular.

   a. Many lives of bishops have been preserved for us in literature.

   b. Einhard's *Life of Charlemagne* is the primary source of our knowledge about this great man.

   c. Asser's *Life of Alfred the Great* is another example.

4. Annals and chronicles are invaluable sources of knowledge.

   a. Annals were chronological listings of events of local or general importance.

   b. Chronicles were generally more connected historical narratives.

      i. *The Anglo-Saxon Chronicle* was kept in the vernacular.

IV. The Arts and music usually were cultivated with a Christian inspiration.

A. Architecture gradually evolved towards the Romanesque style.

1. Basilicas were the first distinctive church structures.
    a. They were rectangular buildings with a central aisle flanked by two lower side aisles.
        i. A transept was sometimes added just ahead of the apse, giving the structure a cruciform shape.
    b. A courtyard (*atrium*) and a porch (*narthex*) served as approaches.
    c. The nave terminated in a slightly elevated, rounded eastern apse.
    d. The interior was usually ornamented with carvings and paintings or mosaics.
2. The rotunda style, either round or polygonal, was occasionally used.
    a. A dome covered the central part of the round church.
    b. The church of San Vitale at Ravenna is an example of the rotunda style.
3. Byzantine architecture evolved into a new form.
    a. It combined the original basilican style in the cruciform shape with the dome-centered rotunda style.
    b. In such churches the dome rose over the intersection of the nave and transept.
        i. The church of Santa Sophia in Constantinople is an example of Byzantine architecture.
4. Proto-Romanesque architecture developed in the later part of the Early Middle Ages.
    a. Charlemagne's cathedral at Aachen exemplified this style, as did several churches in Lombardy.
    b. Stone vaults covered aisles, and piers replaced columns.
        i. The churches were thick-walled.
B. Early Medieval art was dynamic and cosmopolitan.
    1. Contributing influences were Roman, Greek, Hellenistic, Celtic, and Germanic.
    2. Art forms included:
        a. Illuminations in religious books.
        b. Some crude but forceful sculpture.
        c. Metalwork and woodwork, often excellent (as in Hildesheim Cathedral).

3. Early Germanic and Celtic art was ornamental rather than representational.
    a. Linear patterns and stylized life forms were featured.
    b. The "Book of Kells" and the "Lindisfarne Gospels" are good examples.
4. Carolingian and 10th-century illuminations presented movement and narration as well as allegory.

C. <u>Music</u> was widely cultivated both in worship and in recreation.
1. Plain Chant, "prose song" or "talking in song," stressed the sense of the words.
    a. It was employed in the liturgy of the Church throughout Western Europe.
2. Hymns of a more dramatic and popular style also were composed.
    a. The hymn form entered the liturgy in the *tropes* and *sequences* inserted in the Masses.
3. Polyphony, employing parallel harmony, developed by the 10th century.
4. Musical notation was devised to represent pitch and melody and to facilitate music in more than one part.

V. <u>Readings</u> on Early Medieval Culture include:

Artz, Frederick B., *Mind of the Middle Ages* (New York, Knopf, 1953).

Laistner, Max L., *Thought and Letters in Western Europe, 500-900* (New York, Dial Press, 1931).

West, Andrew F., *Alcuin and the Rise of Christian Schools* (New York, Scribners, 1892).

Mullinger, James B., *Schools of Charles the Great* (New York, Steckert, 1932).

Jones, Leslie W., *Medieval Literature in Translation* (New York, Longmans, 1950).

Porter, Arthur K., *Medieval Architecture*, 2 vols. (New Haven, Yale, 1912).

Rice, D. T., *Medieval Art* . . . (New York, Philosophical Library, 1950).

Diringer, David, *The Illuminated Book* . . . (New York, Philosophical Library, 1955).

Reese, Gustave, *Music in the Middle Ages* (New York, Norton, 1940).

Can You Identify?

Cathedral schools	Eusebius of Caesarea
Monastic schools	Orosius
"Liberal arts"	Gregory of Tours
Trivium	Paul the Deacon
Quadrivium	Einhard
"Divine learning"	Asser
scriptoria	*Anglo-Saxon Chronicle*
Boethius	*basilica*
Cassiodorus	*atrium*
Isidore of Seville	transept
Venerable Bede, St.	nave
Alcuin	apse
Rhabanus Maurus	rotunda style
John Scotus Erigena	Byzantine architecture
Lupus of Ferrières	Proto-Romanesque architecture
Gerbert	"Book of Kells"
Fortunatus	"Plain Chant"

PART III

The High Middle Ages (1050-1300)

I. <u>The High Middle Ages</u> were three dynamic centuries of extraordinary progress in almost every field.
   A. <u>The zenith</u> of medieval civilization came during the High Middle Ages (1050-1300).
      1. In comparison, the Early Middle Ages were a period of beginnings, and the Later Middle Ages were a period of dissolution.
      2. The culmination of the "Age of Faith" now occurred.
         a. Religion was the chief inspiration, and the Church the most influential institution.
      3. These years saw the temporary perfection of the "medieval synthesis."
   B. <u>Achievements and contributions</u> of the High Middle Ages include:
      1. Territorial "national" states, which have endured to the present day
      2. Organized, strengthened central governments
      3. Charters of liberty, both urban and national
      4. Representative parliaments
      5. The commercial revolution, with great expansion of trade, industry, and finance
      6. Overseas expansion
      7. Emancipation of labor
      8. Universities
      9. A reformed, vigorous, effective Church
      10. Revival of philosophy and the sciences
      11. Beginnings of modern vernacular literatures
      12. Romanesque and Gothic art and architecture.

II. <u>Readings</u> on Europe in the High Middle Ages include:

Brooke, Zachary N., *A History of Europe from 911 to 1198* (London, Methuen, 1938).

The Cambridge Medieval History, Volumes V and VI.

Haskins, Charles H., *Renaissance of the Twelfth Century* (Cambridge, Mass., Harvard, 1927).

Lyon, Bryce, ed., *The High Middle Ages, 1000-1300* (Toronto, Free Press, 1964).

Previté-Orton, Charles W., *A History of Europe from 1198 to 1378* (London, Methuen, 1937).

Southern, Richard W., *The Making of the Middle Ages* (New Haven, Yale, 1953).

Chapter 17

Economic and Social Progress and Associated Developments in the High Middle Ages

I. Economic advances and prosperity provided a basis for general progress in the High Middle Ages.

A. The Commercial Revolution dawned in the High Middle Ages.

1. Wholesale trade on a large scale became more common.

2. Factors promoting the Commercial Revolution included:

   a. Growing political stability
   b. Western military ascendance
   c. Western naval superiority
   d. The Crusades, with opportunities for increased contact and travel
   e. Western trading posts in the Eastern Mediterranean
   f. The enterprise of the North Italians
   g. Improved ships and navigational aids
   h. Progress in related fields (industrial, financial, agricultural, educational, etc.).

3. Three forms of commerce expanded:

   a. International commerce was carried on among the Western kingdoms, and between East and West.

b. Interregional commerce included trade between different areas.

c. Local commerce grew within and around the rising cities.

4. Maritime routes were the principal avenues of commerce.

   a. The Mediterranean Sea with the adjacent Black Sea was the principal highway.

   b. Atlantic avenues included the English Channel, the Bay of Biscay, the North Sea, and the Baltic Sea.

   c. Rivers were much used, as were the old Roman Roads.

5. Focal centers of commerce included:

   a. Northern Italy, with cities such as Venice, Genoa, Pisa, Milan, and Florence

   b. The Low Countries, with cities such as Ghent, Bruges, and Antwerp

   c. Similar centers in Catalonia, Northwestern France, Southern France, the Rhineland, Northern Germany, and Southern Germany.

6. Cooperative organization was common in commerce.

   a. Merchant-guilds established local monopolies and promoted external trade.

      i. The guilds excluded or minimized foreign competition.

      ii. They established and controlled standards.

      iii. They acted as social and mutual-aid associations.

   b. Hanses were commercial unions of several towns.

      i. Merchants of various cities cooperated to promote, protect, and control regional trade.

   c. Communes were municipal unions formed to obtain status, emancipation, and self-government.

   d. Marketing was done at markets and fairs, as well as by peddlers and from shops.

      i. Markets were held weekly in most towns.

      ii. Fairs, among which the fairs of Champagne were most famous, drew on larger regions and were wholesale.

B. <u>In finance,</u> increased availability of money and development of financial devices aided the economy.
  1. Coinage increased considerably both in volume and in amounts.
     a. Coins of larger denominations reappeared.
        i. Larger silver coins came into use after the Venetians began to coin silver "groats" (12th century).
        ii. Gold coinage was reintroduced (13th century) in the form of Venetian "ducats," Florentine "florins," and Hohenstaufen "augustales."
  2. Capital accumulated through operations such as: trade, investments, loans, tax collecting, coinage, and mining.
     a. Cooperative investment of capital took two principal forms:
        i. *Commenda:* short-term partnerships for particular ventures
        ii. *Compagnias* (companies): continuing family partnerships, such as the Bardi and Peruzzi.
  3. Banking and credit became more sophisticated.
     a. Banks (*banci* or *tavoli*) got their name from the benches or tables used at fairs during monetary transactions.
        i. Exchange was the process of changing one form of money into another for a fee.
     b. Credit existed both in loans and paper transactions, such as letters of credit and bills of exchange.
  4. Interest created a problem.
     a. There was a Church prohibition against it, based on the Old Testament.
        i. But recompense was needed for the risk of capital and the losses involved.
     b. Ways of circumventing prohibitions against usury were:
        i. Penalties for late payment, assured by setting the agreed time of payment too early (*poena conventionalis*)
        ii. Discounting loans at the outset by paying less than the face value of the loan, while expecting payment in full

        iii. Considering each loan as a guaranteed investment in which the lender participated.

    c. The legitimacy of interest came to be accepted under various titles:

        i. *Lucrum cessans:* the interruption of possible gain

        ii. *Periculum sortis:* the risk involved

        iii. *Damnum emergens:* interim losses actually or possibly sustained

        iv. *Poena conventionalis:* (see above, b. i.): an agreed fine for "late" payment.

    d. Rates of interest in the 13th century varied from 10% to 100%.

        i. In Italy rates generally were lower because money was more plentiful and the risk was smaller.

        ii. In France and England rates were correspondingly higher.

C. <u>Industry</u> experienced striking growth and improved organization.

  1. Industry grew rapidly.

    a. Production mounted to meet new demands.

    b. Many techniques were imported from the Near East and Byzantium.

    c. Industrial products and forms included: textiles, metalwork, leatherwork, jewelry, pottery, woodwork and shipbuilding, mining, foods, and alcoholic drinks.

  2. Craft guilds brought improved organization into industry.

    a. These originally split off from the general merchant guilds.

    b. They established standards and prices for products.

    c. They also had rules for training qualified artisans.

        i. Apprenticeships lasted for several (v.g. seven) years.

        ii. A journeyman could work for hire.

        iii. A master, who had demonstrated his command of his craft and paid the required fees, was allowed to hire and train others.

D. <u>Agriculture</u> expanded and adapted itself to the spreading money economy.

    1. Factors in agricultural expansion included:

        a. Increased demand for agricultural products, especially in the growing towns

        b. Increased individual ownership and private enterprise

        c. Improved methods, such as fertilization, greater use of the three-field system, better plows and other tools, use of horses, etc.

    2. Forms of expansion were both internal and external.

        a. External expansion into new areas occurred through conquest and occupation.

        b. Internal expansion occurred through land reclamation, by clearing, drainage, and dikes.

II. <u>Medieval society</u> was transformed with the help of economic changes.

    A. <u>The urban population</u> grew in size and importance.

        1. The population of Western Europe apparently doubled in the High Middle Ages.

        2. Many towns developed in this period.

            a. Many revived on the sites of old Roman towns.

            b. Others resulted from the growth of manorial villages.

            c. Sites of new towns were varied and included:

                i. Harbors and ports

                ii. The mouths of rivers and vicinities of fords

                iii. Crossroads and hilltops (*bergs*)

                iv. Around monasteries and castles (*faubourgs* or *suburbia*)

                v. In connection with fortifications (*burgs*).

        3. Communes won charters and concessions which allowed partial self-government.

            a. Communes were associations of townspeople formed to advance their mutual interests.

            b. Both by charters and proscription, towns began to free themselves from the control of local lords and bishops.

            c. Concessions were gained in various ways: by armed revolts, as rewards for aid in crises, on the payment of cash sums, and by grants from kings who wished to gain town support and to profit from urban revenues.

    d. Privileges won by townspeople included:

        i. Freedom of person and property for inhabitants

        ii. Self-government by their own officials

        iii. Administration of justice by their own judges

        iv. Limited taxes

        v. Immunity from external interference in their municipal affairs

        vi. Recognition of their communes and guilds.

4. The middle class grew and organized.

    a. The middle class included non-aristocratic free people of means.

    b. In the towns they were known as "bourgeoisie," and in the country as "knights" and "squires."

    c. The middle class formed guilds, hanses, communes, *commendas*, and companies.

B. <u>Emancipation of serfs</u> proceeded steadily.

1. Free (non-servile) labor was preferred both by laborers and lords.

    a. In a money-economy, free, hired laborers were more efficient.

    b. Servile obligations were transmuted to money payments such as rents.

2. "Town air makes free" became an accepted principle.

    a. Anyone living in town for a year and a day without challenge was free.

3. Privileges and concessions were used to attract laborers to new, developing areas.

III. <u>Related changes</u> in religion, culture, and government were promoted by economic and social developments.

A. <u>In religion</u> there were many repercussions.

1. New heresies, such as those of the Albigensians and Waldensians, arose in urban areas.

2. The mendicant orders (Franciscans and Dominicans) were formed to cope with urban religious problems.

3. Education of the secular clergy was improved.

4. Theologians advanced economic doctrines such as the permissibility of interest.

B. <u>In the cultural field</u>, increased wealth afforded more time for leisure and learning, while economic advances demanded greater education.

    1. Education shifted from the rural monastic schools to urban cathedral schools.

        a. Cathedral schools improved their offerings.

        b. Public municipal schools arose in some towns.

        c. Literacy among the laity increased.

        d. Universities provided professional education.

    2. Vernacular literatures designed for the literate laity emerged.

    3. Architectural advances were dramatic.

        a. Romanesque and Gothic cathedrals were erected in towns.

        b. Secular architecture grew with the erection of town halls, guild halls, and better private residences.

C. <u>Political progress</u> accompanied the growth of towns and rise of the middle class.

    1. More personal liberties and partial self-government were achieved.

    2. The middle class obtained representation in regional and national assemblies.

    3. The spread of royal justice and evolution of "common" national laws occurred.

    4. Monarchical power and national unity were enhanced.

IV. <u>Readings</u> on Economic and Social Progress in the High Middle Ages include:

Boissonade, Prosper, *Life and Work in Medieval Europe* . . . (New York, Knopf, 1927).

Pirenne, Henri, *Economic and Social History of Medieval Europe* (New York, Harcourt, Brace, 1937) and *Medieval Cities* (Princeton, University, 1937).

Cambridge Economic History of Europe (Vols. I and II (New York, Macmillan, 1941 and 1952).

Baldwin, Summerfield, *Business in the Middle Ages* (New York, Holt, 1937).

Painter, Sidney, *Medieval Society* (Ithaca, Cornell, 1951).
Stephenson, Carl, *Borough and Town* (Cambridge, Mass., Mediaeval Academy, 1933).

Can You Identify?

"High Middle Ages"	*commenda*
The "Commercial Revolution"	*compagnia*
guilds	*poena conventionalis*
merchant guilds	*lucrum cessans*
hanses	*periculum sortis*
communes	*damnum emergens*
fairs	craft guilds
groat	*burg*
ducat	*faubourg*
florin	bourgeoisie

Chapter 18

The Expansion of Europe
and the Crusades

I. <u>Western European expansion</u> began in the High Middle Ages.
   A. <u>Factors</u> included:
      1. Economic progress and prosperity which provided a basis and a motive
      2. Population growth which provided pressure and manpower
      3. Military superiority
      4. A decline in Moslem and Byzantine unity and strength
      5. A spirit of faith which inspired missionary zeal and veneration of the Holy Land.
   B. Expansion occurred in every direction.
      1. The Normans expanded into Southern Italy and Sicily and attempted to expand into the Balkans (11th century).
      2. The Germans expanded eastward, beyond the Elbe, as well as northward into the Baltic area (Teutonic Knights).
      3. The Spaniards were expanding to the south in the Iberian peninsula ("Reconquest").
      4. The Genoese and Venetians were acquiring bases in and about the Mediterranean and Black Seas.
      5. The Crusades were a spectacular form of this general expansion.

II. The Crusades were military, naval, and colonial movements
for the purpose of taking and holding the Holy Land and
adjacent areas in the near East in the name of religion.

A. Causes of the Crusades were complex.
1. The same factors which brought about the general
   expansion of Western Europe were involved, and included "Gospel, glory, and gold."
2. A love of pilgrimages and reverence for the Holy
   Places contributed.
3. The Eastern Schism and Byzantine weakness were
   factors.
4. An appeal for help by the Byzantine Emperor Alexius
   Comnenus, provided the immediate cause.
   a. Seljuk conquests had devoured almost all of By-
      zantium's Asiatic holdings.
   b. Under Alexius Comnenus, the Byzantines rallied,
      and began a limited offensive in Asia Minor.
   c. A shortage of manpower impelled Alexius to ap-
      peal to the Pope (1095).
   d. Urban II preached the First Crusade at the Coun-
      cil of Clermont (1095).
5. Motives of participants and Popes were mixed:
   a. The thought of the Holy Places being in the hands
      of disrespectful infidels was shocking.
   b. Most Crusaders saw the Crusades as "armed pil-
      grimages" and acts of devotion and penance.
   c. The prospect of acquiring land and wealth in the
      Near East appealed to some.
   d. The Crusades provided the Papacy with an op-
      portunity to lead a popular international move-
      ment and enhance its prestige.
   e. The prospect of winning back the Greeks and
      healing the Schism was an added enticement.
   f. The Crusades were also used to divert Western
      Christians from internecine warfare.
   g. For North Italian businessmen, the Crusades pre-
      sented opportunities to acquire valuable trading
      posts and commercial privileges in the Near East.
6. The Crusade was preached throughout the West and
   particularly in France.

B. The First Crusade (1096-99) included two separate movements: the preliminary Peasants' Crusade and the main Crusade of the Princes.

1. The Peasants' Crusade (1096) was inspired by the preaching of Peter the Hermit and Walter the Penniless.

   a. It was an impractical, disorganized expedition of peasants and commoners.

   b. Many attacked Jews.

   c. In the Balkans the Crusaders clashed with the populace.

   d. On arriving at Constantinople they were quickly ferried across the straits.

   e. In Asia Minor their pillaging and looting angered the Turks who destroyed their army.

2. The "Crusade of the Princes" was the first real Crusade.

   a. It was carefully planned and equipped.

   b. The majority of Crusaders were from France.

   c. No crowned heads participated, since the leading rulers were at odds with the Pope.

   d. Participating Princes included: Count Raymond of Toulouse, Duke Robert of Normandy (brother of the English King), Count Hugh of Vermandois (brother of the French King), Count Stephen of Blois, Duke Godfrey of Bouillon, Prince Bohemund of Taranto and his nephew Tancred, and Bishop Adehmar of Le Puy, the Pope's representative.

   e. Various routes were taken to Constantinople, where most leaders were brought to take an oath of allegiance to Alexius.

3. In Asia Minor the Crusaders were successful.

   a. They besieged Nicaea, which then surrendered to the Byzantines.

   b. At Dorylaeum (1097) the Crusaders turned defeat into victory.

      i. They had split up into two armies.

      ii. The first group under Bohemund was attacked by a large Turkish force.

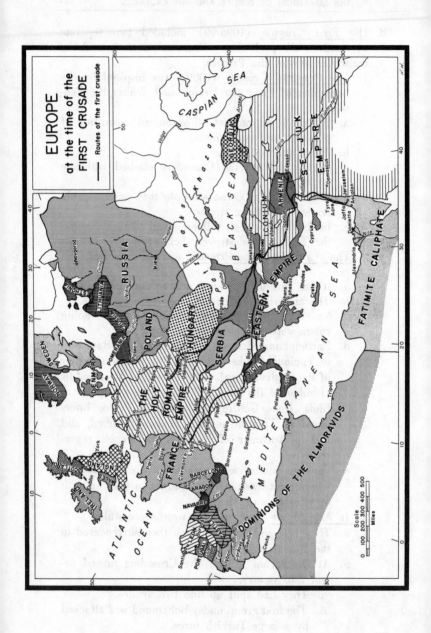

EUROPE
at the time of the
FIRST CRUSADE

Routes of the first crusade

Scale
0 100 200 300 400 500
Miles

       iii. The timely arrival of the second group saved them.

4. <u>Antioch</u> was reached after a difficult and costly march across Asia Minor.
   a. Baldwin meanwhile proceeded to Edessa which he captured and held for himself.
   b. After an eight-month siege, Antioch fell through treachery.
   c. Besieged in turn by Emir Kerbogha, the Crusaders sallied forth, and surprised and routed the Moslems.
   d. Bohemund gained possession of Antioch, and the rest of the Crusaders proceeded to Palestine.

5. <u>Jerusalem</u> was taken in 1099.
   a. It withstood Crusaders attacks for some time.
   b. After a solemn procession around the wall the city was stormed and taken.
      i. A terrible massacre followed.

6. The Kingdom of Jerusalem was established.
   a. Godfrey of Bouillon was elected "Protector of the Holy Sepulchre" (1099).
   b. Baldwin of Edessa, his brother, was elected King after Godfrey's death in 1100.
   c. The Kingdom of Jerusalem was a lay, feudal state, consisting of four virtually autonomous states: The kingdom of Jerusalem itself; the county of Tripoli, just to the north; the principality of Antioch farther north; and the county of Edessa to the northeast.

C. <u>Moslem recovery</u> stimulated the Second and Third Crusades.
   1. <u>Zanghi</u> (d. 1146), Atabeg of Mosul, initiated a westward Moslem expansion.
      a. He took Aleppo in 1128.
      b. Edessa fell to him in 1144.
   2. <u>The Second Crusade</u> (1147-49), preached by St. Bernard, was a fiasco.
      a. Emperor Conrad II and King Louis VII both lost most of their men before reaching Palestine.
      b. They then decided to attack friendly Damascus, but withdrew after a five-day siege (1140).

3. <u>Nurredin</u> (1146-74), who succeeded Zanghi, continued Moslem expansion in Edessa County and Syria at the expense of the Crusader states.

   a. He annexed Damascus in 1155 and soon controlled all of Transjordan and most of Syria.

   b. His attempts to gain Egypt were twice thwarted by the Vizier who summoned Frankish help.

   c. But when King Amalric sought to conquer Egypt for himself the Vizier turned to Nurredin for help.

   d. Nurredin's lieutenant, Shirkuh, drove out the Franks and took over the government (1169).

4. <u>Saladin,</u> Shirkuh's nephew, came to power after the latter's early death (1169).

   a. When the Fatimid Caliph of Egypt died, Saladin did not name a successor but ruled in his own name.

   b. Saladin seized Syria in 1174 after the death of Nurredin.

   c. Temporary peace ended when Reginald of Chatillon raided a caravan which included Saladin's sister.

   d. Saladin set in motion a great *jihad* or "holy war."

      i. He besieged the castle of Tiberias (1187).

      ii. A great Crusader army attempting to relieve Tiberias, was caught without water and annihilated at the Horns of Hattin, an eminence just west of the Sea of Galilee (1187).

      iii. Tiberias, Acre, Gaza, Sidon, Beirut, and Ascalon quickly fell.

   e. Jerusalem itself was taken in September of 1187.

   f. Saladin was now the ruler of most of Palestine and Syria, as well as Egypt and Transjordan.

D. <u>The Later Crusades</u> failed to achieve permanent success.

   1. <u>The Third Crusade</u> (1187-92) was organized in response to the disappointing news of the fall of Jerusalem.

      a. This "Crusade of the Kings" was led by Emperor Frederick I Barbarossa of Germany and Kings Philip II (Augustus) of France and Richard I (Lionheart) of England.

     i. Barbarossa drowned in Asia Minor.

     ii. Richard delayed in Sicily and in Cyprus, which he seized.

    b. Acre was besieged and taken under Richard's leadership, and Philip II returned to France.

    c. The indecisive war between Richard and Saladin continued.

     i. Their mutual respect and gallantry earned for both a place in romance literature.

    d. A peace was finally concluded which gave the Christians possession of a coastal strip from Caesarea to Jaffa and access to Jerusalem.

 2. The Fourth Crusade (1202-04) never reached its proper destination.

    a. It was undertaken at the urgings of Innocent III.

     i. Various lords participated under the leadership of Marquess Conrad of Monferrat.

    b. Venetian ships were used as transports.

    c. Zara was taken to get funds to pay the Venetians.

    d. Then the Crusaders, at the urging of the Venetians, decided to go to Constantinople.

     i. Alexius IV claimed to be the rightful ruler and promised help and rewards if he were restored.

    e. Constantinople was first seized for Alexius.

    f. But when he did not fulfill his promises the Westerners took Constantinople for themselves.

 3. The Latin Empire of Constantinople was established as a result of the Fourth Crusade (1204-61).

    a. It was an intensely feudal state including some of the Byzantine Empire.

    b. But the Byzantines held out in some areas such as Nicaea, Epirus, and Trebizond.

    c. The Byzantines overthrew the Latin Empire in 1261.

 4. Subsequent Crusades in the 13th century achieved little or no success.

    a. There were four additional major crusades and several further minor crusades.

    b. The Children's Crusade of 1215 ended with most

of the children either dying, turning back, or being sold into slavery.

   c. The Fifth Crusade (1217-21) went to Egypt.

       i. It was headed by Cardinal Pelagius, the Papal Legate.

      ii. The Crusaders captured Damietta but declined to make a trade for Jerusalem.

     iii. Using the Nile, the Moslems trapped and routed the Crusaders.

     iv. Damietta was exchanged for prisoners.

   d. The Sixth Crusade (1228-29) was tardily undertaken by the excommunicated Frederick II.

       i. By diplomacy, Frederick obtained the Holy Places and avenues from the Sea.

   e. The Seventh and Eighth Crusades (1248-54) and (1270) were those of Louis IX of France.

       i. The Seventh Crusade went to Egypt, where Damietta was taken, but the Crusaders were trapped and had to be ransomed.

      ii. The Eighth Crusade (1270) was diverted to Tunisia, where Louis fell ill and died.

5. The Fall of Acre (1291), last Crusader stronghold in Palestine, ended serious attempts to regain the Holy Land.

   a. The Mamelukes of Egypt had risen to power in the last half of the thirteenth century.

   b. They defeated the Mongols and then turned on the Christians.

   c. The Mamelukes captured the remaining Crusading strongholds in Palestine, one by one.

III. Evaluations of the Crusades vary.

   A. Failure to achieve original purposes must be admitted.

     1. They did not succeed in holding the Holy Land.

     2. The reunion of the Greeks was not achieved.

     3. Warfare among western Christians was not eradicated.

     4. The cost in human lives, energy, and money was out of proportion to the results achieved.

     5. Though the prestige of the Papacy was temporarily

boosted, it was eventually damaged by the failure of the later Crusades.

6. Influence upon the Christians of the Near East was generally detrimental.

   a. Moslem power was eventually strengthened in the Near East.

   b. Moslem fanaticism against Christians was revived.

   c. The Byzantine Empire was weakened.

      i. The Fourth Crusade, in particular, dealt the Eastern Empire a blow from which it never recovered.

B. Beneficial results occurred in some fields.

1. The economy was stimulated.

   a. Commerce and shipping were greatly increased.

   b. Coinage multiplied, and banking and credit expanded to meet new demands.

2. Social and cultural changes were stimulated.

   a. New luxuries and conveniences, tastes and fashions from the East became popular.

   b. The chivalric ideal became more refined and complex.

   c. New industrial processes and crafts were brought back to the West from the East.

   d. Popular historical writing was stimulated and new themes were introduced into Western prose and poetry.

3. The decline of feudalism was hastened.

   a. Lands were mortgaged or sold to raise cash for crusading expeditions.

   b. Many noble lines were exterminated as a result of deaths in the Holy Land.

   c. Monarchical power grew in the West.

IV. Readings on European Expansion and Crusades include:

Runciman, Steven, *A History of the Crusades*, 3 vols., (New York, Cambridge University, 1951-54).

University of Pennsylvania, *History of the Crusades*, ed. Kenneth M. Setton, 5 volumes planned; (Philadelphia, University of Pennsylvania, 1955).

Munro, Dana C., *The Kingdom of the Crusaders:* (New York, Appleton, 1935).

Krey, August C., *The First Crusade: Accounts of Eye-Witnesses,* (Princeton University, 1921).

Lamb, Harold, *The Crusades* and *The Flame of Islam,* (Garden City, Doubleday, 1930 and 1931).

Treece, Henry, *The Crusades,* (New York, Random House, 1962).

Can You Identify?

Crusades
Alexius Comnenus
Urban II
Clermont (1095)
First Crusade
"Peasant's Crusade"
"Crusade of the Princes"
Dorylaeum (1097)
Bohemund
Kingdom of Jerusalem
Godfrey of Bouillon
Baldwin
Zanghi
Second Crusade

Nurredin
Saladin
Third Crusade
"Crusade of the Kings"
Fourth Crusade
Latin Empire of Constantinople
Children's Crusade
Fifth Crusade (Cardinal Pelagius)
Sixth Crusade (Frederick II)
Seventh Crusade (Louis IX)
Eighth Crusade (Louis IX)
Acre (1291)
Mamelukes

Chapter 19

The Western Empire and the Papacy in the High Middle Ages (1056-1273)

I. <u>The critical period</u> of the Medieval German Empire occurred from 1056 to 1273.

    A. <u>Means</u> used intermittently to bolster monarchical authority included:
1. Control of appointments to high Church offices
2. Increased use of *ministeriales* (officials of servile origin)
3. Expansion and fortification of the crown's direct holdings
4. A "feudal policy" of strengthening the lesser aristocracy
5. Attempted enforcement of more direct, centralized government in Italy
6. Division of the great Duchies into smaller holdings.

    B. <u>Factors</u> which contributed to the ultimate failure of the Empire included:
1. The combined strength of various monarchical opponents.
    a. Included were: the German princes, the freedom-loving Saxons and Bavarians, the prosperous towns of Northern Italy, and the Papacy.
2. Recurrent intervals of civil strife and anarchy
3. The vagaries of imperial policies.
4. Italian preoccupations of Emperors ("Straddling the Alps")
5. The Church-State issue.

II. The Investiture Controversy, combined with princely aspirations for greater autonomy, weakened the later Franconian Emperors (1056-1125).

    A. The central issue in the controversy was the right to appoint men to ecclesiastical positions such as bishoprics.

        1. The Popes and their supporters maintained that this right belonged exclusively to the Church.

            a. The Cluniac-Gregorian Reformers were opposed to lay control of ecclesiastical appointments, since this often meant the appointment of inferior prelates.

        2. The monarchs claimed a right to these appointments since most bishops had civil authority and extensive secular holdings.

            a. The chief monarchical argument was based on tradition and precedents.

        3. A simple solution was impossible since both State and Church had a vital interest in these officials.

            a. Many prelates were governmental officials as well as ecclesiastical leaders.

    B. Henry IV (1056-1106) saw his monarchical authority in both State and Church assailed by the princes and by the papacy.

        1. Henry's minority (1056-65) was a turning point in the fortunes of the Empire.

            a. Monarchical power and rights were usurped and eroded under weak regents.

            b. The Papacy took advantage of this weakness to entrench the Gregorian Reform.

                i. Reform Popes were consistently elected.

                ii. The Electoral Decree of Nicholas II (1059) created the "College of Cardinals," thus withdrawing papal elections from imperial control.

                iii. Reform Popes named Reform Cardinals who in turn elected Reform Popes.

        2. On assuming personal rule (1065), Henry IV attempted to restore monarchical power.

            a. He used various devices to recover control.

            b. The Saxon princes and people resisted and were

joined by others who opposed Henry's centralizing efforts.

3. <u>Eruption of the Investiture Controversy</u> occurred in 1075.

   a. Pope Gregory VII (Hildebrand) strictly forbade the conferral of ecclesiastical offices by laymen (1075).

   b. Henry disregarded papal warnings and continued to appoint unacceptable candidates to bishoprics in both Germany and Italy.

   c. Gregory VII sternly admonished Henry and excommunicated his advisers.

   d. Henry replied by denouncing Gregory VII as an impostor and insisting on the divine source of his own authority.

     i. Henry was supported by his German bishops.

4. <u>Intensification</u> of the struggle was rapid.

   a. Henry was excommunicated by Gregory for his adamance.

   b. Henry was now suspended by the German magnates (1076) in an attempt to diminish his power.

   c. At Canossa early in the following year, Henry submitted or pretended submission and was released by Gregory from his excommunication.

5. <u>Resumption</u> of the struggle soon occurred.

   a. Henry was soon able to recover his authority in Germany, and then defied papal prohibitions anew.

   b. Many German princes supported a series of anti-kings against Henry.

   c. Finally Gregory again excommunicated Henry.

   d. Henry then invaded Italy where he gained ascendancy and besieged the Pope (1085).

     i. Gregory had to call in the Normans before whom Henry retreated.

     ii. Norman depredations incensed the Romans.

     iii. Gregory was forced to accompany the Normans for his own safety and died in exile at Salerno (1085).

   e. The Investiture Struggle continued under succes-

sive Popes, who supported Conrad (1093-1104)
and Henry (1104-06) against their father.

C. <u>Henry V</u> (1106-1125), after the death of his father, resumed the latter's defence of "imperial rights."

    1. <u>Paschal II</u> agreed to cede Church properties and lay
offices acquired since the time of Charlemagne if
Henry would give up lay investiture.

        a. Neither party kept the agreement as Henry proved
insincere and a storm of protest forced Paschal
to retract.

    2. <u>The Concordat of Worms</u> (1122) put an end to the
controversy by a compromise agreement.

        a. In Germany the election of ecclesiastics was to
take place in the presence of the Emperor or his
representative who could thus insist on an accept-
able candidate.

            i. Lay investiture with temporal insignia was to
precede investiture with spiritual insignia by
ecclesiastics.

        b. In Burgundy and Italy elections were to be en-
tirely free.

            i. Bestowal of spiritual insignia by ecclesiastics
was to precede automatic investiture of tem-
poral insignia by the Emperor or his representative.

        c. Considerable power over appointments was left
in the hands of the Emperor.

        d. The real victors were the magnates, who had al-
lied with the Papacy in support of their own interests.

    3. Similar compromises were also arrived at in France
by 1104 and in England by 1107.

    4. Further concessions to the princes were made by
Henry V.

        a. The Emperor was to be elected and was to be
partly dependent on the barons.

III. <u>The Hohenstaufen Versus Guelf Struggle</u> (*ca.* 1125-1250/68)
marked the final state of the contest between the medieval
Empire and the papacy.

A. <u>Party platforms</u> contrasted.

1. The Hohenstaufen faction was pro-imperial and favored a strong central government.
   a. It was anti-papal and anti-baronial.
   b. It also was called the "Ghibelline" party from Waibling, the Hohenstaufen ancestral castle.
   c. Its main adherents were the Hohenstaufens and their supporters, including many Swabians and Franconians.
2. The Guelf party was pro-papal and pro-baronial.
   a. It was opposed to a strong central monarchy.
   b. Its adherents included the Guelf family, the papacy, the great princes, and many Saxons and Bavarians, as well as North Italian cities.

B. Seeds of the struggle were sown in the period 1125-1152.
   1. After the death of Henry V, the magnates asserted their right of election.
      a. Although Henry had designated his nephew, Frederick of Hohenstaufen, Duke of Swabia as his successor, the magnates elected Lothair, Duke of Saxony.
   2. Lothair II (1125-37) aligned himself with the Guelfs.
      a. He was bitterly opposed by the disappointed Hohenstaufens.
      b. Lothair gained needed support by marrying his daughter to Henry the Proud, Duke of Bavaria, a Guelf.
   3. Conrad III (1137-52) was chosen by the magnates instead of Henry who had been designated by Lothair.
      a. Conrad was a Hohenstaufen and the brother of Frederick of Swabia.
      b. The Guelfs opposed Emperor Conrad and his supporters.

C. Frederick I Barbarossa (Red Beard) (1152-1190) united Germany and sought to control Italy and the papacy. Strong imperial rule was his goal.
   1. Frederick and Germany: First Phase (1152-76)
      a. A conciliatory policy characterized the first phase of Barbarossa's rule in Germany.
         i. Frederick let Henry the Lion (a Guelf heir) have both Saxony and Bavaria.
      b. Frederick obtained direct control of Burgundy through marriage to Beatrice of Burgundy.

    c. He was recognized as overlord by states to the east.

2. Frederick and Italy: First Phase (1152-76)

    a. Frederick attempted to assert stronger imperial authority in northern Italy.

    b. The Italian communes had gained many liberties from bishops, overlords, and emperors.

      i. Frederick forcibly subjected Milan and other north Italian towns.

    c. Frederick broke with Pope Adrian IV and his successor, Alexander III.

      i. At Besançon Frederick rejected the idea that the Empire was a "benefice" granted by the Pope.

    d. At the Diet of Roncaglia (1158) the communes were brought to acknowledge Frederick's "royal rights" or *regalia*.

      i. *Podestàs*, responsible to the Emperor, were established in the towns.

    e. The League of Verona and the Lombard League formed in opposition to Frederick enjoyed papal support.

    f. At Legnano (1176) Frederick's forces were decisively defeated by the Lombard League.

3. Frederick and Italy: Second Phase (1176-90)

    a. In the Peace of Venice (1177) Frederick recognized and neutralized Alexander III.

    b. In the Peace of Constance (1183) Frederick made peace with the communes.

      i. The towns regained their customary privileges, but recognized Frederick's imperial overlordship and rural jurisdiction.

      ii. The towns agreed to contribute to the expenses of imperial campaigns in Italy.

    c. The Emperor extended his direct power in Tuscany and the Romagna in compensation.

    d. He also married his son, Henry, to the heiress of Sicily.

4. Frederick and Germany: Second Phase (1176-90)

    a. Frederick overthrew Henry the Lion, and stripped him of his possessions.

        i. Henry had not supported Frederick in his
           Italian campaign.

        ii. Henry refused to appear before the Diet in
           response to Frederick's summons.

       iii. Henry's holdings were declared forfeit and
           forcibly seized.

    b. As a concession to the princes, Henry's holdings
      were divided and distributed as fiefs.

       i. The Duchies of Westphalia and Styria were
           formed from the sides of Saxony and Bavaria.

  5. On the Third Crusade Frederick drowned (1190).

D. **Henry VI** (1190-97), who succeeded his father, was cold
and calculating.

  1. He gained control of the Empire, despite initial difficulties and papal opposition.

  2. He effectively controlled Sicily and much of Italy.

  3. However, he died suddenly while planning a great
Crusade.

E. **Decline** now set in as civil war in the Empire (1197-1215)
involved the kings of England and France.

  1. Philip of Swabia, Henry's brother, was elected by the
Hohenstaufen faction.

  2. Otto of Brunswick, the Guelf heir, was supported by
that party.

  3. Philip was assassinated in 1208 by a personal enemy.

  4. Otto IV was generally accepted, but broke with Innocent III over Church rights in Germany and Italy.

  5. Innocent III now brought forward the Hohenstaufen
heir, Frederick II of Sicily, son of Henry VI.

  6. At Bouvines (1214), Otto, who had allied with John
of England, was defeated by Philip Augustus, Frederick's ally, and Frederick II was now accepted as
King of Germany.

F. **Frederick II** (1215-50) met his greatest opposition in
the papacy.

  1. Frederick was brilliant, skeptical, hard, and shrewd.

    a. His main goal was to acquire strong control in
Italy.

    b. His court at Palermo was a center of culture and
science.

2. <u>Germany</u> was left to itself and enjoyed much autonomy under Frederick.

   a. To gain support for his Italian ventures, Frederick gave extensive privileges to the German prelates and princes in his:

      i Concession in Favor of the Ecclesiastical Princes (1220) and

      ii. Statute in Favor of the Lay Princes (1231).

   b. He left Germany to the weak rule of his sons, first Henry VII and then Conrad IV.

3. <u>Frederick's Italian policy</u> of greater control and centralization was strenuously opposed by the papacy.

   a. Frederick retained direct control of Sicily despite papal opposition.

   b. In the Constitution of Melfi (1231), Frederick organized Sicily in a highly centralized, bureaucratic manner.

   c. He also attempted to subject northern Italy to firm control.

      i. His victory at Cortenuova (1231) brought temporary success.

   d. Frederick II alienated the papacy:

      i. By retaining direct control of Sicily

      ii. By encroaching on papal holdings

      iii. By his delay in going on the promised Crusade.

   e. The papacy and many Italian cities fought Frederick through most of his reign.

      i. He was denounced and excommunicated by Pope Gregory IX, and later by Innocent IV and the Council of Lyons (1245).

4. Failure was Frederick's final lot.

   a. He was defeated at Parma (1248) and La Fossalta (1249).

   b. He died of dysentery in 1250 and his cause was lost.

IV. <u>The Great Interregnum</u> (1250-73) saw the disintegration of the Western Empire.

  A. <u>No effective</u> monarch ruled in Germany during these years.

1. The German princes consolidated their power by crowning nonentities and foreigners.
2. Italy was lost to the Empire.
3. The "viprous brood of the Hohenstaufen" was exterminated when Conrad IV died in Italy (1254), Manfred was killed in Sicily (1266), and Conradin was executed in Naples (1268).
4. William of Holland, Richard of Cornwall, and Alphonso X of Castile were three powerless Emperors at this time.
5. Both Germany and Italy came to consist of several virtually independent states.

B. Rudolph of Hapsburg was elected in 1273.
1. He was a count who possessed scattered domains.
2. He was elected only because the Pope forced the electors to make a choice.

V. <u>Readings</u> on the Western Empire in the High Middle Ages include:

Barraclough, Geoffrey, *Origins of Modern Germany* (Oxford, Blackwell, 1957).

Fisher, Herbert A. L., *The Medieval Empire*, 2 vols. (London, Macmillan, 1898).

Reinhart, Kurt F., *Germany: 2000 years*, Vol. I (New York, Ungar, 1961).

Thompson, James W., *Feudal Germany* (Chicago, University of Chicago, 1928).

Tierney, Brian, *The Crisis of Church and State, 1050-1300* (Englewood, N. J., Prentice-Hall, 1964).

Can You Identify?

ministeriales	Hohenstaufen
Investiture Controversy	Ghibelline
Henry IV, Emperor	Guelf
Gregorian Reform	Lothair II
Gregory VII	Henry the Proud
Canossa (1077)	Conrad III
Henry V, Emperor	Frederick I
Paschal II	Barbarossa
Concordat of Worms (1122)	Henry the Lion

Roncaglia (1158)

podesta

Legnano (1176)

Peace of Venice (1177)

Peace of Constance (1183)

Henry VI, Emperor

Philip of Swabia

Otto IV of Brunswick

Bouvines (1214)

Frederick II

Constitution of Melfi (1231)

Cortenuova (1231)

"Great Interregnum"

Rudolph of Hapsburg

Chapter 20

England in the Middle Ages:
Developing the English Constitution

I. <u>Foundations of the English Constitution</u> were established in the High Middle Ages (1066-1307).

   A. <u>Three general phases</u> occurred:
      1. The strengthening of the monarchy and the organization of government (esp. 1066-1199)
      2. The establishing of rights of Englishmen and limitations of monarchy (esp. 1199-1272)
      3. The beginnings of representative government and the rise of Parliament (1265-1307).

   B. <u>Several factors</u> helped bring about this early development. Among such:
      1. The Norman conquest imposed unity on the country.
      2. Overseas possessions in France afforded a greater integration with continental civilization.
      3. England's limited size and insular nature promoted greater cohesiveness.

II. <u>The Norman Conquest</u> (1066) resulted in a strengthening of the monarchy.

   A. <u>William I, the Conqueror</u> (1066-87) invaded England in 1066.
      1. William was the Duke of Normandy and a rival to the King of France.
      2. William claimed the throne of England because:
         a. He was related to Edward the Confessor.

        b. He had been designated earlier as successor by Edward.

        c. Harold had at one time promised his support.

        d. The Pope had given his blessing.

           i. William had promised to reform the Church in England.

    3. Harold Godwinson was accepted as King by the English Witangemot (1066), but was confronted by two rivals: Harold Hadrada and William.

        a. Harold Godwinson marched north to battle with the invading Scandinavian candidate, Harold Hadrada.

           i. At Stamford Bridge (1066), Godwinson was victorious.

    4. The Battle of Hastings (1066) decided the issue:

        a. William landed in England with an army of volunteers from various parts of France.

        b. Harold Godwinson then marched south to confront William.

        c. At Hastings, William was victorious and Harold was killed.

    5. William was accepted and crowned as king in London.

    6. The conquest was completed by putting down various successive revolts.

B. Strengthening monarchial government was the primary concern of William I.

    1. Lands and offices were redistributed.

        a. Most of the land was confiscated by "right of conquest" or forfeiture and distributed to William's adherents.

        b. Much land also was kept in William's direct possession.

        c. Normans were given important Church offices.

    2. Anglo-Saxon institutions retained as advantageous to the royal government included:

        a. The "*Danegeld*" which provided a direct tax

        b. The *fyrd*: a citizen's militia for local defenses

        c. The sheriffs: royal representatives in the shires

           i. Their position was enhanced when bishops and earls ceased to participate in local government.

    d. Local courts of villages, hundreds, boroughs, and shires

    e. "The Kings Peace" enforced throughout the realm

       i. It provided a legal basis for royal punishment of major crimes.

       ii. Private warfare was outlawed.

3. <u>Norman-French institutions</u> advantageous to the royal government were introduced:

    a. Feudalism in a modified form was established.

       i. Large holdings ordinarily involved vassalage, including oaths, mounted military service, reliefs, aids, etc.

       ii. All fief holders, including rear vassals, were directly bound to the king by oath (Oath of Salisbury).

       iii. Larger baronies were composed of scattered holdings.

       iv. A feudal army of about 5,000 knights thus was made available.

    b. The feudal Great Council (of tenants-in-chief) replaced the Anglo-Saxon Witan.

    c. Inquests (inquiries) into affairs of the realm gave the king accurate information.

       i. Subjects were obliged to answer questions under oaths calling on God to witness.

       ii. *Domesday Book*, the result of such an inquest, was a survey of all income sources, which helped the king get his full dues.

    d. Numerous castles of the "motte and bailey" type were constructed.

4. <u>The English Church</u> was reformed.

    a. Archbishop Lanfranc replaced the usurper Stigand at Canterbury.

    b. Church courts were organized separately from secular courts.

    c. Clerical education was improved.

    d. But William ignored Gregorian reform provisions and continued lay appointments to clerical offices.

C. <u>William's earlier successors</u> followed different policies.

1. <u>William II, Rufus</u> (1087-1100) was imperious and tyrannical, dissolute, and unpopular.

    a. He alienated both nobles and common people by his despotic rule.

    b. He quarreled with Archbishop Anselm over Church-State relations.

    c. William was "accidentally" killed while hunting.

2. <u>Henry I</u>, Beauclerc (1100-1135), Rufus' younger brother, was clever and adroit.

    a. Henry now seized the crown and the royal treasury.

    b. His older brother, Robert Curthose of Normandy, who opposed Henry, was first bought off, then defeated and imprisoned.

    c. A compromise settlement with the Church was reached.

        i. Anselm was reinstated as Archbishop of Canterbury.

        ii. The Concordat of London (1107) allowed the king to supervise and approve episcopal elections, as well as to have the primary right to confer temporal insignia.

    d. The organization of the royal government was improved.

        i. The Exchequer (department of finance) was separated from the *Curia Regis* (general royal court).

        ii. Itinerant justices brought royal justice to the people.

3. <u>Stephen of Blois</u> (1135-54) was a weak feudal king who reigned amidst civil war and anarchy.

    a. The son of a daughter of the Conqueror, Stephen seized the throne on Henry's death.

        i. Many magnates supported Stephen against his rival claimant, the "imperious" Mathilda, daughter of Henry I.

        ii. But Stephen lost much of this support through his incompetence.

    b. Anarchy prevailed for almost two decades.

        i. Mathilda's supporters, who refused to surrender, used the broom plant (*planta genista*) as their symbol, whence the name "Plantagenets."

    c. The civil war ended in 1153, when Stephen agreed to the succession of Mathilda's son, Henry of Anjou.

III. <u>Henry II</u> (1154-89), skillfully ruled a large overseas empire and developed English law and justice.

  A. <u>The Plantagenet Empire</u> included Normandy and its dependencies, Anjou and its dependencies, and Aquitaine, as well as England.

    1. Aquitaine was obtained by Henry's marriage to Eleanor of Aquitaine in 1152.

  B. <u>Establishment of law and order</u> was Henry's first problem.

    1. Forceful direct action was taken against unruly barons and sheriffs.

      a. Rebellious barons were overcome, illegal castles were razed, and unworthy and dishonest sheriffs were dismissed.

    2. Royal justice was expanded.

      a. The use of itinerant justices was renewed and property suits and other cases were brought into the king's court.

    3. Common law spread throughout England.

      a. Common law was general law as opposed to local law.

      b. Common law was precedent law utilizing reason.

      c. Church law, Roman law, and Anglo-Saxon customs also influenced the development of common law.

    4. Writs and assizes played major roles in Henry's legal reform.

      a. "Writs of right" declared the right of royal courts to hear cases.

      b. "Writs of transfer" transferred cases from feudal courts to royal courts.

      c. "Assizes," or hearings by juries, decided cases in royal courts.

        i. Possessory assizes decided the right to present possession of property by simple questions, such as:

          1) Was claimant recently dispossessed (*Novel Diseisin*)?

                2) Did claimant's immediate ancestors hold the title at death (*Mort d'ancestor*)?

    5. The Jury system was established.

        a. Twelve men "tried and true" were summoned from the area and put under oath to declare the truth.

        b. "Grand" juries cited persons seriously suspected of major crimes.

            i. In criminal cases, the actual trial usually was conducted in the old fashioned way, for some time.

        c. "Petit" juries answered to the facts of the case.

    6. The Constitutions of Clarendon (1164) resulted in a contest with Thomas Becket, Archbishop of Canterbury.

        a. According to the constitutions, "criminous clerks" were to be tried in royal courts as well as ecclesiastical courts.

        b. Becket upheld the privilege of canonical immunity until he was slain by followers of the king.

        c. Henry, dismayed by Becket's death, gave up the fight.

    7. Rebellions involving his wife and sons disturbed Henry's later years.

        a. These rebellions were abetted by Philip II of France.

 C. Richard I (1189-99) proved the effectiveness of England's constitution.

    1. Richard was an absentee king.

        a. He participated in the Third Crusade (1189-92).

        b. He was held captive in Germany for two years (1192-94).

        c. After his release he fought in France to regain lands occupied by Philip II during his absence.

    2. Justiciars ruled England throughout Richard's reign.

IV. The Thirteenth Century saw a limiting of the Monarchy under weak, unpopular Kings John and Henry III (1199-1272).

 A. John (1199-1216), fought with Philip II, Innocent III, and his own barons.

1. John Lackland is one of the most infamous of medieval kings.
   a. Although intelligent and crafty, he was cruel, unscrupulous, and erratic.
2. Philip II was appealed to when John married Isabelle of Angouleme (1200) who was betrothed to a rear vassal of Philip.
   a. This marriage, as well as the murder of Arthur, John's nephew, while he was a prisoner, alienated many vassals.
   b. Philip's court declared John's holdings in northwestern France forfeit and Philip successfully occupied them (1202-05).
3. Innocent III (1207) and John were alienated over a disputed election to the see of Canterbury.
   a. Innocent appointed Stephen Langton Archbishop of Canterbury in opposition to John's candidate.
   b. Innocent eventually forced John to accede by interdicting England.
   c. John became a Papal vassal and agreed to pay an annual tribute (1213).
4. John's alliance with Otto IV of Germany, in an attempt to regain his French possessions, failed.
   a. John's cause was lost, along with that of Otto, when the latter was defeated by Philip at Bouvines (1214).
B. Magna Carta (1215), which John was forced to sign at Runnymede, was a landmark in English constitutional history.
   1. Basic rights of Englishmen were guaranteed, though Magna Carta was chiefly a baronial, feudal document.
      a. Liberties of the Church, towns, and freemen were guaranteed.
      b. Punishment without due process of law was forbidden.
      c. The principle that the king is subject to law, and that his subjects have a right to compel him to observe it, was embodied.
   2. Violations of the agreement by both sides soon led to war.

        a. The barons accepted Prince Louis of France as
           their candidate.

        b. John died as the tide began to turn against him
           (1216).

C. <u>Henry III's reign</u> (1216-1272) saw the further limita-
tion of the monarchy and the harbinger of parliamentary
government.

  1. The barons now rejected Louis and accepted John's
     nine-year-old son, Henry (III).

  2. Grievances against Henry's misrule multiplied quickly
     after he assumed personal control in 1232.

     a. Henry showed excessive favoritism to French rel-
        atives and friends.

     b. He lavished great amounts of money on various
        projects, including a vain attempt to regain French
        possessions.

     c. He was subservient to the Papacy.

       i. In the "Sicilian Folly" he undertook to pay
          papal war debts in return for having his son
          appointed to the Sicilian throne.

  3. <u>The Provisions of Oxford</u> (1258) established a com-
     mission of fifteen barons to supervise the government.

     a. When Henry sought more money from his Great-
        Council the barons forced him to accept the Pro-
        visions.

     b. By 1261 the King was strong enough to renounce
        the Provisions of Oxford.

     c. The Mise of Amiens (1264) of arbitrator Louis
        IX declared the Provisions invalid.

  4. Simon de Monfort led a baronial rebellion which de-
     feated the king at the battle of Lewes (1264).

     a. Henry III and his son Edward were held prison-
        ers.

     b. Simon ruled England through baronial council.

  5. <u>Montfort's Parliament</u> was summoned in 1265 to bol-
     ster his cause.

     a. Two knights from each shire and two burgesses
        from each borough were invited, along with the
        usual barons.

       i. But representation was incomplete.

  6. Prince Edward escaped and rallied many of the
     barons to his side.

       a. At Evesham (1265), he defeated and killed Mont-
fort.

       b. Edward was the real ruler for the rest of Henry's
reign (1265-72).

V. The "Edwardian Compromise" gave England a stable, well
organized, conciliatory government.

  A. Edward I (1272-1307) was a capable, statesmanlike
ruler.

    1. Edward consulted with his subjects for the good of
"the community of the realm."

    2. He began the unification of Great Britain by con-
quering Wales.

       a. Scotland was temporarily conquered as a harbin-
ger of its later final incorporation (1603).

    3. Further French advances on the continent were re-
sisted.

  B. Parliament developed during Edward's reign.

    1. Parliament, a joint meeting of lords, churchmen, and
commoners, was called several times.

       a. Edward's principal purpose was to obtain funds
for his foreign ventures and to promulgate statutes.

       b. In return he granted petitions formulated by the
members.

    2. The "Model Parliament" of 1295 included four
houses:

       a. Great lords, lay, and ecclesiastic (the old Great
Council)

       b. Representatives of the lesser clergy

       c. Two knights from each shire and

       d. Two burgesses from each borough.

    3. Eventually, the lesser clergy was to drop out and
the knights and burgesses fused, making only two
houses: Lords and Commons.

    4. Laws issued by the king and approved by Parliament
rounded out the English legal system.

       a. Edward is called the "English Justinian."

  C. Governmental administration was much improved.

    1. Inquests were used extensively to determine exactly
the extent of royal jurisdiction and the limits of
seigniorial jurisdiction.

2. *"Quo Warranto"* writs were employed to bring many matters into royal courts.
3. A civil service was developed.
4. The various departments of the government were clearly distinguished.
5. Three kinds of central royal courts were in operation:
   a. King's Bench for criminal cases
   b. Common Pleas for ordinary civil cases and
   c. The Court of the Exchequer for fiscal cases.
   d. The circuit courts of the itinerant justices continued to operate.
6. *The Confirmation of the Charters* (1297), granted by Edward, agreed not to levy any new taxes without the "common consent of the realm."

VI. Readings on the History of England in the High Middle Ages include:

Lunt, William E., *History of England* (New York, Harper, 1949).

Lyon, Bryce, *Constitutional and Legal History of Medieval England*, (New York, Harper, 1960).

Excellent collaborative multi-volume histories of England have been edited by George N. Clark (Oxford series), Charles W. Oman (Methuen Series), and William Hunt with Reginald Lane Poole (Longmans series).

Thompson, Faith, *Magna Carta* (Minneapolis, U. of Minnesota, 1950), and *Short History of Parliament, 1265-1642* (Minneapolis, U. of Minnesota, 1953).

Contemporary histories of England, available in translations from the Latin, include those written by: William of Malmesbury (to 1142); Roger of Hoveden (to 1201); Roger of Wendover (to 1235); and Matthew Paris (to 1273); all tr. by J. A. Giles.

Can You Identify?

"Norman Conquest"	Stamford Bridge (1066)
1066	Hastings (1066)
William I	*Danegeld*
Harold Godwinson	*fyrd*

"The King's Peace"
Great Council
Domesday Book
Lanfranc
William II
Henry I (Eng.)
Anselm
Robert Curthose
Concordat of London (1107)
Exchequer
Itinerant justices
Stephen of Blois
Mathilda
Henry II
Plantagenets
Eleanor of Aquitaine
Common law
Writs
Assizes
Grand jury
Petit jury
Constitutions of Clarendon
Thomas Becket

Richard I
Justiciar
John (King)
Isabelle of Angouleme
Arthur of Brittany
Innocent III
Stephen Langton
Bouvines (1214)
Magna Carta (1215)
Henry III
"Sicilian Folly" (of Henry III)
Provisions of Oxford (1258)
Simon de Montfort
Mise of Amiens (1264)
Montfort's Parliament (1265)
Evesham (1265)
Edward I
Parliament
"Model Parliament"
Quo Warranto?
King's Bench
Confirmation of the Charters
   (1297)

Chapter 21

France in the High Middle Ages

I. <u>The French Monarchy rose</u> from feudal weakness in the 11th century to strength and leadership in the 13th.
  A. <u>Factors contributing</u> to French strength included:
    1. The geographical advantages of France in Western Europe, (e.g. position, resources, soil, climate, rainfall)
    2. The traditional concept of the monarchy, reinforced by long reigns and uninterrupted succession
    3. A common Romance tongue and a common Catholic Christianity
    4. Church support of the cooperative French monarchy
    5. Alliance of the towns with the French monarchy
    6. Economic expansion and the rise of a strong middle class, friendly to the monarchy
    7. Common external enemies, such as the English and Germans.
  B. <u>Unification</u> of France was promoted by the great Capetians during the High Middle Ages.
    1. Royal domains were expanded and more direct control was established over much of France.
    2. Royal government was better organized and strengthened.

II. <u>Expansion of French royal domains</u> was the work of strong kings (1108-1314).
  A. <u>Louis VI</u> (1108-37) established control over the Ile de France.

1. Louis, the "Fat" (*le Gros*), was the first strong Capetian.
2. He repressed lawlessness and brigandage in the royal domains.
   a. The Ile de France became one of the best governed and most orderly areas in France.
3. Louis VI acquired Aquitaine for his son and heir by arranging his marriage to the heiress, Eleanor of Aquitaine.
4. Royal domains, hitherto scattered, were consolidated and filled out by confiscation, conquest, and purchase.
5. Able ministers, such as Suger, Abbot of St. Denis, aided Louis.

B. Louis VII (1137-1180), called "the Young," managed to hold his own.
   1. He lost Aquitaine when his marriage to Eleanor was annulled.
   2. He intervened successfully in some parts of France.
      a. Louis aided Toulouse (1159) against Henry II of England.
      b. This was an important precedent of royal intervention and defense against the English.
   3. Louis supported the papacy against Frederick I.
      a. He was host to Alexander III during the latter's flight from Italy.

C. Philip II, Augustus (1180-1223) quadrupled the royal domains.
   1. He was called "Augustus" because:
      a. He imitated the Roman Emperor Augustus.
      b. He was born in August.
      c. He increased (*augebat*) royal holdings.
   2. Political sagacity and ability more than made up for Philip's physical weakness.
   3. Philip expanded the royal domains in all directions.
      a. Expansion to the North was accomplished by marriage and conquest.
         i. Artois, Vermandois, and Amiens were added to the royal holdings.
      b. Westward expansion was accomplished at the expense of the Angevin monarchs.

        i. Philip II allied with the sons of Henry II against their father.

       ii. He tried to take Normandy from Richard I, with only temporary success.

     iii. He declared John's French holdings forfeit when John failed to appear in his court to answer charges about Isabelle of Angouleme.

     iv. Normandy, Maine, Anjou, Poitou, and Touraine were occupied and added to the royal domain.

  c. Expansion to the south was begun.

        i. When Philip allowed his son to participate briefly in the Albigensian Crusade, a basis was established for subsequent acquisitions in southern France.

D. Louis VIII (1223-26) expanded royal holdings in the south.

  1. Louis was given Langedoc by Simon's son, Amaury de Montfort, who was unable to control it.

  2. His campaigns in Poitou and Auvergne quieted rebellions and asserted royal control.

E. Louis IX (1226-1270) did not expand the royal domains.

  1. He refrained from seizing Gascony and Guienne from the weak Henry III of England, with whom he concluded the Treaty of Paris (1259).

  2. He created "appanages" for his brothers as his father had directed him to do.

    a. These were important territories (Artois, Anjou, and Poitou), held by members of the royal family in only partial subjection to the crown.

F. Philip III (1270-85) resumed the process of royal expansion.

  1. After Alphonse of Poitou and Toulouse died without heir, Philip incorporated his large holdings into the royal domain.

  2. Philip's son married the heiress of Champagne and Navarre.

  3. Philip dissipated royal energies by invading Aragon in support of Charles of Anjou over Sicily.

G. Philip IV (1285-1314) made several small territorial gains.

1. He obtained Champagne by marriage.
2. He was involved in wars with the English and Flemish.
3. Lille, Douai, and Arras were obtained from Flanders, despite a severe set back at Coutrai in 1302.
4. Some western towns of the Empire, such as Lyons and Toul, were added by purchase and occupation.

III. <u>Improved organization</u> of the French government was the work of these same strong monarchs.

A. <u>A royal civil service</u> apart from the feudal system was initiated by Louis VI and Louis VII.
   1. Men of nonaristocratic origin were employed in the administration.
   2. Philip II continued this practice by using middleclass men as *baillis*.
      a. *Baillis* were royal supervisors appointed over the *prevots* in each territory.
      b. Periodic promotions and rewards encouraged career men.
      c. The office of seneschal was supressed and that of chancellor left vacant.
   3. Louis IX appointed non-aristocratic officials known as *enquêteurs* to supervise the *baillis*.
   4. Philip IV increased the number of civil lawyers in public service and improved governmental organization.

B. <u>Royal justice</u> was organized and extended by Louis IX.
   1. Louis has been called "the French Justinian."
      a. His interest in justice was intense.
   2. Regular judges were assigned to the Parlement of Paris.
   3. Private warfare was forbidden.

C. <u>Departmentalization</u> of the central government was achieved during the High Middle Ages.
   1. The smaller *Curia Regis* or Royal Council appeared as distinct from the larger *Curia Regis* or Great Council.
   2. By the reign of Philip IV the smaller *Curia Regis* was subdivided into specific councils.

a. The Privy Council advised the king on important matters.

b. The *Chambre des Comptes* or Chamber of Accounts dealt with financial matters.

c. The *Parlement* or Royal Judiciary was permanently established at Paris as a High Court.

   i. The Royal Judiciary was originally the *Curia Regis* sitting as a court of justice.

   ii. Louis IX appointed some thirty trained justices to it, while Philip IV improved its organization.

D. Local royal government was improved by stricter supervision.

1. *Prevots* were used as local agents by Louis VI.

2. *Baillis* were set over the *prevots* by Philip II.

   a. The *prevots* had become too autonomous and stricter supervision was necessary.

   b. *Baillis*, known as "Seneschals" in the south, appointed by and dependent on the king, administered justice, collected royal revenues, and assembled contingents for the royal army.

3. *Enquêteurs* or investigators to supervise, judge, and correct the *baillis* were instituted by Louis IX.

E. Extension of royal justice was one aspect of the strengthening of royal government.

1. The *baillis* and *enquêteurs* performed some judicial functions.

2. The *Curia Regis*, both larger and smaller, heard cases in the central government.

3. Louis IX greatly improved and expanded royal justice.

   a. He professionalized and expanded the royal judiciary or Parliament.

   b. He abolished duels and bettered procedures in the courts.

   c. Inquests and evidence supplanted ordeals, although torture was still used.

   d. Local officials were forbidden to acquire property, accept gifts, or enter into marriage in their territories without royal permission.

F. Royal income was substantially increased in the High Middle Ages.

1. Philip II doubled the royal income.
2. Louis IX made royal coinage legal tender throughout France.
3. Philip IV resorted to extortion and other unscrupulous methods to get money.
    a. He imposed a *gabelle* (sales tax) on commercial transactions.
    b. He levied a tariff on wool coming to Flanders from England.
    c. He extorted *decimes* (tenths) and double *decimes* from the clergy for the defense of the realm, without permission of the papacy.
    d. He had the Templars suppressed in order to get his hands on their wealth and to become free of his debts to them.
G. The Estates General or French Parliament was initiated by Philip IV.
    1. The Estates General was first called (1302) to obtain general support against the papacy.
    2. The Estates General included representatives of the towns and lesser nobility as well as feudal magnates and ecclesiastical prelates.
        a. The Estates were again called to approve the suppression of the Templars (1308).
        b. They were later called to raise money for the war with Flanders (1314).
    3. Although often merely a "rubber stamp," the Estates contained the germ of representative government.
H. Other Features of the French monarchy made it strong.
    1. Popular support was gained when charters were granted to communes, serfs were emancipated, and justice was administered.
    2. The Church was a leading pillar of royal power.
        a. French kings cooperated with the papacy.
    1. Louis VII, Philip II, and Louis IX went on Crusades.
        b. Popes frequently took refuge in France.
        c. Philip IV deviated from this policy by defying Pope Boniface VIII.
    3. Limitations on the French monarchy still remained.
        a. Some fiefs of the crown were still virtually autonomous, as in the case of Burgundy, Brittany, Flanders, Anjou, Artois, and Maine.

    b. Guienne and Gascony remained in English hands.

    c. No regular, direct royal tax was maintained.

       i. Feudal immunities were legion.

      ii. The king had to rely on feudal military levies and dues.

     iii. The church enjoyed many exemptions.

IV. <u>Readings</u> on France in the High Middle Ages include:

Guignebert, Charles A., *A Short History of the French People* (New York, Macmillan, 1930).

Funck-Brentano, Jacques C., *The Middle Ages* (New York, Putnam, 1927).

Petit-Dutaillis, Charles, *The Feudal Monarchy in France and England* (London, Routledge, 1949).

Fawtier, Robert, *The Capetian Kings of France* (London, Macmillan, 1960).

Evans, Joan, *Life in Medieval France* (London, Oxford, 1925).

Hutton, William H., *Philip Augustus* (London, Macmillan, 1896).

Sire de Joinville, *The History of St. Louis*, trans. (several editions).

Can You Identify?

Louis VI

Eleanor of Aquitaine

Suger

Louis VII

Philip II

Louis VIII

Louis IX

Treaty of Paris (1259)

"appanages"

Philip III

Philip IV

Curia Regis

baillis

prevots

enquêteurs

Parlement

gabelle

decime

Estates General

Knights Templar

Chapter 22

Other European States in the High Middle Ages

I. The Iberian Peninsula was almost entirely recovered and reorganized by the Christians during the High Middle Ages.

A. Moslem Spain was in decline.

    1. An Era of *Taifas* (small kingdoms) succeeded the deposition of the last Caliph of Cordova (1035).

B. The Christian "Reconquest" (*Reconquista*) was achieved in three stages.

    1. By 1086 the Christians had recovered about two-fifths of the peninsula.

        a. León was occupied early in the 11th century.

        b. Castile, which had become independent of León in the 10th century, expanded at Moslem expense in the 11th century.

           i. Great expansion occurred under Ferdinand I (1035-1065).

           ii. Alphonso VI, the Battler, finally took the old Visigothic capital of Toledo (1085).

    2. A "Moroccan Interlude" (1086-1212) stemmed the tide of Reconquest.

        a. Warlike, fanatical Berber dynasties invited in to halt the Reconquest, now ruled Moslem Spain as well as Morocco.

        b. The Almoravides (1046-1147) routed Alphonso VI at Zalaca (1086).

  c. The Almohades supplanted the Almoravides in Morocco and Spain (*ca.* 1147-1211).

    i. Some expansion was achieved in this period by Aragon and Portugal and, to a lesser extent, Castile.

 3. <u>Virtual completion</u> of the Reconquest (1212-1276) followed defeat of the Almohades at Las Navas de Tolosa (1212).

  a. A composite Christian coalition, led by Alfonso VIII of Castile, and blessed by the Pope, won this victory.

  b. St. Ferdinand III (1217-52) of Castile took Cordova, Seville, Jaen, and part of Murcia.

    i. Granada was spared because of its cooperation with the Christians, and on payment of tribute.

  c. James I, the Conquerer, (1213-76) of Aragon, completed the Reconquest along the east coast and took the adjacent Balearic Isles.

  d. Portugal completed its expansion along the west coast with the occupation of the Algarve district in the south.

C. <u>Castile, Aragon, and Portugal</u> emerged as principal states in the Iberian Peninsula.

 1. Consolidation rather than fragmentation of states followed in the wake of the Reconquest.

 2. <u>Castile</u> was the largest state in the peninsula after its union with León and further expansion.

  a. After several attempts at union, Castile and León were permanently united in 1230.

  b. Castile reached a high point and then relapsed under Alfonso X, the Wise (1252-84).

    i. Alfonso, a great patron of culture, compiled histories, composed *cantigas* (hymns), and codified Spanish and Roman law.

    ii. Civil war broke out over his proposal to follow the Roman rule of being succeeded by the son of his deceased eldest son rather by than by his eldest surviving son.

 3. <u>Aragon</u> consolidated the east coast of Spain and became a leading Mediterranean power.

  a. Tiny Aragon was elevated to the status of a kingdom in 1035 and enjoyed continued expansion.

  b. Aragon was united to the coastal county of Barcelona through intermarriage of their ruling houses in 1135.
  c. Aragon assumed a leading position in the Mediterranean after further expansion along the Coast and into adjacent islands.
  d. Sicily was occupied by the house of Aragon (1276-85) after the "Sicilian Vespers."
    i. This brought Aragon into war with the papacy and France.
4. Portugal arose from the side of León to become first an independent county and then an autonomous kingdom.
  a. The kingdom of Portugal was formally constituted and recognized in the 1140's at the time of Alfonso Enrique.
  b. Portuguese expansion was rapid.
    i. Lisbon was taken with English naval help in 1147.
5. Christian Navarre and Moslem Granada remained smaller, less important states.
D. Iberian political institutions recognized individual human rights, at least among the upper classes, and urban liberties from an early date.
  1. Town charters (fueros or cartas) granted privileges, exemptions, and rights of self-government to municipalities from an early date.
    a. Consejos were town councils composed of aldermen.
    b. Ayuntamientos were general assemblies of townspeople.
    c. Juntas were meetings of representatives of various towns.
  2. Parliaments (Cortes) met in Spain earlier than elsewhere in the West.
    a. Cortes included representatives of the middle class as well as the upper clergy and nobility.
    b. Cortes were held in Aragon as early as 1163, in León in 1188, Catalonia in 1218, and Castile in 1250, according to Spanish historians.
  3. The proud independent Spanish spirit was particularly strong in Aragon.

                 a. A "Union" of nobles and members of the middle class extorted extensive *Privilegios* from Pedro III in 1283 and from Alfonso VII of Aragon in 1287.

        4. Peaceful settlement of disputes between states in the Iberian Peninsula often occurred.

II. The Scandinavian Kingdoms attained greater internal unity and stability during the High Middle Ages.

     A. Political trends included:

        1. Augmentation and consolidation of monarchical power (9th to 11th centuries)

        2. Increased demands by the nobility for greater independence (12th to 13th centuries)

        3. Granting of liberties and holding of representative parliaments.

     B. Expansion took place in the North Atlantic and Baltic regions.

        1. Denmark fashioned a temporary empire which included Norway and England in the early 11th century.

                 a. Denmark later expanded temporarily along the Baltic under Waldemar I and Waldemar II (1157-1241).

        2. Sweden obtained control of Finland and attempted to expand south along the Baltic.

        3. Norway colonized Iceland and Greenland.

     C. Other developments included:

        1. Christianization and civilization emanating from Northern Germany and, to a lesser extent, England

        2. Economic progress and increased trade with the rest of Europe

        3. Growth of an urban middle class and emancipation of the serfs.

III. The States of East Central Europe became civilized Christian kingdoms.

     A. General developments in Poland, Bohemia, and Hungary included:

        1. Attainment of monarchical status recognized by Popes and Emperors (11th to 12th centuries)

        2. Christianization and civilization (10th to 11th centuries)

    3. Continued resistance to German attempts at domination especially in Poland and Hungary (11th to 12th centuries)

       a. Bohemia remained a part of the Holy Roman Empire.

    4. Increased pressures from the East from Mongols, Tartars, Venetians, and Byzantines (13th century).

B. <u>Poland</u> grew strong in the 11th century, but declined in the 12th to 13th centuries.

    1. Christianity was accepted by Duke Mieszco I of Poland in about 966.

    2. Royal power, after a period of growth until 1057, declined thereafter.

       a. Boleslaw I, the Brave, (992-1025) expanded his dominions and took the title of "King."

    3. Anarchy and partition ensued from about 1138 to the end of the High Middle Ages.

    4. The Teutonic Knights cut off Poland from the Baltic Sea in the 13th century.

    5. The Tartars also harassed Poland.

C. <u>Hungary</u> progressed in the 11th to 12th centuries but also encountered difficulties in the 13th century.

    1. The Magyars settled down after their decisive defeat at the hands of Otto I (955).

       a. The Arpad line ruled Hungary for four centuries (*ca.* 900-1301).

    2. St. Stephen, The Hungarian ruler, was baptized in 1000 and recognized as king by the Pope in the following year.

    3. Hungary absorbed Bosnia, Croatia, and Dalmatia in the 11th to 12th centuries.

    4. Hungarian royal power declined in the 13th century under increasing pressures from Venice, Byzantium, and the Tartars.

D. <u>Bohemia</u> was a restless part of the German Empire from the 10th century on.

    1. The conversion of Bohemia began in the later 9th century.

    2. The Premyslid dynasty, of which St. Wenceslaus was a member, ruled Bohemia for about four centuries.

    3. German intervention from time to time resulted in the recognition of German overlordship.

    4. The Duke of Bohemia was made a King by Emperor Frederick I in recognition of his services.

    5. The Bohemians frequently attempted to shake off the German yoke, but without success.

IV. <u>Russia</u>, which developed from the Swedish principality of Kiev in the 9th century, flourished in the High Middle Ages.

  A. <u>The Principality of Kiev</u> pioneered the unification of the Russians in the 9th to 11th centuries.

    1. Swedish adventurers known as "Rus" established the prosperous Principality of Kiev on the middle Dnieper River.

      a. Rurik (*ca.* 862-79), leader of the "Rus," founded the Principality of Novgorod in northern Russia.

      b. Prince Oleg (*ca.* 879-912) united Novgorod with Kiev.

      c. This principality prospered and expanded.

    2. Eastern Christianity was brought to Russia by Byzantine missionaires in the 10th century.

      a. The Grand Duchess Olga was baptized at Constantinople about 957.

      b. Prince Vladimir of Kiev was baptized along with many of his subjects in 988-89.

    3. Byzantine civilization came to Russia along with Christianity.

      a. Strong Byzantine influences existed in the Russian Church as well as in Russian culture.

    4. Russian expansion proceeded in all directions.

      a. Both Sviatoslav (964-972) and Vladimir (978-1015) expanded southward, eventually acquiring the Crimea on the Black Sea.

      b. Sviatoslav occupied Bulgaria after helping the Byzantines overcome it, but was ousted by the Byzantines.

      c. Repeated Russian assaults on Constantinople proved fruitless.

    5. The apogee of Kiev came in the first half of the 11th century, under Yaroslav the Wise (1019-54).

      a. Yaroslav expanded his holding to the west and south.

        b. He issued the first Russian Code of Laws (*Russyska Pravda*).

        c. He arranged marriages for members of his house with the ruling royal houses of France, Hungary, Poland, and Norway, as well as imperial Byzantium.

B. <u>Disintegration</u> prevailed in Russia during the "Age of the Princes" (1054-*ca.* 1217).

    1. The "rota" system of succession unwisely established by Yaroslav, "The Wise," provided that the throne was to go, not to the eldest son of the last Grand Duke, but to the eldest living male member of the ruling dynasty.

        a. Each of Yaroslav's sons received a Russian province, and on the death of the eldest son each moved up a notch toward the throne.

        b. A bitter rivalry resulted among the sons.

    2. Several independent principalities resulted.

        a. The suzerainty of the "Grand Prince" became vague and tenuous.

        b. Various Princes enjoyed successive ascendance.

           i. Moscow gained ascendance in the 14th century.

C. <u>Tartar rule</u> in Russia lasted for over two centuries (*ca.* 1237-1453).

    1. The Tartar conquest of Russia occurred in the first half of the 13th century.

        a. The Tartars were a mixture of Mongols and Turks resulting from Mongol expansion across Asia in the 13th century.

        b. Mongol-Tartar hordes overran Russia under Subatai (1223-7) and again under Batu (1235-40).

           i. The second invasion established Tartar rule in Russia.

    2. Tartar overlordship in Russia remained alien, exploiting, and non-assimilative.

        a. Separation from their subjects was a glaring defect.

           i. They retained their own (Moslem) religion, speech, and customs.

           ii. Their ways were rough, harsh, and cruel.

        b. Collection of tribute was their main concern.

       i.   Native Russian Princes were retained and used as tax-collectors.

       ii.   The Grand Princes of Vladimir were early tax collectors for the Tartars.

       iii.   Prince Alexander Nevski of Novogorod, who eventually became Grand Prince of Vladimir, defeated the Swedes on the Neva River (1240) as well as the Teutonic Knights (1242) and the Lithuanians (1245).

V. The Balkans were in a condition of instability during much of the period.

    A. The Byzantine Empire sank into decline following the death of Basil II (1025).

       1. Petchenegs overran the Balkans and Seljuk Turks the Near East, including Asia Minor, during the "Time of Troubles" (1057-81).

       2. A partial revival was effected under the earlier Comneni until the disastrous battle of Myrocephalon (1176).

       3. Decline continued under the later Comneni and the fratricidal Angeli (1176-1204).

       4. The Latin Empire of Constantinople further sapped the strength of the suffering Empire (1204-61).

       5. The Paleologi (1261 ff.) achieved only a partial revival.

    B. Bulgaria was the main competitor of Byzantium for the Balkans in this period.

       1. The First Bulgarian Empire (*ca.* 893-1014) under Tsars Simeon and Samuel controlled a major part of the Balkans.

       2. Subjection to the Byzantines occurred in the 11th to 12th centuries (1014-1186).

       3. The Second Bulgarian Empire (*ca.* 1186-1257) flourished under Tsars Ivan Asen I and Ivan Asen II.

VI. Readings on various states in Europe in the High Middle Ages include:

    A. On Spain and Portugal:

      Altamira, Rafael, *History of Spain*, tr. (New York, Van Nostrand, 1949).

Livermore, Harold, *A History of Portugal*, (Cambridge, University Press, 1947).

B. On Scandinavia:

Danstrup, John, *History of Denmark*, (Copenhagen, Wivel Press, 1948).

Larsen, Karen, *History of Norway*, (Princeton, U. Press, 1948).

Anderson, Ingvar, *History of Sweden* (London, Weiderfield and Nicolson, 1956).

C. On East Central Europe:

Dvornik, Frantisek, *The Making of Central and Eastern Europe*, (London, Polishe Research Centre, 1949).

Halecki, Oskar, *Borderlands of Western Civilization*, New York, Ronald Press, 1952).

D. On Russia:

Vernadsky, George, *A History of Russia*, Vols. I-III, (New Haven, Yale U. Press, 1943 ff.).

Prawdin, Michael, *The Mongol Empire*, (London, Allen and Unwin, 1940).

Can You Identify?

Reconquista	Waldemar I and II
Toledo (1085)	Boleslaw I, the Brave
Ferdinand I of Castile	Arpad
Alfonso VI, the Battler	St. Stephen
Almohades	Premyslid
Almoravides	Kiev
Las Navas de Tolosa (1212)	Rus
Alfonso VIII of Castile	Rurik
Ferdinand III of Castile	Olga
James I of Aragon	Vladimir
Alfonso X, the Wise	Yaroslav
fueros	"Rota" System
consejos	Tartars
ayuntamientos	Alexander Nevski
juntas	Paleologi
Cortes	Tsars

Chapter 23

The Apogee of the Medieval Church During the High Middle Ages

I. <u>The Papacy</u> provided international leadership in Western Europe during the High Middle Ages.

   A. <u>Reform helped</u> bring the Church to its medieval apogee.

    1. General Church reform evolved out of the Cluniac reform movement by 1049.

      a. Church reform was originally monastic.

      b. Its ambit widened as Cluniacs became bishops and finally Popes.

    2. <u>Leo IX</u> was the first reform Pope (1049 ff.).

      a. Hildebrand, who became Leo's Secretary, later a Cardinal, and finally Gregory VII, was a leading reformer.

        i. From him the fully developed reform movement is often known as "Gregorian" or "Hildebrandine."

    3. Reform aims included abolition of simony, insistence on clerical celibacy, and emancipation of the Church from secular control.

      a. Elimination of simony and enforcement of clerical celibacy were immediately undertaken.

    4. <u>The Gregorian Reform</u> to abolish lay control of the Church began in 1059.

      a. The Electoral Decree of Pope Nicholas II (1059) created a College of Cardinals composed of leading ecclesiastics in the Roman Archdiocese to elect the Pope.

   b. The Investiture Controversy (1075 ff.) resulted from the efforts of Pope Gregory VII to free elections of bishops from lay control.

     i. A compromise was effected in the Empire as elsewhere by 1122. (See: The Western Empire and Papacy in the High Middle Ages).

B. The zenith of Papal secular power was reached during its struggle with the Hohenstaufen.

  1. Alexander III (1159-1181) obtained great prestige by his victory over Frederick I.

  2. Innocent III (1198-1216) brought Papal power to its apogee.

   a. Lothario Conti became Pope Innocent III at the age of 37.

   b. Innocent III became the virtual "Arbiter of Europe."

     i. He forced Philip II of France to give up his mistress.

     ii. He compelled King John of England to accept Lanfranc as Archbishop of Canterbury, and John became a Papal vassal.

     iii. The Kings of Aragon, Portugal, Sicily, and Bulgaria also recognized Innocent's suzerainty.

     iv. Innocent III intervened successfully in the Empire where he put his ward, Frederick II on the throne.

     v. He promoted a Crusade against the Albigensians, as well as the Fourth Crusade which strayed afield.

     vi. Innocent convoked the Fourth Lateran Council (1215) which accepted the legislation he offered.

  3. Subsequent Popes in the 13th century continued to exercise great power.

   a. Gregory IX (1227-1241) and Innocent IV (1243-54) overcame Frederick II.

   b. The Hohenstaufen line was extinguished by a Papal appointee, Charles of Anjou.

        c. Gregory X had Rudolph of Hapsburg elected to the imperial throne (1273).

  C. <u>Excessive secular involvement</u> of the Papacy occurred in the later 13th century.

    1. The Popes continued a policy of opposing foreign domination in Italy.

    2. Martin IV (1281-85) unsuccessfully supported the displaced Angevins against the Aragonese who had seized control of Sicily.

    3. Boniface VIII was humiliated by Philip IV of France.

    4. Preoccupation of the Papacy with temporal matters led many to lose respect and become anti-papal.

II. <u>Opposing Church-State theories</u> were advanced during the High Middle Ages.

  A. <u>Eleventh century theories</u> of Church and State were begotten by the Investiture Controversy.

    1. Gregory VII and Papal supporters argued for indirect power of the Papacy over secular rulers.

        a. They revised and expanded the theories of St. Ambrose and Pope Gelasius.

        b. The Papacy could depose temporal rulers in order to defend the moral law.

        c. Popes could not be judged by kings: they were responsible directly to God.

    2. Henry IV and his adherents denounced the pretensions of the Papacy to depose rulers.

        a. They asserted that secular political power came directly from God and that kings were responsible to Him alone.

        b. Peter Crassus' *Defense of Henry IV* invoked both custom and Roman law.

  B. <u>Twelfth Century Church-State theories</u> were influenced by the revival of both Canon and Civil Law.

    1. Supremacy of the Church was maintained by John of Salisbury and Bernard of Clairvaux.

        a. John insisted that the King received his authority or "sword" via the Church.

    2. Secular supremacy was championed by the *Anonymous (Tractates) of York* which claimed that Christ as King is superior to Christ as Priest.

        a. They asserted that "the power of the King is the

power of God" and that the king has the right
to control the Church.

b. Frederick I also claimed that imperial power is
from God and completely independent of the Papacy.

C. Thirteenth Century theorists espoused extreme positions.

1. "Canonists" or church-lawyers, such as Innocent IV
and Giles of Rome, supported Papal supremacy and
direct Papal power in secular affairs.

a. These men held that the Church exercised a direct overlordship over all men and that temporal
authority came from God through the Church.

2. "Legists" or civil lawyers continued to press for state
supremacy.

a. They were reinforced by Roman law, the actual
power of secular governments, and political doctrines of Aristotle.

b. Peter of Auvergne (d. 1302) and John of Paris
(*De Potestate regia et papali*) stressed that the
state was a natural society, supreme in its sphere.

III. Advanced Church Organization in the High Middle Ages
was one of the reasons for the Church's success.

A. The central government of the Church became a model
for secular governments.

1. The Pope was the head of the Church in the West.

a. The Popes extended elements of administrative
control throughout the Western Church.

b. Papal "provisions" reserved many ecclesiastical
benefices for papal nomination.

c. Papal legates were used to deal with many problems in various parts of Europe.

d. Means for enforcing papal policies included excommunication, interdict, and deposition.

2. The Cardinals provided a papal "cabinet" (or
"curia"), headed various "congregations" (or departments), and constituted an electoral board.

a. Principal subdivisions of the papal government
were:

i. The Chancery: in charge of papal correspond-
ence and implementation of papal policies

ii. The Camera: the financial department

   iii. The Sacred Tribunal, with two subdivisions: the Rota, which judged marriage cases and the Pentitentiary, which considered cases involving excommunications, censures, and dispensations.

  b. Many cases were appealed from local courts to the Papacy.

 3. Ecumenical councils were held on the average of one each half century.

  a. Four of these were held in Rome (Lateran I-IV) and two at Lyons (I and II).

 B. Bishops were the chief religious and administrative officials of the Church on the local level.

  1. Bishops ruled over dioceses with a fullness of apostolic powers.

  2. Archbishops were senior bishops or "metropolitans" in the regions known as "provinces."

  3. Priests, secular and religious, were representatives and delegates of the bishop in caring for the faithful.

  4. Provincial councils were meetings of the bishops of a province under the chairmanship of the Archbishop.

  5. Episcopal synods were meetings of the priests of a diocese, presided over by the Bishop.

IV. Religious Orders contributed to the strength of the Church in the High Middle Ages.

 A. Reforms of old Benedictine monasticism flourished during this period.

  1. The Cluniacs exercised an important influence on monastic life, church reform, and liturgical practices.

   a. They stressed public prayer and liturgy.

  2. The Cistercians, founded in the 11th century by St. Robert of Molesme, and expanded in the 12th by St. Bernard of Clairvaux, returned to Benedict's threefold division of the day: prayer, work, and refection.

   a. They restored monastic manual labor and insisted on austerity in liturgical practices.

   b. Their houses were plain and occupied less desirable places.

    i. They did much clearing and draining of lands.

        ii. They contributed to the agricultural expansion of Europe.

B. Semi-hermitical and quasi-secular orders contrasted.

  1. Semi-hermitical foundations, such as the Camaldolese, Carthusians, and Carmelites, practiced extreme austerities, including almost perpetual silence.

  2. Quasi-secular congregations of "Canons Regular," such as the Premonstratensians and Victorines, lived according to a rule similar to that of monks but ministered regularly to the needs of the faithful.

C. The Mendicant Orders were very popular.

  1. Their way of life was intermediate between that of the old monastic orders and that of the Canons Regular.

    a. They lived according to strict rules of poverty, chastity, and obedience, but they also worked among the people.

    b. They depended on voluntary contributions, whence their name "mendicants" or "beggars."

  2. The Franciscans, or Order of Friars Minor (O.F.M.), were founded by the Italian St. Francis of Assisi in the early 13th century.

    a. Poverty was stressed for the community as well as for its individual members.

    b. Preaching, educational, social, charitable, and missionary services were undertaken by the Franciscans.

      i. Eventually, they also became prominent in the Universities.

      ii. Learned Franciscans included Alexander of Hales, St. Bonaventure, and Roger Bacon.

  3. The Dominicans, or Order of Preachers (O.P.), were founded by the Spaniard St. Dominic de Guzman in 1216.

    a. Their rule resembled that of the Franciscans.

    b. Their primary purpose was preaching and the refutation of heresy.

    c. Education and theology were stressed, and they were soon involved in the universities.

      i. Thomas Aquinas, Albert the Great, and Vincent of Beauvais exemplify their intellectual leadership.

D. Military Orders also were established.
    1. Their members lived according to religious rule, but their external activity consisted of defending and expanding Christendom by the sword.
    2. The Knights Templar, Knights Hospitallers, and Teutonic Knights were founded in the Crusader States.
    3. Military orders also participated in the Germanic expansion along the Baltic and in the Hispanic *Reconquista* of the Iberian Peninsula.

V. Heresies were vigorously combatted.

A. Waldensianism and Albigensianism were the chief heresies of the High Middle Ages.
    1. The Waldensians (founded by Peter Waldo of Lyons) preached poverty, at first, but then went on to deny the necessity of the sacraments and the hierarchical authority of the Church.
    2. The Albigensians (named after the town of Albi where the heresy was strong) revived the ancient Manichaean dualism.
       a. Matter, such as meat and dairy products, and certain physical acts such as sexual intercourse, were considered evil and therefore to be avoided.
       b. The full Albigensian doctrines were put into practice only by the Cathari (Pure Ones) or *Perfecti* (Perfect Ones).
          i. Most of the Albigensians were merely believers.
       c. The Albigensian Crusade was sponsored by Innocent III in order to root out the heresy in Southern France.

B. The Inquisition was established by Pope Gregory IX in 1233 to discover and eradicate heresy, especially Albigensianism.
    1. Roman methods of criminal investigation were used.
       a. Torture was employed to obtain a confession or recantation.
       b. When proven heretics refused to recant they were handed over to the secular authority for punishment.

2. Penalties of fines, confiscation, and corporal punishment, including execution, were meted out.

   a. Death was imposed rarely in extreme cases.

VI. Readings on the Church in the High Middle Ages include:

Hughes, Philip, *A History of the Church*, II (New York, Sheed and Ward, 1949).

Mourret, Fernand, *A History of the Catholic Church*, tr., IV (St. Louis, Herder, 1941).

Flick, Alexander C., *The Rise of the Mediaeval Church* (New York, Putnam's, 1909).

Baldwin, Marshall W., *The Medieval Papacy in Action* (New York, Macmillan, 1940).

Ullmann, Walter, *The Growth of Papal Government in the Middle Ages* (London, Methuen, 1955).

Ehler, Sidney Z., and Morall, John B., *Church and State Through the Centuries* (Westminster Md., Newman, 1947).

Knowles, David, *The Monastic Order in England . . . 934-1216* (Cambridge, University Press, 1940).

Runciman, Steven, *The Medieval Manichee* (Cambridge, 1947).

Vacandard, Elphege, *The Inquisition* (New York, Longmann, 1908).

Can You Identify?

Leo IX	metropolitan (n.)
Hildebrand	Cluniacs
Nicholas II	Cistercians
Cardinals	Canons Regular
Gregory VII	Bernard of Clairvaux
Alexander III	Mendicants
Innocent III	Franciscans
IV Lateran	Francis of Assisi
Martin IV	Dominicans
Boniface VIII	Dominic
John of Salisbury	military orders
Anonymous (Tractates) of York	Waldensians
"Canonists"	Albigensians
"Legists"	Inquisition
Innocent IV	*Cathari*
Chancery	*Perfecti*
Camera	Inquisition (13th century)
Rota	Gregory X

Chapter 24

Intellectual Culture in the
High Middle Ages

I. <u>High Medieval culture</u>, combining and unifying diverse elements, has been characterized as "the medieval synthesis."

A. Aspects of this culture included:
1. Religious inspiration
    a. The Christian faith provided genius and motivation of high medieval culture
2. Universalism: a corollary of religious inspiration
    a. Since all things are governed by God, all have their place in the order of the universe.
    b. All available sources were used.
    c. Medieval culture was cosmopolitan and international despite local differences.
3. Unity, flowing from the conviction that there is a common source and end of all things
4. Dynamic creativity sparked by a vital faith
    a. Great ideals called forth great efforts.

B. <u>Factors</u> in the development of High Medieval culture included:
1. General economic, social, and political progress
2. Commingling of diverse cultural streams
3. Increased availability of translations from Arabic and Greek
4. The rise of universities as nurseries of advanced learning
5. Royal, ecclesiastical, and municipal patronage.

II. Education and learning underwent remarkable expansion in the High Middle Ages.

A. Factors in the progress of education and learning include:
1. The rise of towns and the growth of nations
2. The increasing demand for professional men
3. Advantages of corporate organization.

B. Cathedral schools flourished and expanded.
1. They assumed the leadership once enjoyed by monastic schools.
a. Chartres was noted for its grammar and the quadrivium, Paris for its logic and theology.
2. Other pre-university schools included:
a. Parochial schools
b. Private schools and tutors, as in Italy
c. Municipal schools which appeared in High Middle Ages
d. Professional schools (eg. law at Bologna; medicine at Salerno).
3. Apprenticeship was often used for instruction, as for craftsmen, doctors, surgeon-barbers, and knights.

III. Universities were the most important educational product of the High Middle Ages.

A. Unions of masters and students in higher education for the promotion of common academic interests first appeared about 1200.
1. They were known at first as *studia generalia* and later as "universities."

B. The earliest universities were Bologna and Paris, organized in the late 12th century.
1. The University of Bologna began as a union of law students.
a. Masters were subsequently included in the union.
b. The study of law at Bologna was stimulated by the work of Irnerius and Gratian.
c. Students from related regions organized into "nations," which eventually formed two unions: Cisalpine and Transalpine, which finally united to form one "university."

2. The University of Paris was originally a union of masters of arts, to which students subsequently were admitted.
   a. The union (university) established standards to control the granting of licenses to teach.
      i. Licenses were to be granted for merit and without fees.
   b. Organization of four "nations" arose within the university.
      i. The "rector" of the university was elected by the "proctors" of the nations.
C. University organization and life facilitated the assimilation and expansion of knowledge.
   1. The professions of teaching, medicine, theology, and law — civil and canon — each had its own "faculty."
      a. All the faculties were not necessary at a given university.
   2. Colleges were often organized within Universities as places of residence and study and mutual assistance.
   3. Privileges were granted to the Universities by Church and State.
      a. The university had its own internal government.
      b. The "Privilege of Clergy" was accorded to all masters and students.
         i. They were classed as clerics and could only be judged in ecclesiastical courts.
      c. The *"Jus Ubique Docendi"*—right of teaching anywhere was conferred on all who became masters.
      d. *"Cessatio"* was the right to strike, suspend lectures, and even transfer elsewhere (translation).
   4. Academic organization grew more complex.
      a. Authoritative texts, established as guides, included works of Aristotle, Peter Lombard, Galen, Ptolemy, and Justinian's Code.
      b. Degrees, or progressive steps in the university course, included:
         i. The Bachelor's Degree, which qualified one to be a teaching assistant to a master
         ii. The Licentiate, which conferred the privilege of teaching anywhere in Christendom
         iii. The Master's Degree which was recognition

and certification by other masters of one's qualifications to be a master, and resembled the modern doctorate.

c. Lectures and disputations were means of transmitting knowledge.

    i. In a lecture the text was read and commented on.

    ii. A disputation was a discussion in which a thesis was disputed—pro and con.

d. Satisfactory examinations and defence of a thesis qualified one for degrees.

5. Student recreations were uncontrolled and often radical.

a. Drinking, singing, gaming, and wenching were favorite pastimes.

b. "Town and gown" riots often erupted between students and townspeople.

6. Universities rapidly grew in number, attendance, and influence.

a. There were about twenty universities by 1300 and about eighty universities by 1500.

IV. <u>Scholasticism</u>, which combined philosophy and theology, was a major concern.

A. <u>Shift of emphasis</u> occurred from grammar and rhetoric (11th-12th centuries): to logic (12th century), and finally to philosophy and theology (13th century).

1. The humanism of the 12th century took great interest in classical literature.

a. Bernard of Chartres, Hildebert of Lavardin, and John of Salisbury were humanists of this era.

B. <u>Scholasticism</u> produced a "Golden Age" in medieval thought.

1. Scholasticism is the name given to the joint use of faith and reason (theology and philosophy) in the quest for truth.

2. The initial stage of scholasticism was marked by the ascendancy of logic and natural reason.

a. The study of logic was stimulated by the discovery of Aristotle's logical works, collectively referred to as the *Organon*.

   b. Increased attention to logic precipitated a dis-
      pute over the exact nature of universals.
      i. Roscelin, a nominalist, taught that universals,
         such as justice and man, are merely words.
      ii. William of Champeaux, an extreme realist,
          claimed that universals are more real than
          individuals, and have their own independent
          existence.
      iii. Abelard and John of Salisbury championed
           moderate realism and taught that universals,
           while not real substances, have a basis in
           fact as objective representations of real things.
   c. The beginnings of scholasticism stimulated an in-
      creased effort to apply human reason to matters
      of faith.
   a. St. Anselm's dictum, "I believe so that I may un-
      derstand," asserted the primacy of faith.
      i. Logical arguments and explanations were given
         for the existence of God and the Incarnation.
   b. Abelard's "I doubt in order to understand" was
      a declaration that the dialectic method should be
      pursued.
      i. His *Sic et Non* presented arguments on either
         side of key theological questions and often
         left the solution to the reader.
   c. Peter Lombard, Abelard's pupil, followed his mas-
      ter's method in his *Four Books of Sentences* pre-
      senting conflicting views, but giving orthodox an-
      swers to the problems.
C. Interest in philosophy in general was stimulated at Paris
   and Oxford by the recovery of all of Aristotle's philosophical works.
   1. Aristotle's works were translated first from Arabic,
      then from the Greek.
   2. Integration of philosophy and religious doctrines and
      the reconciliation of reason and faith was a main
      task of thirteenth-century scholasticism.
D. Various schools had different approaches:
   1. The Averroists, following the Moslem philosopher,
      Averroes, were materialistic, pantheistic, and unor-
      thodox.

      a. They taught such doctrines as the double truth and the oneness of the active intellect and the human soul.

      b. Chief proponents of Averroism included David of Dinant and Amaury of Bena.

  2. The Franciscans emphasized Augustinian concepts of intuition, will, and ideal.

      a. Their use of Aristotle was subordinated to Augustine and Neo-Platonism.

      b. Leaders of the Franciscan school included Alexander of Hales, St. Bonaventure, and Duns Scotus.

  3. The Dominicans emphasized reason, intellect, and syllogistic processes.

      a. Reason was put on a par with faith, each having its own sphere.

      b. The eventual primacy of revelation was stressed.

      c. The two greatest Dominicans of the period were Albertus Magnus and Thomas Aquinas.

         i. Aquinas, who is considered the "Prince of thirteenth-century scholastics," authored the famous *Summa Theologica* and *Summa Contra Gentiles.*

V. <u>Social and natural sciences,</u> were looked upon as branches of philosophy.

  A. <u>The social sciences</u> were heavily influenced by philosophy and theology.

    1. Dominant concepts in the social sciences included the existence of God, the supremacy of the moral law, consideration of the general welfare, the goal of eternal life, and the use of material things as means to an end.

    2. Political theory was particularly concerned with Church-State relations.

      a. Thirteenth-century canonists, including Innocent III and Innocent IV, claimed that the fullness of power given to the Pope by Christ included, if and when necessary, the direct control of the state.

      b. Civil lawyers in the later 13th century argued that the state was a natural institution as Aristotle

taught, and that the will of the king was the
source of law.

3. Law was an important field of study.

   a. The civil law text was the *Corpus Juris Civilis*
   codification of Justinian revived by Irnerius.

   b. Legal writers until about 1200 were more elementary and are known as "Glossators," but after
   1200 they were more sophisticated and are known
   as "Post-Glossators."

   c. Canon law was compiled and codified by a
   Camoldolese monk, Gratian in his *Decretum* (or
   Concordance of Discordant Canons) about 1140.

4. In economics the moderation of money-getting and
the stewardship of wealth were taught.

   a. Just prices, truthfulness, faithfulness to contracts,
   legitimate interest rates, etc. were demanded.

B. <u>The natural sciences</u> had many adherents, even though
most medieval savants were clerics.

1. Natural laws and facts were viewed as the footprints
of God.

   a. Science provided the facts for philosophers and
   a way of improving the lot of mankind.

2. The Oxford scientists, including Franciscans, were
particularly progressive in the field of natural sciences.

   a. They used observation and experimentation to
   ascertain natural laws and facts.

   b. Bishop Robert Grosseteste initiated the movement.

   c. Friar Roger Bacon predicted many modern scientific wonders.

3. Other scientists of the High Middle Ages included:
Adelard of Bath (who translated many Arabic scientific works); Alexander Neckham, Bartholomew
the Englishman; Albertus Magnus; Leonard Fibo-
nacci of Pisa (who promoted mathematics).

C. <u>History writing</u> became more logical, better organized,
and more analytical.

1. Englishmen prominent among the best history writers included:

   a. William of Malmesbury who authored a chronicle
   of English history to 1142.

      b. Roger of Wendover who wrote the *Flowers of History* which ended in 1235.

      c. Matthew of Paris, highly esteemed author of a chronicle which reported events until 1259.

   2. Other noted history writers included:

      a. Frenchmen such as Odericus Vitalus of Normandy; Richer, who wrote a history of the bishops of Reims; Suger, who wrote the *Life of Louis VI*; Guibert de Nogent, who wrote an *Autobiography* and a history of the First Crusade: *God's Dealings through the Franks*; and Joinville, the author of a *Life of Louis IX*.

      b. The German Otto of Freising, author of *Two Cities* and *Deeds of Frederick II*.

      c. The Italian Salimbene of Parma, author of a chronicle of Italian history.

VI. Readings on Intellectual Culture in the High Middle Ages include:

A. On Culture in General:

Artz, Frederick B., *The Mind of the Middle Ages* (New York, Knopf, 1953).

Taylor, Henry O., *The Medieval Mind*, 2 vols. (London, Macmillan, 1927).

Haskins, Charles H., *The Renaissance of the Twelfth Century* (Cambridge, Harvard, 1927).

B. On Education and the rise of Universities:

Compayré, Gabriel, *Abelard and the Origin and Early History of Universities* (New York, Scribners, 1897).

Eng, Frederick, and Arrowood, C. F., *History and Philosophy of Education: Ancient and Medieval* (New York, Prentice Hall, 1940).

Daly, Lowrie, *The Medieval University*, 1200-1400 (New York, Sheed and Ward, 1961).

Rashdall, Hastings, *The Universities of Europe in the Middle Ages*, 3 vols. (Oxford, Clarendon, 1936).

C. On Philosophy and Theology:

Gilson, Etienne, *History of Christian Philosophy in the Middle Ages* (New York, Random House, 1955).

Copleston, Frederick, *History of Philosophy*, II and III (New York, Philosophical Library, 1952-3).

DeWulf, Maurice, *History of Medieval Philosophy*, 2 vols. (London, Longmans, 1925-1928).

D. On Political Theory:
   McIlwain, Charles H., *The Growth of Political Thought in the West. . . . to the End of the Middle Ages* (New York, Macmillan, 1933).

E. On Science:
   Crombie, Alstair, *Medieval and Early Modern Science*, 2 vols. (New York, Doubleday, 1959).
   Thorndike, Lynn, *A History of Magic and Experimental Science. . . .* (New York, Macmillan, 1923 ff.).
   Sarton, George, *Introduction to the History of Science*, I, II, and III (Baltimore, Williams and Wilkins, 1927-1947).

Can You Identify?

Chartres	Abelard
Salerno	St. Anselm
studium generale	*Sic et non*
"university" (13th century)	Peter Lombard
University of Bologna	Averroists
University of Paris	Thomas Aquinas
"nations" (academic)	Irnerius
rector (academic)	Glossators
proctor (academic)	Gratian
jus ubique docendi	*Decretum*
cessatio	Roger Bacon
Bachelor (academic)	Adelard of Bath
Licentiate	William of Malmesbury
Master (academic)	Matthew Paris
"Town and gown"	Odericus Vitalis
Scholasticism	Guibert de Nogent
Organon	Joinville
Roscelin	Otto of Freising
William of Champeaux	Salimbene

Chapter 25

Literary and Artistic Expression
in the High Middle Ages

I. Literary and Artistic Expression came to be highly developed in the High Middle Ages.

   A. General features of High Medieval expression were as follows:

     1. Religious inspiration was paramount though not exclusive.

       a. A love of nature and an appreciation of human character was often evident.

     2. Perfectionism was common.

     3. Versatility was widespread.

     4. Anonymity was a sacrificial offering to higher purposes.

   B. Forms of expression included Latin and vernacular literatures, Romanesque and Gothic architecture, and numerous species of arts and varieties of music.

II. Literature of the High Middle Ages was impressive both for its quantity and quality.

   A. Latin literature was produced in rich abundance.

     1. Latin was the universal, international language of scholarship, learning, diplomacy, and the Church.

       a. Though Latin was a living, evolving language, still classical norms, derived from classical literature and grammar, were followed.

     2. Latin prose flourished in a variety of forms.

a. Learned treatises, sermons, letters, histories, and biographies were written in Latin.

3. _Latin drama_ evolved from dramatic representations of scriptural episodes enacted in connection with the liturgy.

   a. When moved outside the Church drama assumed three forms:

      i. Mystery plays which related events in Scripture

      ii. Miracle plays which concerned events in the lives of the saints

      iii. Morality plays, which developed in the Later Middle Ages, portrayed abstract principles as allegorical personages.

4. _Latin poetry_ was the chief form of literary expression.

   a. The superb religious poetry of the era is exemplified by:

      i. *Jesu Dulcis Memoriae* (12th century), *Veni Sancte Spiritus* (13th century), *Dies Irae* (13th century), *Stabat Mater* (13th century), and the Eucharistic hymns of Thomas Aquinas: *Lauda Sion, Verbum Supernum, Pange Linqua,* and *Adoro Te* (13th century).

   b. Secular Latin poetry known as "Goliardic" from a mythical "Bishop Golias," also was produced in large amounts.

      i. It was composed by students and ecclesiastics for light entertainment.

      ii. These gay, satirical, and sometimes ribald poems seldom rose above rhymed doggerel.

      iii. Goliardic poetry included drinking songs, parodies and satires, and sensuous love songs.

B. _Vernacular literature_ struck strong roots in the High Middle Ages.

1. _French literature_ was the leading vernacular literature of the age.

   a. *Chansons de geste*, popular in northern France, were epic poems, narrating, describing, and elaborating heroic events and characters.

      i. The *Chanson de Roland* is one of the best of these epics.
- b. *Chansons d'amour*, originating in the south of France, were love songs composed by troubadours.
- c. *Faiblaux* and fables were also popular.
  - i. *Faiblaux* were amusing short stories.
  - ii. Fables featured animals with human characters and foibles, and were intended to teach a moral.
- d. Romances combined love and adventure in poetic form.
  - i. The British Romances, such as those concerning King Arthur and the Knights of the Round Table, were popular.
  - ii. Allegorical romances such as "The Romance of the Rose," personified abstract qualities.
- e. Vernacular literature in England was composed temporarily almost entirely in French.

2. <u>German literature</u> imitated and adapted French forms and themes to its own inspiration.
- a. A *Rolandslied* (*lied*—song, lay) in German was produced in about 1170.
- b. *Minnesingers* (love—singers) were German troubadours.
- c. German poetry evolved through religious poems (11th-12th centuries), *chansons de geste* (12th century), love poems (12th-13th centuries), "heroic epics," and "court epics" or romances 13th century).
  - i. Leading German poets of the period included: Hartman von Aue, Wolfram von Eschenbach, and Walther von der Vogelweide.

3. <u>Italian literature</u> was influenced by the French and by the Franciscans.
- a. The "sweet new style" (*dolce stil nuovo*) of the troubadours was cultivated by Dante's contemporaries.
- b. Italian versions of the *chansons de geste* also appeared.
- c. The Franciscans promoted religious lyrics.

4. Spanish literature is exemplified by the *Poema del Cid*, a famous Spanish *chanson de geste*, and by religious lyrics, such as the *Cantigas de Santa Maria*, compiled by Alphonso X, the Wise of Castile.

III. The Arts flourished in close association with religion.

   A. Architecture was the chief art form.

    1. Romanesque architecture was the major church design in the earlier part of the period.

        a. It combined features of Christian basilican, Germanic "hall-church," and Proto-Romanesque styles of Lombard origin.

            i. Romanesque architecture flourished in the 11th-12th centuries.

        b. Round arches and stone vaults throughout the church were its chief features.

            i. Stone vaults over nave and aisles were of the 1) tunnel, 2) groined, or 3) ribbed types.

        c. Transepts across the nave toward the apse were also employed.

            i. Both transept and apse became more complex.

        d. Towers were built, sometimes over the juncture of transept and nave, but usually flanking the entrance.

        e. Multicolored frescoes, mosaics, marbles, and sculptures ornamented the interior of the church.

        f. Different regional styles are exemplified by the cathedrals of Pisa, Worms, Autun, and Santiago de Compostella, and by monastic churches at Arles, Toulouse, Cluny, and Caen.

    2. Gothic architecture, which evolved from Romanesque, flourished in the 12th-13th centuries.

        a. Chief features included: pointed arches, ribbed vaults, flying buttresses, stained-glass windows, great height, and integrated organic structure.

            i. The essential structure was skeletal; the rest, such as the great glass windows, "fill-in."

        b. Early Gothic architecture arose in France in the second half of the 12th century, and is exemplified by the Abbey Church of St. Denis.

        c. High Gothic was an epitome of elegance, refinement, and coherence in the 13th century.

          i. In France, the cathedrals of Chartres, Amiens, Reims, and Paris are prime examples.

          ii. In England a more sedate and "squarish" English Gothic arose, as in the Cathedrals of Salisbury and Lincoln.

          iii. Germany produced an imitative High Gothic, and a flamboyant, ornate Late Gothic.

              1) The Cathedral of Cologne imitated that of Amiens.

       d. The late Gothic style of the 14th century ff. was overly ornate, dramatic, and decorative.

    3. Secular architecture was exemplified by castles, town walls with towers, and some town halls.

IV. <u>Art in the High Middle Ages</u> was primarily connected with churches and religious manuscripts.

    A. <u>General features</u> of this art included: unity amidst complexity, impressionism mixed with realism, allegory and symbolism, intellectualism blended with humor, and great originality and imagination.

    B. <u>Sculpture</u> reached a high point.

      1. Thousands of sculptured figures of all sorts adorned the great medieval cathedrals.

      2. Sculpture was an integral aspect of Romanesque and Gothic cathedrals, but was always subordinate to the architecture.

        a. Gothic sculpture displays greater repose than the Romanesque which is often nervous.

      3. Realism and idealism, narration, and symbolism were combined in sculpture.

    C. <u>Painting</u> has survived mainly in manuscript illumination.

      1. Romanesque illumination is bold and inventive.

      2. Gothic illumination is more delicate and refined.

      3. Frescoes were used primarily in Italian churches.

    D. <u>Stained glass</u> achieved great perfection in the High Middle Ages.

      1. Coloring was rich and deep as well as translucent.

      2. Composition of the windows was unparalleled, particularly at Chartres and Canterbury.

    E. <u>Other arts</u> of excellence included tapestry-making, wood-carving, and metalwork.

    1. Tapestries were ingeniously and expertly woven, as, for example, the Bayeaux Tapestry (celebrating the Norman Conquest of England).

    2. Woodcarving was highly developed, especially in the Germanies and in Scandinavia.

F. <u>Music</u> experienced a development similar to that in other fields.

    1. Both religious and secular musical compositions were multiplied.

    2. Polyphony became more complex, evolving through:

        a. Strict *organum* in which the basic melody was paralleled by one or more similar melodies at fixed intervals

        b. Free *organum* or "discant," wherein both the melody and pitch of the parts varied, but the parts were still unmeasured

        c. "Counterpoint" or full "harmony," in which the music of freely composed multiple parts was measured and harmonious

            i. In "motets" the words varied as well as the melodies.

    3. Notation was prompted by the needs of polyphony.

        a. Staffs of five or six lines with intervals were used.

        b. The "clef" or key was used to indicate pitch.

        c. The designation of notes as "full," "half," and "quarter" notes allowed complex measured music.

    4. The integrated complexity of polyphonic counterpoint music resembled the integrated elements in Gothic architecture.

    5. Polyphony also developed in secular music.

    6. Great music masters included Guido of Arezzo, Leonine and Perrotin of Paris, and Franco of Cologne.

V. <u>Readings</u> on Expression in the High Middle Ages include:

    A. <u>On Literature</u>:

        Jones, Charles W., *Medieval Literature in Translation* (New York, Longmans, 1950).

        Walsh, James J., *A Golden Treasury of Medieval Literature* (Boston, Stratford, 1930).

        Jackson, Walter T., *The Literature of the Middle Ages* (New York, Columbia U., 1960).

Holmes, Urban T., *A History of Old French Literature* (New York, Appleton, 1948).

Robertson, John G., *History of German Literature* (Edinburgh, Blackwood, 1959).

B. On Art, Architecture, and Music:

Sewall, John I., *History of Western Art* (New York, Holt, 1953).

Porter, Arthur K., *Medieval Architecture*, 2 vols. (New Haven, Yale, 1912).

Morey, Charles R., *Medieval Art* (New York, Norton, 1943).

Male, Emile, *Religious Art* (New York, Pantheon, 1949).

Reese, Gustav, *Music in the Middle Ages* (New York, Norton, 1940).

Can You Identify?

mystery play

miracle play

morality play

Goliardic

chanson de geste

Chanson de Roland

chanson d' amour

faiblaux

romance (13th century)

"Romance of the Rose"

Minnesinger

dolce stil nuovo

Poema del Cid

Romanesque Architecture

Gothic Architecture

Late Gothic Architecture

strict *organum*

free *organum*

counterpoint

Topographic Map of Europe

PART IV
THE LATER MIDDLE AGES

I. The Later Middle Ages (1300-1500), with their strong cross currents and revolutionary changes, were "An Era of Transition."

   A. Conflicting cross currents were present in almost every phase of life, as in the case of:
      1. Parliamentarianism vs. monarchism
      2. Nationalism vs. internationalism
      3. The proletariat vs. the capitalists
      4. The lower middle class vs. the upper middle class
      5. Commoners vs. aristocrats
      6. Conciliarism vs. papalism
      7. Naturalism vs. supernaturalism
      8. Humanism vs. scholasticism
      9. Renaissance classicism vs. Late Gothic medievalism
        a. The Renaissance was born in Italy.
        b. Late Gothic culture was entrenched beyond the Alps.
        c. The two streams eventually fused in the 15th century.

   B. Revolutionary changes occurred when the equilibrium of the High Middle Ages was upset by these cross currents.

II. The "Question of the Renaissance" continues to be debated and illustrates the relativity of historical judgement.

   A. "Renaissance" proponents maintain that a revolutionary, progressive revival, partly inspired by classical precedents, originated in Italy in the Later Middle Ages, and transformed most aspects of life for the better.

    1. They attribute this "rebirth" to classical inspiration, the salutary environment of historic Italy, and the particular genius of the Italian people.

    2. After transforming Italy, the movement spread to other countries.

    3. Its proponents say that the Renaissance brought about the "birth of modern man" by dispelling the "darkness, superstition, and lethargy" of the middle ages.

    4. Renaissance advocates include Jacob Burckhardt, John A. Symonds, and many others.

B. Opponents of this view include many leading specialists in medieval history.

    1. Most medievalists maintain that the High Middle Ages actually were a period of greater general progress than the Later Middle Ages.

        a. Among such are Henry O. Taylor, Lynn Thorndike, Johann Huizinga, George Sellery, and many others.

    2. Various shades of intermediate opinions exist.

C. A compromise view is that the Later Medieval period simultaneously includes aspects of progress, decline, and continuity.

    1. Progress was exemplified by:

        a. More thorough study and mastery of classical languages and literatures

        b. Broadened interest in such subjects as history, biography, mythology, geography, etc.

        c. Greatly improved techniques and productions in sculpture and painting

        d. More accurate representation of nature in the arts

        e. Increased and improved education of the laity.

    2. Decline was exemplified by:

        a. Eventual decrease of individual political freedom and participation in government.

        b. Economic depression

        c. Social cleavage between upper and lower middle classes as well as between middle class and proletariat

        d. Decline of papal and ecclesiastical leadership.

    3. Continuity was exemplified by:

      a. Continued specialization of production
      b. Continued growth of capitalism
      c. Continued emancipation of the laboring classes in Western Europe
      d. Continued multiplication of universities.

III. <u>Readings</u> on the Later Middle Ages include:

Ferguson, Wallace K., *Europe in Transition* (Boston, Houghton, 1962).

Ferguson, Wallace K., *The Renaissance in Historical Thought* (Boston, Houghton, 1948).

Lucas, Henry S., *Renaissance and Reformation* (New York, Harper, 1960).

Thomson, S. Harrison, *Europe in Renaissance and Reformation* (New York, Harcourt Brace, 1963).

Sellery, George C., *The Renaissance* (Madison, University of Wisconsin, 1950).

Huizinga, Johann, *Waning of the Middle Ages* (London, E. Arnold & Co., 1924).

Burckhardt, Jacob, *Civilization of the Renaissance in Italy* (London, Allen and Unwin, 1937).

Chapter 26

Economic and Social Conditions and Related Developments in The Later Middle Ages

I. <u>Economic cross-currents</u> resulted in a century of recession (1350-1450) counterbalanced against two half centuries of progress (1300-1350 and 1450-1500)

    A. <u>The "Commercial Kaleidoscope"</u> featured:

        1. Commercial decline in the form of a recession from 1350 to 1450

            a. Causes included:

                i. The Hundred Years War (1337-1453)

                ii. Population losses in the Black Death

                iii. Internal conflicts (civil wars)

                iv. Breakup of the Mongol Empire, making trade with the Far East more difficult

                v. Intensified Moslem antipathy for the West, hampering trade with the Near East

                vi. The Ming dynasty in China, which embarked on a "closed door" policy toward the West.

        2. Commercial recovery from 1450 to 1500

            a. Factors included:

                i. End of the Hundred Years War

                ii. Growth of royal absolution and stronger monarchical control.

    B. <u>Industry</u> became more diversified and geared to trade by specialization.

1. Textile manufacturing was the most important industry.
   a. Woolen, silk, linen, and cotton goods of various kinds and grades were produced.
   b. Manufacture of textiles had several stages, such as carding, cleaning, spinning, weaving, fulling, dyeing, and finishing.
   c. Chief centers of the textile industry were in northern Italy and the Low Countries, although Northwestern France, England, and Northeastern Spain also participated.
2. Metal products, such as tools, cutlery, jewelry, hardware, and wagon and carriage parts, were important.
   a. The armorer's art perfected new suits of armor and high-quality swords.
   b. Manufacture of field artillery and firearms gave rise to a new branch of industry after the development of gunpowder.
      i. The manufacture of gunpowder itself was a new industry.
3. Other basic industries included:
   a. Production of hides, leatherwork, tallow, candles, and soap
   b. The making of glass, which came from the East
   c. Papermaking and printing, soon to be of great importance
   d. Shipbuilding at ports such as Venice, Genoa, and Barcelona
   e. Brewing of beer and wine-making
   f. Extractive industries, practiced by much of the population, and including fishing, mining, and lumbering.
C. Agricultural and pastoral activities were still the occupation of most of the population.
   1. Markets for farm products increased with the growth of towns and the trend to specialization.
      a. Cereal production became important in areas such as Poland and Hungary.
      b. Fruit-growing and viniculture were important in southern Europe.

2. Specialization also occurred in pastoral activities.
   a. Sheep-raising was emphasized in England, central Spain, and central Italy.
D. Improved methods were introduced in industry and commerce.
   1. Technological advances in textile-making and mining improved both industries.
      a. Water power was used in fulling cloth and for pumping water out of mines.
      b. Processes for finishing cloth were greatly improved, as in the "*arte di calimala*" in Florence.
      c. Other industrial developments included:
         i. Better blast furnaces
         ii. Making of better paper
         iii. Printing with movable type
         iv. Production of safe and servicable gunpowder and gun barrels.
   2. Commercial improvements were numerous:
      a. Bigger and better ships allowed more cargo to be moved to more distant places.
      b. Improved compasses and astrolabes made possible long-distance navigation out of sight of land.
      c. Advances in cartography and improved geographical knowledge aided maritime developments.
      d. Navigational aids, such as lighthouses and improved harbors, were also important.
      e. Dredging of rivers and construction of canals facilitated inland voyages.
   3. Business aids included:
      a. Assembling of statistics
      b. Double-entry bookkeeping
      c. Use of Arabic numerals
      d. Business education (including commercial correspondence and commercial arithmetic) and
      e. Standardization of merchant law.

II. Capitalistic methods affected almost every aspect of the economy.

   A. Substitution of money payments for dues in goods and services became almost universal.

1. Minting of gold and silver coins in larger denominations increased.
2. Capital accumulated in the hands of shrewd businessmen.
   a. Well known capitalists of this era included: the Bardi, Peruzzi, and Medici families of Florence; Pierre Remi and Jacques Couer of France; Richard Whittington in England; the Fuggers in Germany.

B. <u>Capitalism in commerce</u> was promoted by both permanent and temporary forms of business association.
   1. Permanent associations were generally limited to families or "houses," since limited liability was not yet admitted.
      a. Any additional partners were "adopted" into the family or *compagnia*.
      b. Representative business "houses" were those of the Bardi, Peruzzi, Medici, and Fuggers.
      c. Joint stock companies with limited liability did not appear until the 16th century.
   2. Temporary forms of capitalistic association also developed.
      a. *Commenda* were partnerships for maritime commerce comprising investors and agents receiving various percentages of profit according to particular circumstances.
      b. The *societas terrae* was a similar association for land enterprise.
      c. Commercial loans also became common, and commercial insurance appeared.
   3. The Hanseatic League was a powerful league of towns for commercial and defensive purposes.
      a. It consisted of North German and neighboring towns and originated as a union of merchant guilds in the 13th century.
      b. For a time it dominated trade in the North and Baltic Seas.
   4. Marketing of goods continued to be done in markets, fairs, and shops, as well as by peddlers.
      a. But certain more capitalistic forms of large-scale buying and selling also appeared.

      b. Thus business houses maintained offices and warehouses for year-round buying and selling.

      c. And permanent exchanges or "bourses" developed in commercial centers such as Venice and Antwerp.

         i. Here goods could be bought and sold in wholesale quantities throughout the year.

C. <u>Capitalism in industry</u> developed to a lesser extent:

  1. Most industrial production was still on an individual basis.

  2. Some textile "factories" employing several hundred persons appeared in northern Italy and the Low Countries.

  3. Large-scale mining activities often were conducted, as by the Fuggers in southern Germany, the Tyrol, and Hungary.

  4. The "Putting-out" system was a capitalistic form of production in the textile industry.

      a. Entrepreneurs would purchase large quantities of raw materials, such as wool, which they continued to own after letting them out to various craftsmen, such as weavers, dyers, etc., until the product was finished.

D. <u>Capitalism in agriculture</u> was promoted by conversion of dues and services into money payments.

  1. Feudal lords became rural landlords, and serfs became hired laborers.

  2. Prosperous members of the urban middle class often branched out into capitalistic agriculture by acquiring landed estates.

  3. Large landholding was increased by enclosures and seigniorial appropriation of common pastures, meadows, and woods.

      a. These were used for large-scale pastoral activities or were rented out in smaller units.

      b. Sheep-raising in England became increasingly capitalistic.

E. <u>Banking and credit</u> continued to develop.

  1. Bankers and financiers of the Later Middle Ages engaged in a wide variety of operations involving money and credit.

       a. A certain percentage was always made for "the house."

       b. "Exchange" was a banking operation in which one form of money was converted into another.

       c. "Paper transactions" as substitutes for money-transactions became common.

           i. Among such were "letters of credit" and "bills of exchange."

       d. Banking increased as it became common to deposit money to earn interest and to obtain greater security.

    2. Credit stimulated business.

       a. As credit became more common the old prejudice against interest waned.

       b. Rates of interest were usually high because of the risk involved.

III. <u>Social changes and stresses</u> resulted from the growth of a money economy.

  A. <u>The middle class</u> expanded and divided.

    1. A capitalistic middle class as opposed to the ordinary middle class developed.

       a. The influence of the capitalistic upper middle class increased *pari passu* with their financial power.

       b. The influence of the feudal aristocracy declined.

           i. The importance of cavalry diminished because of changes in warfare.

  B. <u>The propertyless proletariat</u> in both town and country increased.

    1. The majority of the urban populace became day laborers working for hire.

       a. Recessions, unemployment, etc., were particularly hard on them.

       b. They worked for subsistence pay and often had wretched housing, poor food, and minimal clothing.

       c. The urban masses were often worse off than rural laborers.

    2. In the country, most of the proletariat were renters or hired laborers.

      3. The number of indigent, itinerant laborers and beggars increased.

      4. In Eastern Europe the peasants became less free.

C. Social unrest grew.

      1. General factors in uprisings during the Later Middle Ages included:

         a. Glaring inequalities between "haves" and "havenots"

         b. Class distinctions in politics

         c. Social ills caused by wars, unequal taxes, repressive legislation, and economic depressions

         d. Rivalry between the upper and ordinary middle classes in the towns

         e. Grievances and aspirations of the proletariat.

      2. Among famous uprisings were:

         a. The *"Jacquerie"* of 1358 and the *"Tuchins"* of 1378 in France

         b. The "Wat Tyler" Rebellion of 1380-81 and the "Jack Cade" Rebellion ("Peasants' Revolt") of 1450 in England

         c. The great insurrection of 1322-28 in Flanders

         d. The *"Ciompi"* revolt of 1378-82 in Florence.

IV. Political evolution was affected by the growth of a money economy and capitalism.

A. Consolidation of states with greater monarchical control was achieved by monarchs with the help of economic factors.

      1. French kings such as Louis XI gained control over most of modern France.

      2. Ferdinand and Isabella extended their control over most of the Iberian peninsula.

      3. Increased centralization meant:

         a. Diminution of feudal, municipal, and ecclesiastical exemptions

         b. Increased royal control of municipal governments

         c. Spread of royal justice

         d. Abolition of private warfare

         e. Extension of taxation and economic legislation

   f. Maintenance of standing armies

   g. Sponsorship of overseas expansion.

 B. <u>Constitutional evolution</u> through "Parliamentarianism" toward "Monarchism" was aided by the middle class.

  1. The financial importance of the middle class and the need for money prompted kings to call national representative gatherings.

   a. Such gatherings were called Estates General, Parliaments, Diets, etc.

   b. Parliamentary power, based on the ability to withhold money, became very great.

  2. Parliamentary ascendancy did not last.

   a. Conflicting class interests, rivalries, and lack of experience caused the failure.

   b. The nobility were preoccupied with violent contests for power.

   c. The middle class, wanting security, eventually allied with the monarchs.

  3. The monarchs subdued the nobility and emerged supreme with the help of the middle class, regular taxes, and standing armies.

 C. <u>Interstate rivalries</u> and growing nationalism resulted in bitter strife, as in the Hundred Years' War.

  1. Warfare changed in character.

   a. Missiles, such as the long bow, and gunpowder weapons increased in importance.

   b. Knights lost their ascendance with the increase of missile-warfare, and castles became vulnerable to cannonballs.

   c. The mounted feudal aristocracy was gradually replaced by the infantry.

   d. Large paid standing armies replaced the old feudal levy.

 D. <u>Governmental regulation</u> of the economy for national interests developed.

  1. Governments favored the interests of their own citizens.

   a. Withdrawal of privileges from foreigners caused decline of the Hanseatic League.

  2. Domestic industries were encouraged, while competing goods from foreign states were banned.

3. Other governmental aids to the economy included:
   a. Expansion of the coinage
   b. Programs of public works, such as the building and renovation of roads, bridges, and harbors
   c. Establishment of uniform weights and measures
4. Governments attempted fixing of wages and forced labor by laws.
   i. Such laws included the English Statutes of Laborers (1350-1417) and the French Ordinances (1350).

V. <u>Readings</u> on Economic and Social Conditions in the Later Middle Ages include:

Boissonade, Prosper, *Life and Work in Medieval Europe* (London, Kegan, Paul, 1927).

Cambridge Economic History of Europe, I and II

Pirenne, Henri, *Economic and Social History of Mediaeval Europe* (London, K. Paul, French, 1936).

Thompson, James W., *Economic and Social History of Europe in the Later Middle Ages*, 1300-1530 (New York, 1931).

Lopez, Robert S., and Raymond, Irving W., *Mediaeval Trade in the Mediterranean World* (New York, Columbia U. Press, 1955).

Can You Identify?

Later Middle Ages
Renaissance
Late Gothic
"Question of the Renaissance"
arte di calimala
Peruzzi
Medici
Jacques Couer
Fuggers
Hanseatic
commenda
societas terrae

bourse
"factory" (2 meanings)
"Putting Out" system
exchange
proletariat
Jacquerie
Wat Tyler
Ciompi
Parliamentarianism
Monarchism
Statutes of Laborers (1350-1417)

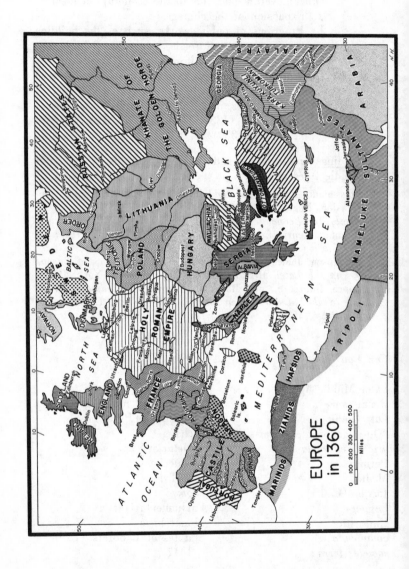

EUROPE
in 1360

0 100 200 300 400 500
Miles

Chapter 27

England and France in the
Later Middle Ages

I. The Hundred Years' War (1337-1453), occupied both England and France during a greater part of the period.

A. England and France had intertwined histories during the Later Middle Ages.
   1. Both were European leaders and rivals.
   2. Similar political problems developed in both countries.
   3. They were locked in mutual warfare during much of the period.

B. Origins of the Hundred Years' War included geographical proximity and interlocked history.
   1. Holdings of the English Kings in southwestern France (Guienne and Gascony) caused much friction.
   2. A running dispute festered over fishing rights in adjacent waters.
   3. The English supported the Flemish against the French king.
      a. Flanders and England were economically interdependent due to reciprocal wool and textile trade.
   4. The French aided the Scots in their struggles against the English.
   5. Edward III claimed the French throne on the grounds that he was a grandson of Philip IV through his mother.

      a. Edward's relation to Philip IV, as a maternal grandson, was closer than that of Philip VI who was a nephew.

      b. But Salian custom was against inheritance through the female line.

C. <u>The initial advantage</u> in the war lay with the English.

  1. Although France was much larger than England and had greater resources and population, its potential strength was not actualized.

      a. Much French territory was in English hands.

  2. England was more compact and better united.

  3. A larger monetary income helped make the English monarchy stronger.

  4. The English king had a standing army which was better coordinated and well trained in the use of "combined tactics."

      a. The latter involved joint use of infantry, cavalry, and the longbow.

  5. France was enfeebled by feudal factionalism and weak Valois monarchs.

D. <u>The First Phase</u> (1337-1360) saw a series of dramatic English victories.

  1. English success was the result of:

      a. Use of the longbow and "combined tactics."

      b. French conservatism, obtuseness, and exaggerated chivalry.

  2. At Sluys (1337), off the coast of Flanders, the English won a naval victory in which English longbowmen swept the decks of the French ships.

  3. At Crécy (1346) the English defeated a French force three times as large as its own.

      a. From a defensive position on a hillside, arrows from English longbows cut down the charging French cavalry.

  4. Calais was taken by the English (1347) after being besieged for a year.

  5. A truce and the Black Death temporarily halted the War.

  6. At Poitiers (1356):

      a. The Black Prince repeated the tactics of Crécy, to which he added cavalry charges with devastating results.

      b. King John II and many French nobles were taken prisoners.

   7. By the Treaty of Brétigny (1360) King John was to be ransomed for three million gold marks and England received most of southwestern France with Calais, Ponthieu, and Guisnes in northwestern France.

E. The Second Phase (1360-1380) saw the French gain the upper hand.

   1. Charles V, the Wise, (1364-1380) was a capable administrator whereas Edward III (d. 1377) was in his dotage.

   2. Charles' general, Du Guesclin recaptured stronghold after stronghold using guerilla tactics and avoiding major engagements.

      a. The English were distracted in Spain.

   3. By 1380 the English were confined to coastal holdings of Brest, Calais, Cherbourg, and a narrow strip from Bordeaux to Bayonne.

F. The Third Phase (1380-1415) was without decisive results, due to domestic distractions on both sides.

   1. England was preoccupied with the "Wat Tyler Rebellion" (1381) and the Lancastrian Revolution (1399).

   2. In France Charles VI went mad (1399 ff.) and a struggle for control between Burgundian and Orleanist (or Armagnac) factions ensued.

G. The Fourth Phase (1415-1429) was a period of great English successes.

   1. Energetic Henry V resumed the war with a promise of Burgundian assistance.

   2. At Agincourt (1415) Henry defeated a superior French force with the familiar combined tactics.

   3. By the Treaty of Troyes (1420), Henry V married the daughter of Charles VI, and became his designated heir.

      a. The Dauphin Charles was disinherited.

   4. The Dauphin Charles resisted with support from southern France, he was dominated by favorites and generally listless.

   5. The deaths of both Henry V and Charles VI in 1422 altered the situation.

      a. The infant Henry VI succeeded to the English throne under a regency.

      b. The Duke of Bedford, English regent in France, advanced the cause of his king.

      c. Bedford moved southward and besieged Orleans (1428 ff.) while the Dauphin remained idle.

H. The Fifth Phase (1429-1453), initiated by Joan of Arc, conclusively turned the tables.

   1. Joan of Arc rallied the French (1429).

      a. Prompted by visions, Joan, a peasant maid, came to the Dauphin at Chinon and urged action.

      b. Accompanied by Joan, the French army relieved Orleans (1429).

      c. At Joan's persuasion, the Dauphin was conducted to Reims where he was crowned as Charles VII.

      d. A siege of Paris failed.

      e. Joan was captured and tried and executed for heresy by the English in 1431.

   2. Factors for final French success included:

      a. France's greater population and resources

      b. The fact that the war was fought on French soil

         i. This made the French logistical problem simpler.

         ii. It also helped to unite the French people against the foreign English.

      c. Rising nationalism and a patriotic spirit, helped by the example of Joan of Arc.

      d. A direct tax (taille) granted by the Estates General gave the crown the necessary funds to fight a "modern" war.

      e. Professional, mercenary soldiers served in the reorganized French army, which was provided with the best gunpowder artillery.

      f. English weakness aided the French.

         i. The long and turbulent regency (1422-1437) and Yorkist vs. Lancastrian quarrels distracted England.

   3. Ultimate French victory ensued.

      a. The French successfully recovered the Ile de France, Normandy, and Aquitaine, town by town, castle by castle.

        i. Entrance was usually gained by gunpowder or voluntary surrender.

    b. By 1453 all English holdings on French soil except Calais were retaken by the French.

    c. England was expelled from all of France save Calais.

4. <u>Results</u> of the war ultimately benefited both countries.

    a. The French monarchy was guiding the country to unification.

    b. England began to grow stronger and more unified since it no longer squandered time and money on continental possessions and claims.

II. <u>England in the Later Middle Ages</u> saw the initial growth of a Parliamentary tradition (to *c.* 1455), and final national consolidation under a strong monarchy (*c.* 1455 ff.).

A. <u>Parliamentary Ascendance</u> (1307-1455) was fostered by the weakness of kings, disputed successions, and demands of the Hundred Years' War.

1. <u>Edward II</u> (1307-27) was weak, sensuous, and excessively dependent on favorites.

    a. Parliament for a time curtailed the king, and Lords Ordainers ran the government.

    b. Scotland was lost with the English defeat by Robert Bruce at Bannockburn (1314).

    c. After a moderate royalist party restored Edward to power in 1322, he ruled in a reckless manner.

    d. Queen Isabelle and her lover Mortimer returned to lead a rebellion which overthrew and deposed the king, who was later murdered.

2. <u>Edward III</u> (1327-77) was energetic, able, and chivalrous, but also vain, extravagant, and impractical.

    a. Edward led his country into the costly Hundred Years' War, wherein his initial success was followed by later losses.

    b. Parliament gained growing ascendancy through its power over the purse strings.

        i. It was summoned on the average of once a year.

        ii. It controlled taxation, using the principle

that new taxes must have the consent of the "commonality of the realm."

   iii. Parliament began to initiate legislation by bargaining with the king for desired laws.

   iv. It acquired the right to impeach the king's ministers for misconduct.

   v. It restricted Papal intervention by the Statutes of *Provisors* (1351) and *Premunire* (1353) which curtailed Papal jurisdiction over English clergy.

3. Richard II (1377-99) was proud, impetuous, and absolutistic, as well as a prey of favorites.

  a. Discontent under the regency broke out into violence with the "Wat Tyler Rebellion" (1381).

   i. The peasants wanted repeal of servile dues and relief from exploitation.

   ii. Richard temporarily calmed the peasants, after which the barons repressed the rebellion.

  b. Richard ruled despotically and arbitrarily when he came of age.

   i. Both barons and middle class were alienated by his caprices, favoritism, and despotism.

  c. Henry of Lancaster, whose property had been confiscated, led a successful revolt against Richard (1399), who was later murdered.

  d. The Later Plantagenets (1307-1399), who left much to be desired, were now succeeded by the Lancastrians.

4. Henry IV (1399-1413) of Lancaster, "King by the grace of Parliament," spent most of his reign establishing peace and order.

  a. He supressed rebellions and followed a conciliatory foreign policy.

  b. Parliament supervised royal finances and presented "bills" rather than petitions.

   i. Henry could not change the wording of these bills.

5. Henry V (1413-22) was energetic, ambitious, and principled.

  a. He obtained control of northern France and the recognized right to succeed to the French throne.

b. Government in England was carried on by his brothers, Gloucester and Bedford.

c. His early death was a blow to English interests.

6. Henry VI (1422-61) was periodically unbalanced and one of the weakest of English kings.

   a. A long regency under the Duke of Gloucester in England and the Duke of Bedford in France ensued until 1437.

   b. Henry assumed weak personal rule in 1437 but went insane in 1453.

7. The "Wars of the Roses" (1455-85) were a struggle for control between the Houses of Lancaster and York.

   a. Red and white roses were the symbols of the houses.

   b. The wars were almost entirely aristocratic.

      i. They helped to discredit the aristocracy.

8. Parliament grew in power during the Later Middle Ages.

   a. It gained experience with politics, legislation, and financial questions.

   b. Its original four houses were reduced to two.

      i. The knights and the burgesses formed one house (Commons), and the lower clergy dropped out to form their own convocation.

      ii. Many parliamentary powers came to be accepted, including those of taxation, legislation (in union with the king), the deposition and installation of monarchs, and the impeachment of royal officials, as well as immunities of speech and passage.

B. Monarchical power increased at the expense of that of Parliament in the Yorkist and Tudor periods (ca. 1455 ff.).

1. Edward IV (1461-83) of York was a strong and able monarch.

   a. His action at Mortimer's Cross forced Henry VI to flee to Scotland.

   b. Edward IV refused to bow either to the Earl of Warwick or to Parliament.

      c. Warwick and Henry VI joined forces, and for a short time in 1471 Henry regained the throne.

      d. Edward was victorious at Barnet and Tewkesbury (1471).

         i. Henry VI died and other members of the royal family were eliminated.

  2. <u>Richard III</u> (Duke of Gloucester), Edward IV's brother who became regent, imprisoned his royal nephews in the Tower, and usurped the throne.

      a. The young Edward V and his brother were done away with, and Richard III was declared king by Parliament (1483).

      b. The Lancastrian heir, Henry Tudor, overthrew Richard on Bosworth field in 1485.

  3. <u>Henry VII</u> (1485-1517) initiated "Tudor absolutism."

      a. Henry was shrewd, thrifty, and conciliatory.

         i. He married Elizabeth of York.

         ii. He refrained from judicial murders and vindictiveness.

      b. A moderate absolutism prevailed during his reign.

         i. He restricted the nobility by "Livery and Maintenance Statutes" which limited the number and garb of retainers they were allowed.

         ii. The "Court of the Star Chamber" was inaugurated to try the magnates.

III. <u>France</u> experienced an initial decline of royal power (1314-1429), followed by a growth of monarchical absolutism (1429 ff.).

  A. <u>French monarchical decline</u> (1314-1429) was fostered by weak kings and serious losses in the Hundred Years' War.

    1. The last direct Capetians (1314-28) were the three sons of Philip IV, who ruled briefly without leaving male heirs, thus weakening the monarchy.

    2. <u>Philip VI</u> (1328-50) initiated the House of Valois.

      a. Philip was cultured and chivalrous but impractical and extravagant.

      b. He suffered grave reverses in the Hundred Years' War.

    3. <u>John II</u> (the Good) (1350-56/64) was carefree, pleasure loving, and chivalric, but foolish.

    a. He spent the last years of his life as an English prisoner after his defeat at Poitiers (1356).

    b. He gave Burgundy as an appanage to his son Philip the Bold.

4. <u>Charles V</u>, the Wise ruled first as regent for his absent father (1356-64) and then as king (1364-80).

    a. Charles' frailty was offset by his intelligence and energy.

    b. As regent he protected the throne by overcoming the rebellions of Etienne Marcel (1356-58) and Charles the Bad, as well as by surmounting the Jacquerie Revolt of the peasants.

    c. Charles V strengthened royal power.

        i. He obtained from the Estates General a direct tax known as the *fouage* or hearth tax.

        ii. He built up a royal army and pressed the predatory "Free Companies" roaming about France.

        iii. He gradually won back most of the French land held by the English.

5. <u>Charles VI</u>, "the Mad" (1380-1422) soon lost his sanity and with it the advantages won by his predecessor.

    a. Charles was under the regency of his grasping and quarreling uncles for the first eight years of his reign.

    b. He assumed personal rule in 1388, only to go mad in 1392.

    c. A struggle for power ensued between the Armagnac-Orleanist and Burgundian factions.

    d. The Burgundians aspired either to rule France or to build up an autonomous middle kingdom.

B. <u>French monarchical power grew</u> rapidly after 1429.

1. <u>Charles VII</u>, the "Well Served," (1422/29-61) was weak and pliant, but lucky in his able servants.

    a. He was dominated by selfish favorites during the initial years of his reign as "King of Bourges" (to 1429).

    b. After the advent of Joan of Arc (1429), worthy and able ministers took over, reorganized the government, and successfully expelled the English from French soil.

    c. The monarchy meanwhile waxed strong from:
      i. A direct tax (*taille*) granted by the Estates General to win the war
      ii. Indirect taxes (*aides*)
      iii. A regular standing army
      iv. Control of Church appointments, acquired in the *Pragmatic Sanction of Bourges* (1438).

2. <u>Louis XI</u>, the "Spider King" (1461-83) was crafty, shrewd, and deceitful.

    a. He dealt with his rivals separately and indirectly, as far as possible.

    b. Louis thus managed to subvert the "League of Common Weal" (composed of leading nobles).
      i. The ambitious Charles the Bold of Burgundy was enmeshed in a web of intrigues and killed by adversaries subsidized with French gold (1477).

    c. Suppression of feudal autonomy and promotion of French unity were Louis' great works.
      i. Burgundy and Picardy were acquired, along with a right to Artois and Franche Comté.
      ii. Louis also acquired the appanages of Anjou, Orleans, Berry, and Bourbon, with their dependencies.

    d. French absolutism was built up by Louis.
      i. Strict supervision of collection and tight economic policies increased royal revenues.
      ii. The middle class was both favored and used.
      iii. French courts were employed as royal instruments.

3. <u>Charles VIII</u> (1483-98) was the last of the Valois line.

    a. Anne of Beaujeu, his sister, was regent for Charles during much of his reign (to 1492).
      i. Anne acquired Britanny, last of the great feudal duchies, for Charles, by forcing the heiress Anne of Britanny to marry him.

    b. Charles' invasion of Italy (1495-6) was a failure.
      i. He first bought neutrality from Emperor Maximilian and King Ferdinand of Spain by ceding lands to both.

      ii. He promenaded through Italy and occupied Naples without opposition.

     iii. But a coalition called the "League of Venice" forced Charles to withdraw to France.

IV. <u>Readings</u> on England and France in the Later Middle Ages include:

A. <u>On the Hundred Years' War:</u>

Perroy, Edward, *The Hundred Years' War*, (London, Eyre & Spottiswoode, 1951).

Oman, Charles W., *A History of the Art of War in the Middle Ages*, 2 vols., Vol. I, (Boston, Houghton Mifflin, 1924).

B. <u>On England:</u>

Vickers, Kenneth H., *England in the Later Middle Ages*, (London, Metheun, 1921).

Lyons, Bryce, *A Constitutional and Legal History of England*, (New York, Harper, 1960).

C. <u>On France:</u>

Guignebert, Charles A., *A Short History of the French People* (New York, Macmillan, 1930).

Funck-Brentano, Jacques C., *The Middle Ages* (New York, Putnam, 1927).

Also Froissart, Jean, *Chronicles of England, France, Spain, and the Adjoining Countries*, (New York, Colonial Press, 1901).

And Philip de Commines, *Memoirs*, tr. (London, G. Bell, 1896).

Can You Identify?

Hundred Years War	Dauphin Charles
"combined tactics"	Duke of Bedford
Sluys (1337)	Joan of Arc
Crecy (1346)	*taille*
Calais (1346-7)	Edward II
Poitiers (1356)	"Lords Ordainers"
Treaty of Bretigny (1360)	Mortimer
Du Guesclin	Edward III
Agincourt (1415)	Richard II
Treaty of Troyes (1420)	Henry of Lancaster

Lancastrians
Henry V
Henry VI
"Wars of the Roses"
Edward IV
Richard III
Henry VII
"Tudor Absolutism"
Philip VI
John II, the Good

Charles V, the Wise
"Free Companies"
Charles VI
Charles VII
aides
Louis XI
"League of the Common Weal"
Charles the Bold
Charles VII
"League of Venice"

Chapter 28

Southern Europe in the
Later Middle Ages

I. <u>Southern Europe</u> (Italy, Spain, and Portugal) came to the fore in the Later Middle Ages.

    A. <u>Factors</u> in this rise included:
        1. The distractions and difficulties of England, France, and the German Empire
        2. Continued importance of the Mediterranean as the main artery of long-distance commerce.

II. Italy in the Later Middle Ages was composed of numerous independent states, of which the North Italian city-states were the most dynamic and progressive.

    A. <u>General developments in Italy</u> included:
        1. Independence of foreign control, except for foreign dynasties in southern Italy and Sicily
        2. Keen, unremitting interstate rivalries
        3. Use of *condottieri*, hired military captains with mercenary armies, for defence and security
        4. Enthusiastic promotion of a cultural "Renaissance," stressing a revival of classical forms, standards, and spirit.
        5. Italy was divided into three main areas:
           a. The North Italian city-states
           b. The Papal States
           c. The kingdoms of Naples and Sicily.

B. The North Italian city-states displayed exceptional enterprise and vigor.

 1. Political evolution of the North Italian city-state in the High and Later Middle Ages typically included successive stages of:

   a. Seigniorial rule of bishops or feudal lords

   b. Democratic (communal or republican) government

   c. Oligarchical rule challenged by internal strife

   d. Dictatorships ("tyrannies" or "despotisms") which soon became hereditary

   e. Foreign intervention and domination at the close of the period (1494 ff.).

 2. Prosperity, though continuing, was diminishing, and internal stresses were developing.

   a. Frequent revolutions of the proletariat against the middle class, or of the proletariat and ordinary middle class against the upper middle class, occurred.

   b. Such fruitless uprisings only made dictatorship appear more attractive and inevitable.

 3. Individual, civic, and peninsular pride were strong stimulants to the cultural Renaissance.

 4. Milan was a typical dictatorship which became a hereditary despotism or *signoria* under the Visconti (to 1447) and the Sforzas (1450 ff.).

   a. It was the largest, strongest state in the Po Valley.

 5. Similar despotisms developed in Verona, Ferrara, Mantua, Rimini, Urbino, and most other north Italian states.

 6. Venice was a stable, conservative, prosperous state, ruled by a hereditary merchant oligarchy.

   a. Family heads of the merchant oligarchy composed the Council of Five Hundred.

     i. The Council of Ten was the Executive Committee, and the Doge was the chief executive.

   b. Venice developed a far-flung overseas empire as well as an expanding territorial state in Italy.

   c. Venetian interests were primarily commercial.

        d. A strong, efficient, strict, practical administration allowed the Venetian government to last until 1797.

    7. <u>Genoa</u> was also governed by a merchant oligarchy.

        a. The Genoese triumphed over their commercial and naval rivals, the Pisans by 1280.

        b. The Genoese were in turn defeated by the Venetians by 1381.

    8. <u>Florence</u> has been properly called "the Athens of Renaissance Italy."

        a. Florence clung longest to its democratic aspirations.

        b. Fluctuating power usually gravitated to the capitalistic middle class (*populo grasso*).

           i. Numerous revolutions and changes in government occurred.

           ii. The *"Ciompi* Revolt" of 1378 is one such uprising.

        c. Eventually the Medici established a hereditary dictatorship, initially under the cloak of democratic forms (1434 ff.).

           i. Cosimo de Medici (1435 ff.) came to power as the leader of the popular party.

           ii. Lorenzo the Magnificent (1469 ff.) was a generous patron of the Renaissance.

        d. Temporary restoration of the Florentine Republic occurred as late as 1494 to 1512 and 1527 to 1531.

        e. Florence was a leading textile producing, commercial, and financial center.

        f. From Florence came both the initial and the greatest leaders of the Renaissance in literature, painting, sculpture, and architecture.

C. <u>The Papal States</u> were a disjunctive, turbulent, theocratic polity stretching across central Italy.

    1. Difficulties besetting the Papal States included:

        a. The primarily spiritual and religious office of their "prince," the Pope

        b. Their mountainous, compartmentalized terrain

        c. Ambitions of local communities

       d. The fact that many Popes were older men with short reigns and failing faculties

       e. Territorial encroachments by neighbors such as Venice, Naples, etc.

       f. Foreign intervention from beyond the Alps.

     2. Virtual anarchy prevailed in the Papal States during the absence of the Avignon Popes (1309-78) and the Great Western Schism (1378-1417).

     3. Recovery and retention of the Papal States preoccupied Renaissance Popes such as Alexander VI (1492-1503) and Julius II (1503-1515).

  D. <u>Southern Italy and Sicily</u> became the dual kingdoms of Naples and Sicily after the "Sicilian Vespers" (1282).

     1. Charles of Anjou, at papal invitation, took over the crown of Sicily and control of both the island and mainland in the 1260's.

     2. The "Sicilian Vespers" (1282) was a general revolt against the French by the islanders, apparently as a result of Aragonese and Byzantine intrigues and accumulated grievances.

     3. The Aragonese occupied the island and took over the government.

     4. A prolonged war against the Aragonese and Genoese was waged by the Angevins and French with Papal support.

       a. But it failed to dislodge the Aragonese from Sicily.

     5. King Alfonso V, the Magnanimous (1443-58) temporarily united the two crowns and encouraged a Neapolitan Renaissance.

     6. French intervention in Naples (1494 ff.) was warded off by Ferdinand of Spain who retained Sicily and seized Naples in 1503.

III. <u>Spain</u> (1276-1516) after two centuries of division and strife was strengthened and united under Ferdinand and Isabella (1474-1516).

  A. <u>Civil wars</u> preceded unification.

     1. Factors which contributed to division included:

       a. Disputed successions

       b. Aristocratic pretensions and revolts

   c. Foreign intervention from both within and without the peninsula

    i. Peninsular states intervened in each other's affairs.

    ii. France and England intervened in peninsular matters.

   d. Occasional weak or misguided rulers.

B. <u>Castile</u> (1284-1474) had a stormy history marked by internal conflicts.

 1. Civil Wars included those of:

  a. The de la Cerda heirs vs. Sancho IV (d. 1295)

  b. Henry II Trastamara vs. Pedro I the Cruel (d. 1369)

  c. The nobles against Juan II (d. 1454) and Henry IV (d. 1474).

 2. Castilian overseas expansion in the Atlantic began with the taking of the Canary Islands in the 15th century.

 3. The Castilian *Cortes* or Parliament enjoyed considerable power in this period.

C. <u>Aragon</u> (1276-1479) made remarkable progress despite a similarly disturbed history.

 1. Civil wars raged repeatedly.

 2. Extensive privileges for nobles and townspeople were won by their "Union" in the so called "General Privilege" (1283) and "Privilege of the Union" (1287).

  a. Pedro IV defeated the Union at Epila in 1348, repealed the privileges, and exacted severe vengeance.

 3. Love of freedom and insistence on personal rights continued to be vigorous in Aragon and Catalonia where the Cortes were strong.

 4. Great progress was made in Aragonese expansion into the Mediterranean.

  a. The Conquest of the Balearic Islands was completed.

  b. Sicily was taken from the house of Anjou in the "Sicilian Vespers" (1282).

   i. Aragonese rule of Sicily was generally indirect so that the two crowns were separate.

      c. Sardinia was also occupied.

      d. Naples was taken and ruled directly along with Sicily by Alfonso V, the Magnanimous (1435-58) and later by Ferdinand I (1503 ff.).

    5. Aragonese commerce was well developed.

      a. The Catalonian *Consulado del Mar* (*Consulat del Mar*) was a body of maritime and commercial law that gained wide acceptance.

D. <u>Ferdinand and Isabella</u> (1474/9-1516) unified and strengthened Spain.

    1. Unification of Spain was made possible by the marriage of Ferdinand and Isabella in 1469.

      a. Isabella succeeded her brother, Henry IV, on the throne of Castile after defeating the supporters of Henry's daughter (1474).

      b. Ferdinand succeeded to his father's throne in Aragon in 1479.

    2. Royal power grew as "the Catholic Monarchs" worked together to strengthen the monarchy and to forge a permanent union of the two crowns.

      a. Ferdinand and Isabella established the principle that each was the other's equal, at least in Castile.

      b. They organized a general militia or *Santa Hermandad* under royal control, which superceded the old local *hermandades*.

      c. They appointed royal supervisors or *corregidores* to superintend the towns.

      d. Close cooperation with the Church gained them the title of "Catholic Monarchs" as well as considerable control of the Church in the "Real Patronato" and the "Spanish Inquisition."

      e. They ordered the conversion or expulsion of Jews and Moslems, and used the Inquisition to ensure the genuineness of such conversions.

    3. Expansion of their territories was vigorously promoted.

      a. Granada was taken in 1492, thus ending the last Moslem enclave on the peninsula.

      b. Rousillon and Cerdagne were regained from Charles VIII of France by diplomacy.

      c. Navarre was annexed (1512 ff.).

d. The kingdom of Naples was added to that of Sicily as direct possessions of the crown (1503).

e. New world expansion was begun by the explorations of Columbus, Vespucci, de la Cosa, and Ponce de Leon (1492-1516).

f. Dynastic ascendancy in Europe was arranged by the marriage of princess Juana to the Hapsburg heir, Philip of Austria.

IV. Portugal rose to power and prosperity in the Later Middle Ages.

A. Evolution of Portugal from a county (*ca.* 1095) to a kingdom (by 1143) and completion of the Portuguese "Reconquest" (1143-1250) occurred in the High Middle Ages.

B. Main developments in Portuguese History in the Later Middle Ages included:

1. Consolidation of the monarchy
2. Resistance to absorption by Castile
3. Alliance with England for defence and commerce
4. Beginnings of significant Portuguese overseas expansion and empire
5. Growth of royal absolutism.

C. Consolidation of the Monarchy was achieved from 1279 to 1385.

1. Diniz, "the Farmer King," (1279-1325) set the pace by promoting internal progress in numerous ways.

a. He encouraged agriculture, industry, and commerce.

b. He established the University of Coimbra.

2. Alliance with England (1373 ff.) against Castile contributed to Portuguese security.

3. Ferdinand I (1367-83) gave his daughter in marriage to John I of Castile in the hope of uniting the two countries.

D. Exploration highlighted the progressive rule of the house of Aviz in the following century (1385-1481).

1. John I (1385-1433), founder of the house of Aviz, came to the throne at the head of an English-supported revolution to avoid absorption by Castile.

a. The Treaty of Windsor (1386) brought Portugal

into close commercial and political alliance with England.

   b. Ceuta in Morocco was taken by Portugal.

2. Prince Henry, the Navigator promoted overseas exploration both during the reign of his father John I and that of his brother Alfonso V.

   a. Henry established a navigational school at Sagres.

   b. He encouraged exploration down the African coast.

   c. Alfonso V (1438-81) came to be known as "the African" from his fruitless "crusades" in Africa.

3. Portuguese exploration reached the Madeiras Islands by 1420, Sierra Leone by 1452, Santarem by 1471.

E. The "Age of Empire" or "Heroic Age" (1481-1580) brought Portugal to the apex of its power and wealth.

1. João (John) II, "the Perfect," (1481-95) was wise, just, and capable.

   a. He kept peace with Castile and maintained a close alliance with England.

   b. Royal absolutism grew as the power of the nobles was crushed.

   c. John II patronized both the Renaissance and overseas expansion.

      i. The "Cabo Tormentoso" or Cape of Good Hope was rounded by Bartholomew Diaz in 1486.

2. Emanuel (Manuel) I, "the Fortunate," (1495-1521) reigned during the period when Portugal found the sea route to India and obtained control of "half the world."

   a. Vasco de Gama opened a sea route to India (1497-8).

   b. Cabral reached Brazil and claimed it for Portugal in 1500.

   c. A Portuguese Empire in the Orient was founded by Viceroys Almeida (1500-08) and Albuquerque (1508-15).

      i. They gained control of the Indian Ocean and established bases about it which they fortified, such as Goa (1510), Malacca (1511), and Ormuz (1515).

V. <u>Readings</u> on Southern Europe in the Later Middle Ages in-
   A. <u>On Italy</u>:
       Cotterill, Henry B., *Italy from Dante to Tasso: 1300-1600*,
           (New York, Stokes, 1919).
       Schevill, Ferdinand, *History of Florence*, (New York, Har-
           court Brace, 1936).
   B. <u>On the Iberian Peninsula</u>:
       Altamira, Rafael, *History of Spain*, tr. M. Lee, (New York,
           Van Nostrand, 1949 ff.).
       Merriman, Roger B., *Rise of the Spanish Empire in the
           Old World and the New*, 4 vols. (New York, Macmil-
           lan, 1918-1934).
       Livermore, Harold V., *A History of Portugal*, (Cambridge,
           University Press, 1947).

Can You Identify?

condottieri	Isabella of Castile
signoria	Ferdinand of Aragon
Visconti	*Santa Hermandad*
Sforzas	*corregidores*
"Council of the Five Hundred"	Granada (1492)
Doge	John (João I)
populo grasso	Aviz
Cosimo de Medici	Henry the Navigator
Lorenzo the Magnificent	John (João) II
Charles of Anjou	Manoel I, the Fortunate
"Sicilian Vespers"	*Cabo Tormentoso*
Alfonso V, the Magnanimous	Vasco da Gama
Privilege of the Union (1287)	Cabral
Consulado del Mar	Albuquerque

Chapter 29

Other European States in the Later Middle Ages

I. <u>The German Empire</u> in the Later Middle Ages (1273-1519) was a loose union of virtually independent states.

  A. <u>Political disintegration</u> of the Empire was the result of the long Hohenstaufen (centralizing) vs. Guelf (decentralizing) struggle which the latter finally won.

    1. This period was the "Age of the Princes."

    2. Their independence was based on their acquisition of such prerogatives as:

      a. Coinage of money

      b. Final justice

      c. Mineral rights

      d. Indivisibility of territories

      e. Succession by primogeniture.

    3. Some 200 to 300 practically sovereign states existed in the Empire, including:

      a. Territorial principalities: dukedoms, counties, and margravates, such as Bavaria, the Palatinate, and Brandenbury

      b. Prince-bishoprics, such as Mainz, Cologne, and Magdeburg

      c. Free cities, such as Lubeck, Bremen, and Augsburg.

    4. The imperial title, after passing from house to house, came to reside temporarily with the Luxemburgers and finally with the Hapsburgs.

      a. Imperial incumbents usually followed a policy of *Hauspolitik*: building up the possessions and power of their own house regardless of national interests.

    5. Italy was no longer a part of the Empire.

B. Rotation of the crown (1273-1347) resulted from the determination of the electors to control and weaken the monarchy and to secure their own privileges.

    1. Rudolph of Hapsburg (1273-9), first Emperor of this famous line, acquired Austria and neighboring lands as a base for his house.

    2. Adolph of Nassau (1292-98) was slain in his attempt to wrest territories from the Wittens of Saxony.

    3. Albrecht of Austria (Hapsburg) (1298-1308) attempted to appropriate several territories before he was assassinated.

    4. Henry VII of Luxemburg (1309-1313) obtained Bohemia for his house.

    5. Louis IV of Bavaria (1313-47) temporarily acquired extensive territories but was deposed after quarreling with the Pope and the Princes.

C. The Luxemburg house came to the throne again in 1347 and ruled until 1437 with one brief interruption.

    1. Charles IV of Bohemia (1347-78) was of German-Czech origin.

        a. He sponsored a Czech Renaissance which included the foundation of the University of Prague.

        b. *The Golden Bull* (1356), a constitution issued by Charles IV, established the Empire as a loose association of practically sovereign states.

           i. Seven electors were designated ex officio to elect the Emperor:

              1) The three prince-bishops of Mainz, Trier, and Cologne, and

              2) Four secular Princes: the King of Bohemia, the Duke of Saxony, the Margrave of Brandenburg, and the Count Palatine of the Rhine.

           ii. The Pope was excluded from any part in the election.

           iii. Extensive privileges were extended to the electors, including: the right of coinage, sub-soil mineral rights, high justice, primogeniture, indivisibility of territories, and inviolability of person.

    iv. These privileges, which amounted to virtual sovereignty, were soon assumed by other secular princes.

2. Wenzel the Drunkard (1378-1400) was eventually deposed and temporarily replaced by the feeble Ruprecht of the Palatinate (1400-1410).

3. <u>Sigismund</u> (1410-37), last of the restored Luxemburgers, was an energetic ruler of wide interests.

    a. He ruled Hungary, Bohemia, and other territories.

    b. He crusaded against the Turks at Nicopolis (1396).

    c. He helped end the Great Western Schism at Constance (1414-18).

D. <u>The Hapsburgs</u> now returned to the imperial throne (which they held from 1437 to 1806 in Germany, to 1918 in Austria).

1. Albrecht II of Hapsburg (1437-40) was designated by his father-in-law Sigismund as his successor, but soon died.

2. <u>Frederick III</u> (1440-93) was a weak, indolent ruler who lost Hungary and Bohemia while dreaming of world domination.

3. <u>Maximilian I</u> (1493-1519) promoted Hapsburg fortunes by advantageous marriages.

    a. His marriage to Mary of Burgundy gained him the County of Burgundy and the (Belgian and Dutch) Low Countries.

    b. The marriage of his son Philip to Juana the Mad, daughter of Ferdinand and Isabella, eventually brought Spain and the Spanish overseas Empire into Hapsburg hands.

E. <u>German progress</u> in the Later Middle Ages was achieved mainly on the local level.

1. Efforts at greater centralization of government failed.

    a. Institutions that developed in the later 15th century, and temporarily gave some hope of unity, included:

      i. An imperial *Diet* or *Reichstag* that included representatives of the middle class

      ii. A *"Reichskammergericht"* or imperial law court

      iii. A *"Reichsregiment"* or supreme administrative council

      iv. Division of the Empire into *"Kreise"* (districts) for administrative purposes

      v. The *"Holy Vehm,"* a type of *vigilantes* to enforce law and order.

    b. These plans failed when Maximilian became suspicious and jealous and refused to cooperate.

  2. Meanwhile local German principalities became stronger and better organized during the Later Middle Ages.

    a. The authority of the Princes was increased and confirmed by local diets.

  3. Commerce expanded and industry flourished.

  4. Universities multiplied, and printing with movable type spread from the Rhineland.

F. The Teutonic Knights developed a strong military state along the eastern shores of the Baltic.

  1. Originally a religious military order, founded for crusading in the 13th century, they transferred their activity to the Baltic area in the early 13th century.

  2. They defeated and subjected the fierce, warlike but backward tribes in Prussia, Samatien, Courland, Livonia, and Estonia, as far north as the Gulf of Finland during the 13th and earlier 14th centuries.

  3. They thus cut the Poles and Lithuanians off from the Baltic Sea.

  4. German rural landlords operated large estates with native serfs while German businessmen developed prosperous cities.

  5. A decline set in during the 15th century.

G. The Swiss established an independent democratic state in the Later Middle Ages.

  1. The hardy Swiss successfully opposed Hapsburg overlords in the 13th to 14th centuries.

    a. The "forest" (rural) "cantons" (counties) of Schwyz, Unterwalden, and Uri formed a "Perpetual Pact" of alliance and resistance in 1291.

      b. This resistance movement was subsequently joined by the other cantons, both rural and urban.

      c. Hapsburg military efforts to subdue them met continued defeat in the 14th century at Mortgarten, Sempach, and Näfels.

      d. Swiss independence was formally recognized by the treaties of Basel (1499) and Westphalia (1648).

  H. __Bohemia__ made strenuous efforts to throw off the German yoke during this period.

    1. The bitter Hussite Wars (1419-36) of the Bohemians against their German overlords were inspired both by religious differences and nationalistic aspirations.

    2. A native dynasty ruled an independent Bohemia from 1457 to 1526.

  I. __The Hanseatic League__ was a well organized association of German cities united to promote their common economic interests by every available means.

    1. Leading cities included Lübeck, Hamburg, and Bremen.

    2. At its height in the 14th century the League included some seventy cities.

    3. "Factories" or agencies were established abroad at such centers as London, Bruges, Bergen, and Novgorod.

    4. For some time the League controlled trade in the Baltic and North Sea areas, and was commercially powerful in England, Denmark, and the Low Countries.

    5. The League waged war against King Waldemar IV of Denmark and obtained the favorable treaty of Stralsund (1378).

    6. The Hanseatic League declined in the 15th century in the face of strong national states and principalities.

II. __Borderland States__ of Western Christendom included Poland-Lithuania, Hungary, and the Scandinavian Kingdoms.

  A. __Poland-Lithuania__ was one of the larger, stronger borderland states in the Later Middle Ages.

    1. The union of Poland and Lithuania was effected in

1386 by the marriage of the Lithuanian prince Jagiello to the Polish Queen Jadwiga.

  a. Jagiello became a Christian and took the name Ladislas (V) (1386-1434).

2. The Teutonic Knights were repeatedly defeated by Ladislas and his successor, Casimir IV.

  a. By the Second Peace of Thorn (1466), West Prussia was ceded to the Poles, while East Prussia was to be held by the Knights as a vassal state.

3. Some eastern territories were lost to the Russians by the Lithuanians.

4. The great power and privileges of the nobility constituted a grave flaw in the Polish constitution.

B. Hungary prospered and expanded in the 14th century, but declined and contracted in the 15th century.

1. The Angevin dynasty (from French Anjou) (1308-86) brought prosperity, expansion, and progress to Hungary.

2. The German rule (1387-1437) of Sigismund and his Hapsburg successors caused confusion and bitterness.

3. Native rule (1458-90) under Matthias Corvinus Hunyadi revived Hungarian vigor.

4. Civil war and chaos followed the death of Hunyadi (1490 ff.).

5. The aggressive Ottoman Turks conquered much of Hungary in the early 16th century.

  a. Their victory at Mohacs (1526) gave the Turks temporary mastery over most of Hungary.

C. The Scandinavian States of Denmark, Norway, and Sweden were united by the Union of Kalmar (1397).

1. Scandinavian monarchs were hard pressed by German intrusions and the pretensions of their own nobility.

2. Queen Margaret of Denmark, who first came to rule over Denmark and Norway, obtained the throne of Sweden by the Union of Kalmar (1397).

3. The Swedes were restive under Danish rule.

III. Russia in the Later Middle Ages was under Tartar rule until Mongol power was supplanted by that of the Princes of Moscow in the later 15th century.

A. Tartar domination for two and a half centuries (*ca.* 1237-

1480) left an indelible impression on the Russian character.

1. The Tartars (Mongols and Turks) conquered Russia in the 13th century (1237-40).
    a. They were cruel and destructive.
    b. Sarai, in southeast Russia, became their capital.
2. Their Moslem faith created a chasm between them and their Christian subjects.
3. Tartar rule was both indirect and unconstructive in most of Russia.
    a. They governed through Russian princes who acted as their representatives and tax collectors.
        i. Their hold on southern Russia was more direct.
    b. They were interested in little other than the collection of taxes.
4. Tartar governmental and military methods came to be imitated to some extent by their Russian lieutenants.

B. The Rise of Moscow to power in central and northern Russia began in 1328.
1. Ivan Khalita (John Moneybags) (1328-41) became chief tax collector for the Tartars and the Russian Grand Prince in 1328.
2. Muscovite influence began to spread.
3. Vasili II (1425-62) subjected many neighboring principalities, including: Sudzal, Vladimir, and Novgorod, to his control.
    a. He gained partial independence from the Tartars.
4. Ivan III (1462-1505) secured complete independence of Moscow from the Tartars.
    a. He refused to pay taxes and successfully defied a large Tartar army in 1480.
    b. He took the titles of "Tsar" (Caesar) and "Autocrat of All the Russians."
        i. He married a Byzantine princess and claimed to be heir to the Byzantine Empire, now overrun by the Turks.
        ii. Many now regarded Moscow as the "third Rome," as Constantinople had been previously called the "second Rome."

IV. <u>The Balkans</u> were conquered by the Ottoman Turks in the Later Middle Ages.

   A. <u>The Byzantine Empire</u> under the native Paleologi (1261-1453) grew steadily smaller and weaker.
      1. The Paleologi were distracted by internal strife.
      2. Religious dissent over such questions as reunion with Rome caused further division.
      3. Ottoman pressure eventually resulted in the downfall of Byzantium and the capture of Constantinople (1453).

   B. <u>Serbia</u> built up a Balkan Empire in the 14th century.
      1. Serbian unification came under Stephen Nemanja in the later 12th century.
      2. Stephen Dushan (1331-55) ruled much of the Balkans and took the title of "Tsar."

   C. <u>The Ottoman Turks</u> conquered Asia Minor and the Balkans during the 13th to 15th centuries.
      1. The Ottoman Turks were settled in northwestern Asia Minor as vassals by the Seljuk Sultan of Rum in the 13th century.
      2. They steadily increased their territory in Asia Minor at Byzantine expense.
      3. Invited into the Balkans by the Byzantine usurper, John VI, Cantacuzene, the Ottoman Turks seized Gallipoli in 1354 and refused to withdraw.
         a. They also seized Adrianople (1366), which became their capital.
      4. By the end of the 14th century the Ottomans had overcome both Serbia and Bulgaria and made great inroads into failing Byzantium.
         a. Crusades from the west were repelled at Nicopolis in 1396 and Varna in 1444.
      5. Constantinople was taken in 1453 despite Byzantine heroism.
         a. The Turks outnumbered the defenders ten to one.
         b. Huge cannons were used to breach the walls of Constantinople.
      6. Turkish operations clearing enemy combatants in the Balkans were completed by 1500.

V. _Readings_ on the Rest of Europe in the Later Middle Ages
   include:

A. On the German Empire:
   Barraclough, Geoffrey, _Origins of Modern Germany_ (Oxford, Blackwell, 1947).
   Reinhardt, Kurt F., _Germany: 2000 Years_, (New York, Ungar, 1961) (Also: Milwaukee, Bruce, 1950).
   Janssen, Johannes, _History of the German People at the Close of the Middle Ages_, (London, K. Paul Trench, 1896 ff.).
   Zimmern, Helen, _Hanse Towns_ (New York, Putnam, 1889).
   Lutzow, Franz, H., _Bohemia_, (London, Chapman, 1896).

B. On Peripheral States:
   Halecki, Oscar, _History of Poland_ (New York, Roy Publishers, 1956).
   Kosary, Dominic G., _History of Hungary_ (New York, Benjamin Franklin Society, 1941).
   Danstrup J., _History of Denmark_ (Copenhagen, Wivel, 1948).

C. On Russia and the Balkans:
   Vernadsky, George, _History of Russia_ (New Haven, Yale, 1943 ff.).
   Schevill, Ferdinand, _History of the Balkan Peninsula_ (New York, Harcourt Brace, 1922).
   Vasiliev, Alexander, _History of the Byzantine Empire_, (Madison, Wis., University of Wisconsin Press, 1952).

Can You Identify?

Hauspolitik	"Perpetual Pact" (Swiss: 1291)
Rudolph of Hapsburg	Hussite Wars
Henry VII of Luxembourg	Hanseatic
Charles IV of Bohemia	Poland-Lithuania
"Golden Bull" (1356)	Second Peace of Thorn (1466)
Sigismund	Hunyadi
Frederick III of Hapsburg	Mohacs (1526)
Maximilian I	Union of Kalmar (1397)
Reichstag	Tartars
Holy Vehm	Ivan Khalita
Teutonic Knights	Vasili II
"Forest Cantons"	Ivan III

Tsar	Adrianople (1366)
Paleologi	Nicopolis (1396)
Stephen Dushan	Varna (1444)
Ottoman Turks	1453

Chapter 30

The Decline of the Church in the Later Middle Ages

I. Decline in the status of the Church and Papacy occurred in the Later Middle Ages.

    A. External factors in this decline included:
1. Rise of nationalism and monarchism in opposition to the internationalism of the Church
2. A growing desire of the people to participate in the running of government (Parliamentarianism), including that of the Church (Conciliarism)
3. The spreading money-economy and capitalism which created a competition for money between Church, State, and people
4. A secularistic, skeptical, individualistic attitude on the part of members of the middle class
5. A growing humanism which glorified the naturalistic spirit of ancient pagan writers
6. Excessive defeatism and obscurantism in philosophy, as in Ockhamism and Neo-Platonism.

    B. Internal factors included:
1. Contemporary crises which undermined the Papacy:
   a. The Avignon Residence of the Popes
   b. The Great Western Schism
   c. The Conciliar Movement.
2. Papal preoccupation with problems such as:
   a. The government and defence of the Papal states
   b. The reconstruction of Rome.

3. Worldliness of the clergy, which was increasing.
   a. Popes often acted in a very secular manner.
   b. Cardinals often became mercenary in order to support their princely way of life.
   c. Bishops acting as government officials often led half-worldly lives.
   d. Parish priests frequently were inadequately educated and poorly trained.
4. Religious orders declined as a result of the Black Death, lack of new vocations, and corruption engendered by excessive wealth.
5. Many ecclesiastical procedures were outmoded and many deforming accretions existed.
6. Excessive faith in externals, such as pilgrimages and relics, sometimes bordered on superstition.

II. A Contest between Boniface VIII and Philip IV of France (1296-1303) contributed to a decline in Papal prestige and influence.

A. A powerful French monarchy confronted the Papacy which had eliminated the Hohenstaufen.
   1. Philip IV, advised by his civil lawyers, pursued a policy of centralization, absolutism, and money-grasping.
   2. Boniface VIII (1294-1303), who was energetic and intelligent, but also stubborn and irascible, took issue with Philip.

B. The initial struggle centered on the right of the French King to tax the clergy without Papal consent (1296-97).
   1. Philip levied a tax on the clergy without getting papal approval.
   2. Boniface VIII replied with the bull *Clericis Laicos* (1296) which condemned this innovation, also practiced by Edward III.
   3. After both kings took strong measures against the Pope, Boniface gradually retreated and the quarrel subsided.

C. The second stage of the struggle (1301-3) concerned the King's jurisdiction over clerics.

1. Philip had tried and condemned the Bishop of Pamiers for treason.
2. Boniface replied with the bull *Ausculti Fili* (1301), reproving Philip in a fatherly manner, and reminding him of papal jurisdiction over kings.
3. The French Estates-General, provoked by a partly fabricated version of the bull, sharply rebuked the Pope.
4. *Unam Sanctum* (1302) was issued by Boniface, asserting papal superiority over "every human creature."
5. William of Nogaret broke in on the Pope at Agnani, insulting and manhandling him (1303).
   a. Boniface died from the shock three weeks later.
6. Subsequent popes abandoned the contest.

III. The Avignon Residence of the Papacy for seven decades (1309-1378) lessened papal prestige.

  A. Clement V (1305-14) introduced a period of French ascendance in the papacy.
   1. As Bishop of Bourdeaux, a French subject of the English King, Clement was a compromise choice, supported by Philip IV.
      a. He censured Boniface VIII.
      b. He condemned and eventually dissolved the Knights Templar, on the urging of Philip IV who sought their wealth.
   2. Clement V and his cardinals took up residence at Avignon in 1309.
      a. They alleged as reasons:
         i. Current rebellions in Rome and the Papal States
         ii. The location of Avignon, which made it a convenient place for mediation in the Hundred Years' War.
      b. Clement created twenty-two French cardinals.
  B. Seven French popes, including Clement V, occupied the Papal throne at Avignon.
   1. John XXII organized new Papal bureaus and revamped the finances of the Church.

2. Benedict XII issued reform decrees for religious orders.
3. Clement VI (1342-52) depleted the papal treasury by his luxurious living and munificence.
4. Innocent VI (1352-62) sent Cardinal Albornoz to reconquer the Papal states.
5. Urban V (1362-70) took the curia back to Rome, but returned to Avignon after three years.
6. Gregory XI (1370-78) returned to Rome, where he died shortly afterwards.

C. Centralization of papal government was increased and papal taxation was expanded by the Avignon Popes.
1. Building expenses and running costs demanded increased revenues.
2. Among financial sources tapped were:
   a. Expectations: fees for the promise of a future beneficed appointment
   b. Services: fees for papal services
   c. Annates: a portion of the first years' revenues of a benefice
   d. Also, benefice-tithes, legal fees, and gratuities.

IV. The Great Western Schism divided Western Christendom for forty years (1378-1417).

A. The origin of the Schism traces to a disputed election following the sudden death of Gregory XI (1378).
1. Rioting Romans demanded that the Cardinals elect "a Roman or at least an Italian" as Pope.
2. The Cardinals selected the Archbishop of Bari, a Neapolitan, who was neither a Roman nor a Frenchman, but an Italian who was an Angevin subject.
3. The latter took the name of Urban VI and received the acknowledgment and support of the Cardinals for three months.
4. When Urban turned on the Cardinals, threatening them with reform and correction, most of them withdrew from Rome to Anagni.
5. The dissident Cardinals, a majority, declared the first election invalid because of threats of force and lack of freedom of choice, and elected Robert of Geneva who became Clement VII.

B. <u>Perpetuation of the Schism</u> resulted from various factors:

  1. The double election cast a cloud of uncertainty over the legitimate succession.
  2. Both "Popes" succeeded in setting up courts complete with their own cardinals.
     a. Urban VI held Rome.
     b. Clement VII ruled from Avignon.
  3. Each "pope" was succeeded by another, thus continuing the lines.
  4. Continuing national support on either side prolonged the schism.
     a. Support for the rival "popes" followed nationalistic lines.
        i. The Avignon "popes" were supported by the French, together with the Scots and Castilians, as French allies.
        ii. The Roman popes were supported by the English, who were joined by their allies, the Portuguese and Flemish, and by most Italians and Germans.

C. <u>Great harm</u> to papal prestige resulted.

  1. Confusion and chaos arose from conflicting "papal" decrees and double appointments.
  2. Secular princes easily wrested new privileges from their dependent popes.
  3. The division of Christendom saddened the pious faithful.
  4. The continued demand for money by each claimant irritated many.

D. <u>Efforts to end the Schism</u> were made by secular and ecclesiastical leaders, as well as by saints.

  1. <u>The Conciliar movement</u> was partly a result of such efforts to end the schism.
     a. The Conciliar theory claimed that a general council could depose a pope.
     b. This theory was promoted by Conrad of Gelnhausen, John Gerson, Pierre d'Ailly, and, for a time, Nicholas of Cusa.
  2. <u>The Council of Pisa</u> (1409) was a fruit of the Conciliar Movement.
     a. It was attended by the majority of cardinals

from both camps as well as by 500 prelates or their proxies.

    b. Neither existing pope approved it and neither resigned.

    c. When the Council elected Alexander V, there were three popes.

E. The Council of Constance (1414-1418) terminated the Schism.

    1. It was convoked by Emperor Sigismund and approved by John XXIII (Pisa) and Gregory XII (Rome).

    2. John resigned and Gregory, after convoking the council, abdicated.

        a. Only old Benedict XIII of Avignon, now at Perpignan, refused to cooperate, though his successor submitted.

    3. Election of Martin V (1417) ended the Schism.

    4. A new nationalism was evidenced in the council.

        a. Voting was done by nations.

           i. The members were apportioned into five linguistically related groups or "nations," each with one vote.

        b. Separate concordats were arrived at by the Papacy, with the various nations in attendance.

V. The Renaissance Papacy (1417-1534) became excessively involved in secular pursuits.

A. The Papacy from 1417 to 1534 was occupied mainly by churchmen who were in large part princes and humanists.

    1. Most of the Popes of this era were involved in restoring the Church materially as well as spiritually.

        a. Martin V (1417-31) ended the Schism and began the architectural restoration of Rome.

        b. Eugene IV (1431-47) convoked a council which moved from Basle to Ferrara to Florence to Rome.

           i. It arranged a settlement with the Hussites and seeming reunion with the Byzantines.

        c. Nicholas V (1447-55) refounded the Vatican library and was a notable Renaissance patron.

        d. Pius II (1458-64) a former humanist, issued the

bull *Execrabilis* (1460) condemning the conciliar theory.
   e. Other Popes, such as Sixtus IV (1471-84) and
      Alexander VI (1492-1503), pursued a "family
      policy" in their administration.
   2. In the spiritual arena, Renaissance Popes:
   a. Insisted on papal prerogatives and maintained
      the deposit of faith
   b. Supported missionary activities
   c. Made modest reforms in some areas and patron-
      ized the better aspects of the Renaissance.

VI. Revolutionary theories and movements arising out of the
flux of the Later Middle Ages included:

A. Theories challenging the constitution of the Church:
   1. Pierre Dubois, in his *Recovery of the Holy Land*,
      acknowledged the spiritual supremacy of the
      Church, but advocated monarchical control of its
      temporalities.
   2. Marsiglio of Padua, in his *Defender of the Peace*,
      claimed that authority in both state and church
      flowed from the will of the people.
   a. As a democratic society, the church was an as-
      sociation of the faithful.
   b. The general council, which represents the people,
      is superior to the pope, who is only a sort of
      president.
   3. The Conciliar Movement adopted some of these ideas
      (See above).

B. Theories undermining doctrine and discipline:
   1. Ockhamism endangered the rational basis of Chris-
      tianity.
   a. William of Ockham denied valid knowledge of
      anything except individual existences experi-
      enced by sense perception and intuition.
      i. Abstract universal concepts are uncertain, ac-
         cording to Ockham.
   2. Mysticism stressed the direct experience of God.
   a. An emotional anti-intellectual brand of Christian-
      ity was fostered by some mystics, such as Gerald
      Groote, probable author of the *Imitation of
      Christ*.

C. <u>Heresies</u> which developed out of the ferment of the Later Middle Ages attacked existing Church organization and practices.

1. <u>The Wycliffites</u> or "Lollards" were early English Protestants.

   a. John Wycliff began by attacking the wealth and luxury of prelates.

   b. Eventually he denied the hierarchical constitution of the Church, the primacy of the Pope, and the authority of bishops.

   c. He advocated private interpretation of the Scriptures and repudiated some sacraments.

   d. Wycliff's followers, the Lollards or "poor Priests," continued preaching his doctrines.

2. <u>The Hussites</u> were early Bohemian Protestants.

   a. John Hus took up Wycliff's teachings at the University of Prague, and added the necessity of receiving the Eucharist under both forms: bread and wine.

   b. The Hussite movement became a nationalistic revolt against German dominance.

   c. After Hus was executed by the Council of Constance (1415), the movement developed into bitter warfare which lasted for two decades.

D. <u>Borderline radicals and extremists</u> also flourished.

1. "Spiritual Franciscans" taught the necessity of absolute poverty.

   a. They were condemned by John XXII.

2. The "Beghards" and "Beguines" were lay religious who practiced poverty and lived as mendicants spending their time in good works.

3. The "Flagellants" were extreme and dramatic penitents who were heavily influenced by Manichaean concepts.

E. <u>Popular religion,</u> however, continued to be a strong factor in Europe.

1. It was often excessively confident of the efficacy of externals, and sometimes superstitious or pessimistic.

2. The aspirations of many of the faithful remained high.

   a. Many saints and blessed lived in this period.

b. The majority of the people and religious were good and desired religious reform and had high standards of piety.

VII. <u>Readings</u> on the Church in the Later Middle Ages include:

Hughes, Philip, *History of the Church*, III (New York, Sheed and Ward, 1947).

Flick, Alexander C., *Decline of the Mediaeval Church* (New York, G. P. Putnam's, 1930).

Creighton, Mandell, *A History of the Papacy From the Great Schism. . .* , 6 vols. (London, Longmans, 1919).

Salembier, Louis, *The Great Schism of the West* (London, K. Paul, Trench, 1907).

Can You Identify?

Conciliarism	Martin V
Boniface VIII	Nicholas V
Clericis laicos (1296)	Pius II
Unam Sanctam (1302)	Alexander VI
Avignon	Pierre Dubois
Clement V	Marsiglio of Padua
John XXII	*Defender of the Peace*
Cardinal Albornoz	William of Ockham
Gregory XI	Ockhamism
Great Western Schism	Gerard Groote
Urban VI	John Wyclif
Clement VII	Lollards
Conciliar theory	John Hus
Council of Pisa (1409)	"Spiritual Franciscans"
Council of Constance (1414-18)	Beghards
	Beguines

Chapter 31

Renaissance and Late Gothic
Culture in the Later Middle Ages

I. <u>Two major cultures</u> coexisted and converged in the later Middle Ages.

  A. <u>"Italian Renaissance"</u> culture was more classical, naturalistic, lay, and "modern."

    1. It first arose and flourished in Italy, whence it gradually spread beyond the Alps.

  B. <u>"Late Gothic"</u> culture was more Christian, supernatural, clerical, and "medieval."

    1. It gradually began to be influenced by Italian Renaissance culture, especially in the 15th century.

II. <u>Italian learning and literature</u> were primarily humanistic in spirit and tone in the Later Middle Ages.

  A. <u>Humanism</u> stressed the study and imitation of classical literature and imbibed the spirit of the classical authors.

    1. The name derives from the "more specifically human learning" (*litterae humaniores*) advocated by Cicero for the orator and political leader.

    2. The humanistic spirit was secular, urbane, tolerant, civilized, and keenly appreciative of this world and present life.

    3. The glorification of the human person, which was an aspect of humanism, was in part a reaction against

273

the supernaturalism, otherworldliness, abstraction, and intellectualism of Later Scholasticism.

    a. Typical humanistic activities included: careful mastery of Latin and (to a lesser extent) Greek; intensive study and appreciation and imitation of classical literature; collection, collation, and correction of manuscript copies of classical works; and cultivation of related studies such as history, geography, and philology.

B. <u>Early Italian humanists</u> included: Dante, Petrarch, Boccaccio and Salutati.

    1. <u>Dante</u> (d. 1321) was a transitional figure: half medieval and half Renaissance, half scholastic and half classical.

        a. Dante Alighieri was a student and admirer of classical authors, especially Vergil, whose *Aeneid* he knew by heart.

           i. His works are full of classical references.

        b. He was also a follower of Aristotle and of Thomas Aquinas.

        c. He wrote in both Latin and the vernacular. (See below, H, 1.).

    2. <u>Petrarch</u> (d. 1374) is known as "Father of the Italian Renaissance."

        a. Francesco Petrarch, like Dante, was a Florentine by birth.

        b. Study and admiration of the Latin classics were his great delight.

        c. He traveled widely and promoted classical studies by personal contacts as well as by extensive correspondence.

        d. In addition to voluminous, influential correspondence, Petrarch composed a long epic poem, *Africa*, celebrating the exploits of Scipio Africanus and the beginnings of the Roman Empire.

        e. He wrote *Familiar Letters* to classical authors.

        f. Petrarch also wrote in the vernacular. (See below, H, 2.).

    3. <u>Boccaccio</u> (d. 1374), already a distinguished author in the vernacular. (See below, H, 3.) was "converted" to humanistic pursuits by Petrarch.

      a. Giovanni Boccaccio, as a humanist, composed works in Latin on mythology and antique biography, and attempted to study Greek.

   4. Salutati (d. 1406), whose first name was Coluccio, was an extremely competent humanistic chancellor of Florence for three decades.

      a. One of his letters was said to be worth two brigades of soldiers.

C. <u>Greek studies</u> soon became a part of the humanistic program.

   1. Renaissance humanists followed Latin classical authors in recognizing the Greeks as masters and models.

   2. Petrarch and Boccaccio attempted to study Greek without much success.

   3. Manuel Chrysoloras, a great Byzantine scholar and diplomat, taught Greek at Florence (1395 ff.).

   4. Cardinal Bessarion, another learned Byzantine, stayed on in Italy and promoted Greek studies as well as the attempted reunion of the churches after the Council of Ferrara-Florence (1448-49).

   5. Western scholars brought back numerous Greek manuscripts from tottering Constantinople.

D. <u>Later Italian humanists</u> (of the "Quattrocento" or 15th century) were numerous, versatile, and erudite. They included:

   1. Leonardo Bruni, historian, translator of Greek, and prolific author

   2. Aeneas Sylvius Piccolomini, copious, many-faceted author, who became Pope Pius II

   3. Leon Battista Alberti, a "universal man," who was at once architect, artist, musician, philosopher, mathematician, historian, poet, and dramatist

   4. Lorenzo Valla, great grammarian and textual critic, who discredited the "Apostles' Creed" and the "Donation of Constantine" on philological grounds

   5. Collectors of Greek manuscripts, such as Poggio Bracciolini and Giovanni Aurispa

   6. Patrons of humanism, such as the wealthy Niccolo Niccoli; the Florentine dictator Lorenzo de Medici, "the Magnificent"; and Pope Nicholas V

7. Teachers, such as Vittorino da Feltre and Guarino da Verona.

E. <u>Humanistic Educational Theory</u> referred mainly to the general (liberal: non-professional) education of the upper-class laity, and advocated:

    1. Extensive study of classical languages and literatures (primarily Latin, secondarily Greek) as the "core of the curriculum"

    2. Broad education, including many subjects, both academic and social, (such as Latin grammar, rhetoric, literature, logic, mathematics, geometry, astronomy, and music; as well as Greek grammar and literature, the vernacular, history, archeology, geography, philosophy, and the natural sciences; along with drawing, riding, dancing, military training, etc.)

    3. Religion and moral training were included.

    4. Humanistic educational theorists included: P. P. Vergerio, M. Vegius, B. da Guarino, Aeneas Sylvius, L. B. Alberti, L. Bruni, and others.

F. <u>Humanist Philosophers</u> inclined towards neo-Platonism.

    1. Plato's idealism, figurative expression, and literary presentation appealed to them more than Aristotle's matter-of-fact syllogisms and technical language.

    2. Plethon was a Byzantine who propogated Neo-Platonism in Italy.

    3. Marsilio Ficino, a brilliant pupil of Plethon, succeeded him and translated Plato's works into Latin.

    4. Pico della Mirandola taught a type of universal eclecticism.

G. <u>Renaissance Social Sciences</u> were influenced by classical examples.

    1. Political theorists included Dante, who urged political unity under the emperor (*De Monarchia*); Salutati, who attacked dictatorships (*De Tyranno*); Marsiglio of Padua, who argued for popular sovereignty in both state and church (*Defensor Pacis*); and Machiavelli, who would exempt lay rulers from the ordinary restrictions of the moral law (*The Prince*).

    2. Historians who were humanists, such as L. Bruni and F. Biondo, wrote history in more formal Latin;

while others, such as Villani and Machiavelli, wrote in the freer vernacular.

3. Natural sciences were in decline, although progress was made in geography and anatomy.

H. Italian Vernacular Literature had much more creativeness and ultimate value than the Latin literature of the humanists.

1. Dante's *Divine Comedy*, with its universal outlook, is still considered the greatest Italian classic.

a. Dante's sonnets to Beatrice (*Vita Nuova*) and his *Banquet* are also held in high regard.

2. Petrarch's sonnets to his "lady-love" Laura, written in the vernacular, are more admired than his lumbering *Africa* in Latin.

3. Boccaccio's *Decameron* was a pioneer work of vernacular prose-fiction with its hundred short stories told by ten Florentine men and women on ten successive nights.

4. Lorenzo de Medici helped revive Italian poetry in the 15th century by his popular songs in the vernacular.

5. The Carolingian "Roland-theme" was converted to new forms by Pulci in his humorous *Morgante* concerning a giant; by Boiardo in his romantic *The Enamored Roland*; and by Ariosto in his sarcastic *Roland Driven Mad*.

III. Transalpine Learning and Literature in the Later Middle Ages were affected by Late Gothic and Renaissance influences.

A. Late Gothic continuations and elaborations of High Medieval precedents still prevailed in Transalpine education and learning, philosophy and literature, architecture and art.

B. Humanism was gradually diffused beyond the Alps.

1. Renaissance humanism was brought north by Italian churchmen and secretaries as well as by Transalpine students and travelers who returned from Italy.

a. Circulation of written works, particularly after the development of printing, promoted the spread of humanism.

C. Early German Humanism was fostered at the University
   of Heidelberg and in the Schools of the Brethren of the
   Common Life (15th century ff.).

   1. Professor Rudolph Agricola (d. 1485) promoted
      classical studies at Heidelberg, where Johann Reuchlin
      (d. 1522) also added the study of Hebrew to Human-
      istic pursuits.

   2. At Deventer, Headmaster Alexander Heguis (d. 1498)
      introduced a humanistic curriculum, and here Desi-
      derius Erasmus (d. 1536) imbibed classical compe-
      tence and interests.

   3. Erasmus became "the Prince of Northern Human-
      ists," a veritable "new Petrarch," who spread human-
      istic interests and techniques throughout much of
      Western Europe.

      a. The works of Erasmus include his *Adages, Praise
         of Folly*, and *Familiar Colloquies*, as well as a
         critical edition and translation of the Greek New
         Testament.

D. Other Transalpine Countries accepted humanism in the
   15th and 16th centuries.

   1. Early English humanists included bishops such as
      William Grey; lords such as Earl Tiptopf; and Ox-
      ford savants such as William Grocyn; as well as
      Chancellor Sir Thomas More, aided by his friend
      Erasmus.

   2. Early French humanists included the Trinitarian
      head, Robert Gaguin, and the profound scholar, Le-
      fevre d' Etaples.

   3. Early Spanish humanists included Cardinal Jiménez
      de Cisneros, founder of the University of Alcalá.

E. Diffusion of Learning beyond the Alps was promoted by:

   1. Multiplication of humanistic schools, such as those of
      the Brethren of the Common Life, and the English
      "public" (private) "grammar schools."

   2. Foundation of new universities, more sensitive to
      "modern" trends.

   3. The invention of printing with movable type in the
      Rhineland, 1430-50.

      a. Early printing presses were those of Lawrence
         Cöster and Johann Gutenberg.

F. Miscellaneous branches of Transalpine learning had varying fortunes in the Later Middle Ages.

1. Philosophy declined with the subtlety of later Scholasticism, the anti-intellectualism of Ockhamism, and
the eclecticism of Raymond Lull and Nicholas of
Cusa.

2. In political theory, Jean of Jandun concurred with
the popular sovereignty of Marsiglio of Padua; Pierre Dubois promoted monarchism; John Fortescue
lauded limited monarchy; and Philip de Commines
advocated an amoral pragmatism on the part of
monarchs.

3. In science, the laws of motion were investigated by
Nicholas Oresme and John Buridan, while geographical knowledge was promoted by Henry the Navigator
and his seamen.

4. The old and the new in history writing were represented by the chivalric interests of Jean Froissart in
his work on the Hundred Years' War, and the realism
of Philip de Commines concerning Louis XI.

G. Vernacular literature beyond the Alps was represented by the works of Geoffrey Chaucer, Francois Villon, and Juan del Encina.

1. Chaucer is famous especially for his vivid, realistic
English masterpiece, the *Canterbury Tales.*

2. Villon is noted for his French poetry concerning the
life of the lower classes in Paris, such as his *Ballad
of the Hanged.*

3. Juan del Encina is regarded as "the Father of Spanish Comedy."

IV. Italian Renaissance Arts are famous for their mastery and
perfection, as well as for their classicism.

A. General features of Italian Renaissance Arts include:

1. Classicism: as in the imitation of classical models,
and use of classical elements, themes, and standards

2. Naturalism and realism: as in the careful study and
representation of human anatomy, linear perspective, light and shadow, etc.

3. Secularism and laicization: as in the employment of

living models and the depiction of non-religious scenes

4. Perfectionism and "art for the sake of art," as in the painstaking and untiring improvement of the work at hand

   a. Ghiberti took two decades for his first pair of baptistry doors for the Cathedral of Florence and two and a half decades for the second pair.

5. Schools of art with special characteristics developed in various cities at different times.

B. Painting was the leading art form of the Renaissance. This was called the "Age of the Masters."

1. Cimabue (d. 1302) began to break with the formalistic Byzantine style in his *Madonnas*.

2. Giotto (d. 1336) initiated the "new painting" with the naturalism and narrative style of his *Life of St. Francis* (Assisi) and *Life of Christ and the Virgin Mother* (Padua).

3. Massaccio (d. 1448) heightened the naturalism and forcefulness of his work by the use of perspective and chiaroscuro (light and shadows), as well as by skillful composition, as in his *Expulsion of Adam and Eve* and *Tribute Money*.

4. Boticelli (d. 1510) favored classic Platonic idealism and spiritualized nudes, as his *Birth of Venus* and *Springtime*.

5. The Bellinis (Jacobo, Gentile, and Giovanni) (d. 1470-1516) used rich colors for story scenes and portraits such as those of *Doge, Loredano*, and *Sultan Mahomet*.

6. Leonardo da Vinci (d. 1519), a many-sided genius, combined psychological insight, intellectual perception, and technical perfection in his *Last Supper, Mona Lisa*, and *Madonna of the Rocks*.

C. Sculpture initially imitated classical models and anticipated early developments in painting.

1. Classical sculpture was imitated by the Pisanos (Nicola, Giovanni, and Andrea) (d. 1278-1348) in bas-reliefs on pulpits, sarcophogi, doors, etc.

2. Ghiberti (d. 1455) brought bas-relief to a new height with his exquisite sculptures for the doors of the baptistry at Florence.

3. Donatello (d. 1466) emancipated sculpture from architecture with his excellent free-standing *David*, his equestrian *Gattamelata*, and other works.

4. Verocchio (d. 1488) continued this style with his statues such as *The Boy and the Dolphin* and the equestrian *Bartolomeo Colleoni*.

D. <u>Architecture</u> employed classical elements and features, but also achieved originality.

1. Classical elements included columns, capitals, pediments, entablatures, rounded arches, and domes.

2. Classical features included classical norms and proportions, such as those expounded in Vitruvius' *On Architecture*.

3. Some originality was demanded by the diverse nature of Renaissance churches, dwellings, and other buildings.

4. Renaissance architects in Italy included:

   a. Brunelleschi, who studied classical ruins and produced the tremendous dome of the Cathedral of Florence, as well as the Pitti Palace, Pazzi Chapel, etc.

   b. Leon Alberti, who wrote *On Architecture* and designed several churches as well as the Rucellae Palace

   c. Bramante, the original designer of St. Peter's Cathedral in Rome.

V. <u>Transalpine Arts</u> were primarily Late Gothic, though the Italian Renaissance style gradually began to exert an influence.

A. <u>Late Gothic Art</u> was more ornate, dramatic, and detailed than the restrained, idealized, selective Renaissance work.

1. Late Gothic realism was more particularized and realistic, as in the paintings of the Van Eyck brothers.

   a. Among Van Eyck paintings were *The Adoration of the Lamb* (Ghent) and *Jan Arnolfini and his Wife*.

   b. Members of the Van Eyck school who began to show Renaissance influences were Roger Van der Weyden, Hugo Van der Goes, and Hans Memling.

2. Late Gothic mannerism was more generalized and idealistic.

a. It is exemplified by the *Très Riches Heures* of the Duke of Berry and the *Madonnas* of Stephen Lochner of Cologne.

B. Late Gothic sculpture is exemplified by the manneristic figure of Notre Dame de Paris at the Cathedral of Paris and the realistic figures of *The Well of Moses* at Dijon by Claus Sluter.

C. Late Gothic architecture was elaborate and ornate.
   1. Styles included the Flamboyant, Decorative, Perpendicular, and Rayonnant.
   2. Among examples of this style are several cathedrals and chapels in England and elsewhere, as well as town halls and guild halls in Belgium and northern Germany.

D. Music of the Late Middle Ages was increasingly polyphonic.
   1. Religious music was more complex, dramatic, and free.
   2. Secular music also became polyphonic, as in rondels, madrigals, etc.

VI. Readings on Late Medieval Culture include:

A. General works on the period as already recommended, such as those of Ferguson, Lucas, Thomson, Symonds, etc.

B. On Learning and Literature:
   Whitfield, John H., *Literary Source Book of the Italian Renaissance* (Philadelphia, University of Pennsylvania, 1903).
   The Portable Renaissance Reader, ed. James B. Ross et al. (New York, Viking, 1953).
   Tilley, Arthur A., *The French Renaissance* (New York, Macmillan, 1919).
   Robb, N. A., *Neoplatonism of the Italian Renaissance* (London, Allen and Unwin, 1935).
   Butler, Pierce, *The Origins of Printing in Europe* (Chicago, University Press, 1940).
   Works of writers mentioned in this chapter, found in various translated editions.

C. On the Arts and Music:
   Wölfflin, Heinrich, *Classic Art: An Introduction to the Italian Renaissance*, tr. (London, Phaidon, 1959).

Benesch, Otto, *The Art of the Renaissance in Northern Europe*, Cambridge, Mass., Harvard University Press, 1945).

Gregory, Padraic, *When Painting Was in Glory*, (Milwaukee, Bruce, 1941).

Reese, Gustave, *Music in the Renaissance* (New York, Norton, 1954).

Vasari, Giorgio, *Lives of the Most Eminent Painters, Sculptors, and Architects* (various translated editions).

Can You Identify?

Italian Renaissance (culture)
Late Gothic (culture)
humanism
Dante
Petrarch
C. Salutati
Manuel Chrysoloras
Cardinal Bessarion
Leonardo Bruni
Aeneas Sylvius Piccolomini
L. B. Alberti
Lorenzo Valla
Niccolo Niccoli
P. P. Vergerio
Marsilio Ficino
Machiavelli
The Prince
Divine Comedy
Boccaccio
Decameron
Rudolph Agricola
Alexander Hegius
Erasmus

Cardinal Jiménez de Cisneros
Brethren of the Common Life
John Fortesque
Jean Froissart
Philip de Commines
classicism (artistic)
Cimabue
Giotto
Massaccio
Boticelli
The Bellinis
Leonardo da Vinci
Ghiberti
Donatello
Verrochio
Renaissance architectural style
Brunelleschi
Bramante
Late Gothic painting
The Van Eycks
Tres Riches Heures
Claus Sluter
Late Gothic architectural style

INDEX

284